ALSO BY TIMOTHY W. RYBACK

Hitler's Private Library: The Books That Shaped His Life

The Last Survivor: Legacies of Dachau

HITLER'S
FIRST
VICTIMS

HITLER'S FIRST VICTIMS

The Quest for Justice

TIMOTHY W. RYBACK

ALFRED A. KNOPF   NEW YORK

2014

THIS IS A BORZOI BOOK
PUBLISHED BY ALFRED A. KNOPF

Copyright © 2014 by Timothy W. Ryback

All rights reserved. Published in the United States by Alfred A. Knopf, a division of Random House LLC, New York, and in Canada by Random House of Canada Limited, Toronto, Penguin Random House companies.

www.aaknopf.com

Knopf, Borzoi Books, and the colophon are registered trademarks of Random House LLC.

Library of Congress Cataloging-in-Publication Data
Ryback, Timothy W., author.
First victims : the quest for justice / Timothy W. Ryback. — First edition.
pages cm.
Includes bibliographical references and index.
ISBN 978-0-385-35291-8 (hardcover)—ISBN 978-0-385-35292-5 (eBook)
1. Hartinger, Josef, 1883–1984. 2. Public prosecutors—Germany—
Biography. 3. Nuremberg Trial of Major German War Criminals,
Nuremberg, Germany, 1945–1946—Sources. 4. Special prosecutors—
United States—History. 5. Governmental investigations—
United States—History. 6. Holocaust, Jewish (1939–1945)
7. National socialism—Germany—History. I. Title.
KK185.H33R93 2014   341.6'90268—dc23   2013050971

Jacket photograph: University of Munich Archives
Jacket design by Oliver Munday

Manufactured in the United States of America
First Edition

IN MEMORY OF THE FIRST FOUR VICTIMS
OF THE HOLOCAUST

Rudolf Benario, age 24, d. April 12, 1933
Ernst Goldmann, age 24, d. April 12, 1933
Arthur Kahn, age 21, d. April 12, 1933
Erwin Kahn, age 32, d. April 16, 1933

How are such things possible in a country that was once so orderly, that once belonged to the leading cultural nations of our era and that, according to its constitution is a free, democratic republic?

E. J. GUMBEL, *Four Years of Political Murder*

CONTENTS

PART III Guilty

HITLER'S
FIRST
VICTIMS

Prelude to Justice

O N THE AFTERNOON OF Wednesday, December 19, 1945, shortly after the midday recess, Major Warren F. Farr, a Harvard-educated lawyer, took the podium before the International Military Tribunal in Nuremberg to make a case for applying the dubious legal concept of collective guilt. The assistant trial counsel of the American prosecution team intended to prove, he told the tribunal, that the *Schutzstaffel*, Adolf Hitler's black-uniformed "protection squads," was a "criminal organization" and that its members should be held collectively responsible for the myriad atrocities perpetrated in its name.

"During the past weeks the Tribunal has heard evidence of the conspirators' criminal program for aggressive war, for concentration camps, for the extermination of the Jews, for enslavement of foreign labor and illegal use of prisoners-of-war, for deportation and Germanization of conquered territories," Major Farr crisply reprised. "Through all this evidence the name of the SS ran like a thread. Again and again"—throughout his discourse Farr jabbed the air with his pencil—"that organization and its components were referred to. It is my purpose to show why it performed a responsible role in every one of these criminal activities, why it was—and, indeed, had to be—a criminal organization."

Farr spoke in a voice that was firm and resolute, but noticeably restrained, seeking to retain the solemnity with which Robert H. Jackson, chief prosecutor for the United States, had opened the prosecution four weeks earlier. "The wrongs which we seek to condemn and punish have been so calculated, so malignant, and so devastating," Jackson had observed, "that civilization cannot tolerate their being ignored, because it cannot survive their being repeated." Jackson enumerated a triad of transgressions—crimes against peace, war crimes, and crimes against humanity—as the phalanx of twenty-one defendants watched from the dock. They seethed defiant indifference, belligerence, and arrogance. Former Luftwaffe chief Hermann Göring slouched in the corner beside Rudolf Hess. The statuesque Nazi ideologue Alfred Rosenberg appeared in a three-piece suit, as did the Third Reich's banker, Hjalmar Schacht. The military high command donned uniforms. Wilhelm Keitel blamed Hitler. "Hitler gave us orders—and we believed in him," Keitel said. "Then he commits suicide and leaves us to bear the guilt." Julius Streicher, the virulently anti-Semitic editor of *Der Stürmer*, blamed the Jews. Ernst Kaltenbrunner, the highest-ranking SS officer to stand trial at Nuremberg, objected to being forced "to serve as an ersatz for Himmler," who had sidestepped justice with the snap of a cyanide capsule. Only Hans Frank, the former governor-general of occupied Poland—"a lawyer by profession, I say with shame," Jackson noted—readily admitted to his own guilt and that of his country. After viewing film footage of the liberated concentration camps, Frank said to his fellow defendants, "May God have mercy on our souls." He was equally contrite before the tribunal. "A thousand years will pass," he would tell the court, "and the guilt of Germany will not be erased." But Jackson knew that crime as well as punishment was on trial in Nuremberg. "We must never forget that the record on which we judge these defendants today," he reminded the court, "is the record on which history will judge us tomorrow."

Now, on the twenty-third day of the trial, as Farr prepared to leave his mark on judicial history, the courtroom solemnity that had greeted Jackson gave way to distraction. Farr's fellow jurists shuffled papers. The defendants chatted among themselves or stared blankly into the distance. Göring planted his jowled face on the dock rail like a bored schoolboy. Frank, in dark glasses, sat in shaded, sinister silence. Previously, the tribunal president, Sir Geoffrey Lawrence, had grown noticeably impatient as Colonel Robert Storey, executive trial counsel, presented a meticulously researched case against the Nazi *Sturmabteilung*, the brownshirt SA storm troopers. Telford Taylor, Jackson's deputy and eventual successor, recalled that the defendants had "roared with laughter" each time the tribunal president interrupted Storey. Now it was Farr's turn. "Farr had his troubles with the tribunal," Taylor remembered. "Its members were still nursing the irritation Storey had aroused and perhaps wanted to avoid giving the impression that he had been singled out for criticism." In addition, Taylor noted, "it was the next-to-last day before the Christmas break, and everyone was tired and eager to get away."

Farr forged into the courtroom fatigue. "About a week or ten days ago there appeared in a newspaper circulated in Nuremberg an account of a visit by that paper's correspondent to a camp in which SS prisoners of war were confined," he said. "The thing that particularly struck the correspondent was the one question asked by the SS prisoners. Why are we charged as war criminals? What have we done except our normal duty?" It was his intention that afternoon, Farr informed Sir Geoffrey and his fellow judges, to answer that question with evidence that proved the SS was "the very essence of Nazism." But as Farr began detailing the structure and nature of the SS, pointing his pencil toward the wall-size chart of this hydra-headed monster—the General SS, the Gestapo, the

Security Department, the Death's Head Unit, the Waffen SS—with SS Reichsführer Heinrich Himmler as its leader, Sir Geoffrey grew peevish. "Major Farr," he said. "To go into this degree of detail about the organization of the SS?"

The American judge, Francis Biddle, joined the sniping. When Farr read a top-secret order from Hitler relating to the structure, membership, and responsibilities of the SS, dated August 17, 1938, then quoted a speech by Himmler from October 1943 in Poznan on the militarized SS police in the occupied territories and quoted an article by Himmler, Biddle intervened. "What has what you just read got to do with what you are presenting?" he asked irritably. Farr insisted on the need to establish the SS as a "criminal weapon" of the National Socialist regime. "Yes, but Major Farr, what you have to show is not the criminality of the people who used the weapon," Sir Geoffrey objected, "but the criminality of the people who composed the weapon."

Farr did not budge. "I quite agree I have to show that," he said. "I suppose I have to show, before showing the persons involved knew of the criminal aims of the organization, what those criminal aims were." This, Farr knew, was the core of his case. For the last twenty-three days, the prosecution had presented hundreds of pages of evidence, citations from speeches, directives, and top-secret memoranda. They had shown nightmare footage from the concentration camps. They had introduced as evidence tattooed flesh and a shrunken human head. "It is unnecessary to repeat the evidence of wholesale brutality, torture, and murder committed by SS guards," Farr said. "They were not the sporadic crimes committed by irresponsible individuals but a part of a definite and calculated policy, a policy necessarily resulting from SS philosophy, a policy which was carried out from the initial creation of the camps."

Farr cited verbatim and without apology a Himmler speech from 1942, Document 1919-PS, on the necessity of the concentration camps. "We shall be able to see after the war what a blessing it was for Germany that," Farr quoted Himmler, "in spite of all the silly talk about humanitarianism, we imprisoned all this criminal sub-stratum of the German people in concentration camps. I'll answer for that." Farr paused. He looked to the defendants' dock, from which Himmler was absent.

"But he is not here to answer," Farr said. He turned to Sir Geoffrey. "Certainly there was no 'silly humanitarianism' in the manner in which SS men performed their tasks," he told the British aristocrat. "Just an illustration," he said. "I have four reports, relating to the deaths of four different inmates of the Concentration Camp Dachau between 16 and 27 May, 1933." Farr held a sheaf of evidence collected in the spring of 1933 by the Munich prosecutor's office. "Each report is signed by the Public Prosecutor of the District Court in Munich and is addressed to the Public Prosecutor of the Supreme Court in Munich. These four reports show that during that two-week period in 1933, at the time when the concentration camps had barely started, SS men had murdered—a different guard each time—an inmate of the camp."

These were not manuals or speeches or directives or confidential memoranda. This was hard evidence, the stuff on which successful criminal prosecutions were built: signed depositions; police reports; crime scene sketches; forensic reports; autopsies; original black-and-white photographs of abused human bodies with lacerated backs and buttocks, cracked necks, and deeply gashed flesh with dangling sinews and glimpses of bone; and, most important, the names of the SS personnel indicted for these murders. This was "an illustration of the sort of thing that happened in the concentration camps at the earliest possible date, in 1933. I am prepared to offer those four reports in evidence and to quote from them"—and here Farr paused to observe acidly—"if the Tribunal thinks that the point is not too insignificant."

"Where are they?" Sir Geoffrey asked.

"I have them here," Farr said. "I will offer them in evidence. The first is our Document 641-PS."

THE DOCUMENTS THAT Farr offered Sir Geoffrey on that late December afternoon contain some of the earliest forensic evidence of the systematic execution of Jews by the Nazis. While these initial Dachau killings do not represent the homicidal process in its full horrific scope, the murder of Jewish detainees in Dachau that spring involved the constituent parts of the genocidal process—intentionality, chain of command, selection, execution—we have come to know as the Holocaust.

I first became aware of the Dachau murders while on assignment as a "far-flung correspondent" for *The New Yorker* in the early 1990s. At the time, Hans-Günter Richardi had already detailed the killings in his superb account of the early Dachau Concentration Camp, *Schule der Gewalt* (School of Violence), as had Prof. Dr. Lothar Gruchmann in his fascinating though daunting twelve-hundred-page compendium, *Justiz im Dritten Reich* (Justice in the Third Reich). I felt there was little left to add.

Later, I discovered in a Munich archive the unpublished, and seemingly forgotten, account of these incidents by Josef Hartinger, the Bavarian deputy state prosecutor who had collected the forensic evidence that Farr was to present in Nuremberg twelve and a half years later. In two extended letters, one dated January 16, 1984, and the other dated February 11, 1984, Hartinger, ninety years old at the time, revealed an astonishingly bold plan to have the camp commandant, Hilmar Wäckerle, arrested on murder charges, and the SS guard units evicted from the concentration camp system.

At the time, Hartinger was a thirty-nine-year-old Munich prosecutor and a rising star in the state civil service. Like many that spring, he sensed the horrific nature of the Hitler regime, but like few others, he recognized its fissures and early fragility, and like fewer still, he willingly risked everything—his career, his welfare, even his life—in the unflinching pursuit of justice. While Hartinger's fight for accountability couldn't stem the tide of Nazi atrocity, his story suggests how vastly different history might have been had more Germans acted with equal courage and conviction in that time of collective human failure.

PART I

INNOCENT

1

Crimes of the Spring

T HURSDAY MORNING OF Easter Week 1933, April 13, saw clearing skies that held much promise for the upcoming holiday weekend. Mild temperatures were foreseen for Bavaria as they were throughout southern Germany, with a few rain showers predicted for Friday, but brilliant, sunny skies for the Easter weekend. Previous generations hailed such days as *Kaiserwetter*, weather fit for a kaiser, a playful gibe at the former monarch's father, who appeared *en plein air* only when sufficient sunlight permitted his presence to be recorded by photographers. In the spring of 1933, some now spoke in higher-spirited and more reverential tones of *Führerwetter*. It was Adolf Hitler's first spring as chancellor.

Shortly after nine o'clock that morning, Josef Hartinger was in his second-floor office at Prielmayrstrasse 5, just off Karlsplatz in central Munich, when he received a call informing him that four men had been shot in a failed escape attempt from a recently erected detention facility for political prisoners in the moorlands near the town of Dachau. As deputy prosecutor for one of Bavaria's largest jurisdictions—Munich II—Hartinger was responsible for investigating potential crimes in a sprawling sweep of countryside outside Munich's urban periphery. "My responsibilities included, along with the district courts in Garmisch and Dachau, all juvenile and major financial criminal matters for the entire jurisdiction, as well as all the so-called political crimes. Thus, for the Dachau camp, I had dual responsibilities," he later wrote.

Deputy Prosecutor Hartinger was a model Bavarian civil servant. He was conservative in his faith and politics, a devout Roman Catholic and a registered member of the Bavarian People's Party, the centrist "people's party" of the Free State of Bavaria, founded by Dr. Heinrich Held, a fellow jurist and a fierce advocate of Bavarian autonomy. In April 1933, Hartinger was thirty-nine years old and belonged to the first generation of state prosecutors trained in the processes and values of a democratic republic. He pursued communists and National Socialists with equal vigor, and since Hitler's appointment as chancellor had watched the ensuing chaos and abuses with the confidence that such a government could not long endure. The Reich president, Paul von Hindenburg, had dismissed four chancellors in the past ten months: Heinrich Brüning in May, Franz von Papen in November, and Kurt von Schleicher just that past January. There was nothing preventing Hindenburg from doing the same with his latest chancellor Adolf Hitler.

Until then, Hartinger's daily commerce in crime involved burned barns, a petty larceny, an occasional assault, and, based on the remnant entries in the departmental case register, all too frequent incidents of adult transgressions against minors. Forty-one-year-old Max Lackner, for example, was institutionalized for two years for "sexual abuse of children under fourteen." Ilya Malic, a salesman from Yugoslavia, was arrested after he "forced a fourteen-year-old to French-kiss." Hartinger spoke discreetly of "juvenile matters." Homicides were rare. The only registered murder for those years was a crime of passion committed by forty-seven-year-old Alfons Graf, who put four bullets into the head of his companion, Frau Reitinger, when he discovered her in the back of his company car with another man.

But that year, following Hitler's January appointment as chancellor and the dramatic arson attack a month later that saw the stately Berlin Reichstag consumed in a nightmare conflagration of crashing glass, twisted steel, and surging flames, the jurisdiction was swept by an unprecedented wave of arrests in the name of national security. In Untergrünberg, the farmer Franz Sales Mendler was arrested for making disparaging remarks about the new government. Maria Strohle, the wife of a power plant owner in Hergensweiler, told a neighbor that she heard Hitler had paid 50,000 reichsmarks to stage the arson attack on the Reichstag; she was sentenced to three months in prison, as was Franz Schliersmaier in Bösenreutin, who put the amount at 500,000. One Bavarian was indicted for comparing Hitler to Stalin, and another for calling him a homosexual, and still another for suggesting he did not "look" German. "Hitler is a foreigner who smuggled himself into the country," Julie Kolmeder said at a Munich beer garden a few streets from Hartinger's office. "Just look at his face." A Munich coachman crossed the law with the indelicate aside, *"Hitler kann mich im Arsch lecken."* Euphemistically: Hitler can kiss my ass. More than one person was prosecuted for calling a Nazi a *"Bazi."** Thousands of others were taken into *Schutzhaft*, or protective custody, for no apparent reason at all.

The shooting of four men in a failed escape from the Dachau Concentration Camp must have struck Hartinger's Roman Catholic sensibilities as particularly unfortunate, coming as it did just two days before Good Friday and amid an appeal by the archbishop of Munich and Freising for an Easter amnesty. "In the name of, and on behalf of, the Bavarian bishops, I have the honor, Your Excellency, to extend the following request," the stately and imperious Cardinal Faulhaber had written Bavaria's Reich governor on April 3,

---

* The word *Bazi* can be translated as "swindler" or "scoundrel," and derives from the Bavarian dialect, as does the word *Nazi*, a shortening of the word *Nationalsozialist*, but also an old nickname for Ignatius, a popular Bavarian name commonly associated with a country bumpkin, and applied disparagingly to Hitler followers. A Nazi never called another Nazi a "Nazi." They referred to each other as National Socialists or "party comrades."

"that the investigation procedure for those in protective custody be expedited as quickly as possible in order to relieve the detainees and their families from emotional torment." Faulhaber expressed the desire that the detainees could be home in time for the Easter weekend, reminding the governor that there was no occasion more sacred to Christians than the Eastertide. "If because of time constraints the investigations cannot be completed by Good Friday," Faulhaber proposed, "then perhaps out of pure Christian and humanitarian grounds, an Easter amnesty can be granted from Good Friday until the end of Easter." The cardinal reminded the governor that in December 1914 Pope Benedict XV had invoked a Christmas armistice that stilled weapons on both sides of the front. What worked in a time of war must certainly work in peacetime, was the suggestion. Indeed, the previous month Chancellor Hitler himself had stated that his "greatest ambition" was to "bring back to the nation the millions who had been misled, rather than to destroy them." What better way to instill a sense of national loyalty than through a gesture of Christian clemency on the holiday celebrating the resurrection of Jesus Christ? In this deeply Catholic corner of the country, when the archbishop of Munich and Freising, the oldest and most powerful of the state's bishoprics, spoke, the vast majority of Bavaria's four million Catholics listened, and on this occasion so did its political leadership.

A week later, the state interior minister, Gauleiter Adolf Wagner, responded on the Reich governor's behalf.* "Most Honorable Herr Cardinal, I have the honor of responding to your letter to the governor of April 3, 1933," he wrote, "to inform Your Eminence that we are in the process of reviewing the cases of everyone currently in detention, and that by Easter more than a thousand individuals

---

* The Gauleiter, or district leader, was the Nazi Party official responsible for local affairs. These Nazi Party districts corresponded to the thirty-three voting districts for the Reichstag elections. In 1941, the number of Gauleiter and corresponding districts was increased to forty-three.

will be released from protective custody." Wagner conveyed additional good news. The state government would permit Easter Mass to be celebrated among those practicing Roman Catholics who remained in detention as long as it did not constitute "a burden to the state budget." Wagner recommended that "the responsible religious authorities should be directly in contact with the administration of the individual detention camps, whom I will provide corresponding instructions as to how to deal with this matter."

But now, amid heartening news of the Easter amnesty, came news of the deaths at Dachau. The call to Hartinger that Thursday morning was conducted in conformity with Paragraph 159 of the *Strafprozessordnung,* or Criminal Procedure Code, which required police officers "to report immediately to the prosecutor or local magistrate" any case in which "a person has died from causes other than natural ones." Paragraph 160, in turn, obligated Hartinger to take immediate action: "As soon as the prosecutor is informed of a suspected criminal act, either through a report or by other means, he is to investigate the matter until he has determined whether an indictment is to be issued." In compliance with his Paragraph 160 responsibilities, Hartinger called Dr. Moritz Flamm, the Munich II medical examiner, who was responsible for conducting postmortem examinations and autopsies in criminal investigations.

Hartinger liked Dr. Flamm. Both men had previously worked in Munich I, Hartinger as an assistant prosecutor and Flamm as a part-time assistant medical examiner. Like Hartinger, he was a man of keen intelligence who had earned perfect grades in school. And like Hartinger, Flamm was a man of sterling professionalism. Flamm autopsies were models of precision and efficiency—not a moment wasted, not a detail overlooked. Often thirty pages in length, they could withstand the most rigorous scrutiny in a court of law. Flamm was particularly proficient in bullet wounds. He had completed his medical training at the Ludwig Maximilian University of Munich in July 1914, just in time to join the 2nd

Bavarian Infantry Regiment. He was dispatched to the front in August 1916 with the 3rd Medical Company, where he served meritoriously, earning an Iron Cross, the Bavarian Military Order, and the Friedrich August Cross. "Particularly noteworthy is his absolute reliability and his medical professionalism that make him, without question, suited for any type of service," the company surgeon had commented after the war. "At the front [Flamm] became virtually indispensable as the situation with medical supplies deteriorated," he wrote, "all the while demonstrating a seemingly inexhaustible dedication to his work." The surgeon observed that Flamm was notably "modest" and "by nature rather sensitive," but possessed of intelligence, sound judgment, and humor even "in the most desperate situations." The surgeon said he had come to know in Flamm a physician "for whom one seldom can wish full and well-deserved recognition and in good conscience can provide unqualified praise." Flamm's handwriting, precise and refined, with playful, elegant flourishes, reflects his calm and easy competence.

Flamm also demonstrated a fierce independence and willingness to act on his conscience when circumstances demanded. In the spring of 1919, amid a failed Bolshevik coup that saw thousands taken into protective custody—with and without cause—he exercised his authority as chief physician of a military hospital to order the release of two patients who were being detained on suspicion of collaborating with communists. Flamm was accused of Bolshevik sympathies, but was taken into "personal protection" by his superior, who vouched for him "administratively, professionally, and politically" and insisted that he was a man free of "any personal, moral, or political blemish." After two years with Flamm in Munich II, Hartinger had come to share the same high regard. In addition, Flamm had a driver's license and his own motorcar.

———

DACHAU WAS an easy twenty-minute drive north of Munich, first
to the town of Allach, where BMW had an assembly plant, then
into the Dachau moorlands along tree-lined country lanes and
across open fields. The town, whose name derived from *dah,* for
"mud," and *au,* for "meadow"—the "muddy meadow"—was in fact
a charming weave of cobblestone streets and cross-timber façades
situated on a prominent rise that overlooked the surrounding
moorlands. The local residents, a sturdy rural Bavarian stock
reputed to be particularly *geschert*—rough-cut and provincial—
took their history in stride, managing over the centuries to till their
fields and peddle their wares in the service of monarchs, communists, constitutionalists, and now National Socialists.

In the eighteenth century, the Wittelsbachs, who had ruled
Bavaria for more than eight hundred years, built their summer residence there, a cheerful rococo palace with a splay of windows along
its southern façade that still glint splendidly in the afternoon sunlight. In the late nineteenth century, landscape artists discovered
the Dachau moors, whose soft hues complemented the impressionist style that was all the rage of the era. In the 1890s, Dachau was
awarded two stars by the Michelin Guide. Munich received only
one. By the end of the century, more than a thousand artists were
said to be living and working around Dachau.

During the Great War, the Royal Powder and Munitions Factory was constructed just east of town in a swampy woodland fed
by the Würm Mill Creek, isolated enough to protect the local population from an industrial accident but accessible to the Dachau train
station along the main rail line between Munich and Stuttgart and
beyond to the fighting fronts. For the next several years, the factory
produced millions of projectiles that were adapted to the changing fashions of the front. In addition to standard bullets for pistols,
rifles, and machine guns, specialized munitions for slicing barbed
wire, shooting down observation balloons, and piercing armor
were developed. After the war, in April 1919, the Bolsheviks won a

military victory here during the rule of the ill-fated Soviet Republic of Bavaria, when Bavaria broke briefly from the Reich, only to return to the longer-lived but equally tumultuous and ultimately equally ill-fated Weimar Republic.

The Treaty of Versailles idled munitions production, stranding thousands of workers. For the next decade, the facility stood as a haunting reminder not just of military defeat and political humiliation but also of the ruinous impact on the local economy. "Since 1920, the numerous work sites have stood empty," the *Dachauer Zeitung* reported, "the many buildings and work halls, constructed at such expense, stand dead and abandoned." A local author, Eugen Mondt, who circulated within distinguished literary circles—he was a friend of the poet Rainer Maria Rilke and attended a reading by Franz Kafka*—lived adjacent to the abandoned facility. As Mondt watched the vacant building fall into decay, an eerie and seemingly Kafkaesque ruin emerged in his mind. "The facility seemed uncanny to me," he wrote. "It was like a city of the dead."

No one was quite certain who selected the moldering ruin as the site for a detention center. Some thought it was the new thirty-two-year-old chief of police, Heinrich Himmler, whose first job had been with an agricultural fertilizer business in the nearby town of Oberschleissheim. Some thought it might have been Dachau's own town fathers. In January 1933, a few weeks before Hitler came to power, the *Amper-Bote (Amper Messenger)* published an ambitious plan to retool the abandoned industrial facility into a public work camp for the unemployed. The offices could be reequipped, the cooking and sanitation facilities renovated, the barracks refurbished. The camp residents would be put to work cultivating the

---

* On the evening of March 22, 1922, Mondt was among the fifty or so guests who attended a reading in Munich by Kafka, who presented his short story "In the Penal Colony," a chilling tale about a nightmare facility where men are held in indeterminate detention for unknown reasons and ultimately destroyed in murderous machinery. "The words left the audience stunned," Mondt wrote. Kafka himself thought the evening a failure and never again read in public outside his native Prague.

ter had been officially designated the *Konzentrationslager Dachau,* but it was in fact situated in the district of Prittlbach, a town so obscure and isolated that the Nazis had borrowed the name from the neighboring rail-linked town of Dachau. It was Hartinger's first visit to this remote corner of his jurisdiction since Himmler had announced the camp's opening three weeks earlier.

Hartinger was troubled from the outset. There was not a single green uniform of a state police officer in sight. Instead, the entrance was guarded by a clutch of armed men in brown storm trooper uniforms with black kepis indicating their elevated status into the elite SS. Hartinger knew that the Reich governor had issued a special ordinance on March 10 permitting storm troopers to help manage the surge of protective-custody detentions—"These are to be armed by the police with pistols"—but it made provision for these guards to serve under state police supervision.

Hartinger demanded entrance. A call was made. The iron gate swung open. Flamm steered his motorcar through the narrow entrance. As they drove past boarded-up buildings and work details of detainees in gray dungarees, their heads shaven, guarded by rifle-toting storm troopers, Hartinger's disquiet deepened. He knew something about detention facilities. His position after university had been as a prison assessor with the attorney general's office in his hometown of Amberg. At a glance, Hartinger knew this place violated virtually every regulation for a state facility.

At the camp commandant's headquarters, a two-story building, the judicial commission was received not by a state police officer but by an SS captain, SS Hauptsturmführer Hilmar Wäckerle. He was dressed in a crisp black SS uniform with flawlessly polished knee-high riding boots and a peaked black kepi, a veritable poster boy of Aryan superiority. With one hand, Wäckerle held a leashed and muzzled attack dog. In the other, he gripped a pizzle. He exuded cruelty and arrogance. Wäckerle was evidently a man who understood the trappings of brute force but possessed little appreciation fields, shoring up the banks of the Amper River, and rebuilding roads. "Naturally, it would be necessary to develop this orgation carefully and in the greatest detail," the article said, "so in every respect the best orderliness, security and pleasant w[...] ing conditions would be provided for those wishing to work her[...] The only issue that remained to be clarified was whether residen[...] in the facility was to be "forced" or "voluntary." The proposal wa[...] taken under consideration by the Munich authorities.

On Thursday, March 13, Interior Minister Wagner dispatched a team to Dachau to assess the site's potential for concentrating in one place the thousands of political prisoners glutting Bavaria's jails, prisons, and makeshift detention centers. The following Sunday, a column of trucks loaded with Nazi "volunteers" rolled into the abandoned facility and hoisted a swastika banner. "On the water tower of the former gunpowder factory, visible from far away, the black-white-and-red flag flutters in the wind," the *Dachauer Zeitung* reported, "a sign that new life has moved into the once desolate compound of the big Dachau gunpowder factory." On Monday, March 20, Police Chief Heinrich Himmler announced the opening of the Dachau Concentration Camp. Two days later, a bus delivered the first detainees.

HARTINGER AND FLAMM ARRIVED at the camp, along with a note taker, shortly before ten o'clock that morning.* The facility was enclosed by the ten-foot-high perimeter wall that once protected the industrial park from sabotage; the stone escutcheons of Wittelsbach heraldry still graced the entrance gate. The detention cen-

---

* The three-man team was known as a *Gerichtskommission*, or judicial commission, and operated in cooperation with an investigation team from the state police, known as a *Mordkommission*, or homicide commission, which was responsible for collecting evidence, taking depositions, making sketches of the crime scene, and so on. The prosecutor prepared criminal indictments that were then presented to a judge who could issue arrest warrants that would be executed by the police.

for the less overt, more subtle sources of power. He did not understand that the middle-aged, slightly balding civil servant with thick-
rimmed eyeglasses, a man of modest appearance and stature—in
the office, Hartinger was known as the "short, dark guy"—carried
with him the full legal authority of the Bavarian state.

Hartinger had entered the facility not on the SS captain's beneficence but through the force of Paragraph 160 of the Criminal
Procedure Code. For his part, Wäckerle was obligated under Paragraph 161 to cooperate fully with "authorities and officials of the
police and security services" and adhere to "all regulations in order
to avoid obscuring the facts of the case." The Dachau Concentration Camp may have been Wäckerle's concentration camp, but it
remained in Hartinger's legal jurisdiction.

Hartinger was led to the scene of the shooting across a small
footbridge over the Würm Mill Creek and along a wooded path
to a remote area that was being clear-cut for a shooting range for
the camp guards. He was told that the four detainees had been
equipped with picks and shovels the previous afternoon around
five o'clock and had been led to the clearing to remove stubble
and underbrush by SS lieutenant Robert Erspenmüller, a former
police officer, who was serving as the deputy camp commandant.
According to Erspenmüller, the four men had been noticeably "lax"
in their comportment and needed to be prodded repeatedly. They
had been at the site for only a few moments when the youngest,
a twenty-one-year-old medical student from Würzburg named
Arthur Kahn, allegedly sprinted for the trees. The accompanying
guards, Hans Bürner and Max Schmidt, said they had shouted for
Kahn to halt. Suddenly, it was said, two other detainees, Rudolf
Benario and Ernst Goldmann, both twenty-four and both from the
town of Fürth, near Nuremberg, also bolted. The two guards said
they shouted again, then opened fire.

Erspenmüller had been standing at a distance, overseeing the
work. He too drew his pistol and began firing. According to Erspen-

müller, the fourth detainee, Erwin Kahn (not related to Arthur), a thirty-two-year-old salesman from Munich who looked as if he was about to run back toward the camp, stepped into the line of fire, taking several bullets to the face. Erspenmüller said he pursued Arthur Kahn, firing as he went, eventually bringing him down a hundred meters or so into the woods. Back in the clearing, Benario and Goldmann lay facedown, both dead. Erwin Kahn was still conscious but delirious. He was carried on a stretcher by two SS men to the camp infirmary and placed on a table. "One of the stretcher-bearers was a short SS man from Grünwald who was not strong enough to lift him," one witness later recalled, "so I had to jump in to help place the wounded man on the table." A bullet had penetrated his cheekbone, just below the left eye, and exited the back of his skull. Bone fragments were visible, but Kahn was lucid. He asked to see a rabbi. Kahn was bandaged and dispatched to the local hospital.

Standing in the dank moorland chill of this April morning, blood marking the places where the men had been shot, it was perhaps easy to understand the young men's temptation to bolt. The provisional nature of the detention facility and the proximity of the trees, not to mention the evident inexperience of the guards, could have proved to be a fatal combination. One could easily attribute these deaths to a tragic underestimation of the seriousness of the circumstances. But there was no excuse for the treatment of the young men's bodies. The corpses had been unceremoniously dumped, like slain game, on the floor of a nearby ammunition shed. Their heads were shorn but they were still fully clothed. Basic human decency would have demanded a more respectful treatment of the slain young men. Hartinger began to sense that something was terribly wrong here.

The corpses were stripped of their bloodied clothing, and Dr. Flamm set to work on the forensic examination. Arthur Kahn, the medical student who was said to have first attempted to escape, had taken five bullets. One had cut through his upper right torso, a second through his upper right arm, a third through his right thigh; a fourth was lodged in his right heel, and the fifth—the one that killed him—had traversed his skull from behind and exited through the frontal lobe. Dr. Rudolf Benario, a political scientist, had been shot twice. Benario appeared to be of a fragile constitution, with delicate hands and well-groomed nails. One bullet had clipped his left ring finger, and the second entered his skull from behind. Ernst Goldmann, more robust, with thick limbs and coarse hands, had been shot through his lower left arm and his right hand, and had taken three more bullets in the back of his head. Flamm counted fifteen bullet wounds in total. There were certainly more shots fired, but these had found their mark. When he finished, Dr. Flamm turned to Hartinger. There was no need for an autopsy, he said. The cause of death was clear in each case: a bullet to the back of the head. Flamm then turned to Wäckerle. "Your guards are very good shots with their pistols," he observed pointedly.

Hartinger demanded to see the men's quarters. He was led by a young SS man, Hans Steinbrenner, into the "inner camp," a barbed-wire compound with a dozen or so one-story barracks, little more than a human cage within a sprawling industrial wasteland. Steinbrenner led Hartinger to Barrack II, where Hartinger entered on his own.

We do not know specifically with whom Hartinger spoke or the details that were relayed to him, but a number of detainees were witness to the events leading up to the shooting. Willi Gesell had been with Benario, Goldmann, and Arthur Kahn on the transport of thirty men who had arrived the day before the shootings. Gesell remembered long afterward that Wäckerle had called Benario, Goldmann, and Kahn to step forward on arrival in the camp, then ordered Steinbrenner and several other guards to set upon them. "They started beating the Jews wildly and kicking them," Gesell recalled. When the brown-uniformed swarm cleared, Gesell saw

Benario, Goldmann, and Kahn writhing in the dirt, "bleeding from their nose and mouth and other parts of their bodies." Steinbrenner ordered them to their feet and marched them to Barrack II, all the time lashing them with his pizzle. The three men were barely settled in the barrack when Steinbrenner came back. He ordered them, along with Erwin Kahn, to a work detail with about thirty other detainees. The four Jews were put to work emptying enormous trash bins outside the barracks. "While they were doing this, they were beaten horrifically by Steinbrenner, who was charged with overseeing the work," another detainee, Horst Scharnagel, would later recall. When Steinbrenner saw Scharnagel looking on, he pressed him into service as well, whipping and beating the five men as they struggled with the containers. The men returned to the barrack that evening bloodied and exhausted.

Around three o'clock in the morning, Steinbrenner appeared in the barrack with three other SS guards, all of them evidently drunk. Steinbrenner fired his pistol into the ceiling, then assembled all the men outside for roll call. Names were called. The men were dismissed. Four hours later, Steinbrenner was back yet again. This time, he summoned Benario, Goldmann, and Arthur Kahn, then added Willi Gesell. He ordered them to fill a container with trash and haul it to a nearby gravel pit that was being used as the camp garbage dump. "It was only with the greatest effort that we were able to lift the container and drag it a few meters," Gesell remembered. "We were constantly being beaten along the way." Steinbrenner worked the men for four hours, then returned them to their quarters.

At two o'clock that afternoon, Steinbrenner summoned Benario, Goldmann, and the two Kahns yet again. He marched them outside the wire enclosure to work on clear-cutting the SS shooting range beyond the camp perimeter. The men returned at four o'clock. Exactly what happened next is unclear. One detainee, Heinrich Ultsch, recalled resting outside with Benario, Goldmann, and Arthur Kahn. "On the critical day during the afternoon—it was gradually getting dark—we were lying on the grass between Barracks II and III," Ultsch recalled. "We were talking about money and Kahn said that he had smuggled a dollar bill into the camp and was afraid." Ultsch offered to hide the bill for him. Arthur Kahn, who had been preparing to attend medical school in Scotland, went into the barrack to get the money. At that moment, Steinbrenner appeared and called for Kahn, Goldmann, and Benario. "The last two, who were right there, answered immediately, and in the meantime we started calling for [Arthur] Kahn, who had gone into the barracks. He came out just at the moment when another answered that his name was Kahn and that he came from Munich. When Steinbrenner heard this, he said, 'You come along too.'" He handed the four of them spades and picks, marched them to the footbridge over the Würm Mill Creek, and turned them over to Erspenmüller.

Willi Gesell remembered the incident differently. He recalled that the detainees were standing in line for the daily distribution of letters and packages when Steinbrenner suddenly appeared.

"Everybody stop!" he is said to have barked. "Where is Kahn?"

"Here!"

"Another Kahn!"

"Here!"

"And Goldmann?"

An older man stepped forward.

"No, not you, the Jew there."

Ernst Goldmann stepped forward.

"Benario!"

"Here!"

"You four, come with me!"

According to Gesell, Steinbrenner handed the men spades, marched them to the footbridge over the Würm Mill Creek, and turned them over to Erspenmüller, who led them into the woods. A few minutes later, just after five o'clock, a series of gunshots pierced the late afternoon stillness, accompanied by screams. There were no witnesses to the actual shooting.

Hartinger sensed the fear and tension in the barrack. "I have a clear recollection that a terrified young man pressed hard through the crowd," Hartinger recalled. "He was sobbing and told me that he was afraid he was going to be murdered." Hartinger tried to calm him. He told him not to worry, everything would be fine. Then he departed.

On the drive back to their offices in Munich, Hartinger told Flamm he suspected that the men had been intentionally shot on explicit orders of the commandant. "My reasons were based not only on the physical circumstances but in particular on my assessment of the personalities I encountered in the camp, and especially on my evaluation of the nature of the camp commandant Wäckerle, who made a devastating impression on me," Hartinger later wrote. "I also had to include in my deliberations the fact that all those who had been shot were Jews."

2

Late Afternoon News

WHILE HARTINGER AND FLAMM were investigating the shootings in the Würm Mill Creek Woods, a hundred miles to the north in the town of Fürth, an easy ten-minute tram ride from Nuremberg, Leo and Maria Benario were preparing a package of provisions to send their son, Rudolf. He had been transferred two days earlier, suddenly and unexpectedly, from a makeshift detention facility in Fürth to the recently erected Dachau Concentration Camp.

For the past several weeks, the Benarios had been shuttling fresh changes of clothing and other necessities to their son, especially medication for the chronic bronchitis from which he had been suffering. He had been taken into protective custody by a group of storm troopers in the early morning hours of March 10 during a roundup of a dozen local political activists who included his friend Ernst Goldmann. Since the town jail was too small to accommodate all the prisoners, the men were detained in the local sports hall.

The problem with protective custody, of course, was the uncertainty. *Schutzhaft* was a security measure dating back to the mid-nineteenth century in which a person could be detained without cause.* It was a double-edged legal instrument, as the name suggested, used either to protect an individual from intimidation or threat by an angry mob, or to secure the public at large from a potential threat. Since there were no indictments or arrest warrants, there were no charges to challenge, no recourse for appeal. Judges were irrelevant, lawyers useless. The Benarios' son had fallen into a legal gray zone beyond the reach of normal judicial process.

The Benarios had taken some comfort in the provisional and proximate nature of Rudolf's detention and the assumption that he had ceased political activity in the past year to focus on completing his doctoral dissertation in political economy at the Friedrich Alexander University in Erlangen. Indeed, just that November, when the Bavarian political police had approached the university rector about communist activities on campus, he had cleared Benario of any suspicion. "Among the individual students to be noted is a former student political economics student Benario, who according to information given to me by the political police was determined to have been actively involved with communist activities," the rector wrote in a memorandum dated December 12, 1932. The rector had seen Benario at the university just that autumn—most likely for Rudolf's dissertation defense—and was firm in his conviction that Benario "had no affiliation" with the communist movement.

Rudolf had been involved with political activists in Fürth but had distanced himself from those elements, announcing his engagement and preparing for a settled life that suited his family station and his officially recognized status as *Doctor rerum politicarum,* or

---

* The legal term *Schutzhaft* dates back to Prussia's 1850 Law for the Protection of Personal Freedom (*Gesetz zum Schutze der persönlichen Freiheit*), which stipulated that detainees could be held without cause, but had to "be released at the latest the following day" or handed over to "proper authorities." The parameters for *Schutzhaft* were expanded in 1916 in response to wartime security concerns, then curtailed in the Weimar Republic, only to be radically applied under the Nazis.

doctor of political economy. But his transfer to the Dachau Concentration Camp dashed any hope of immediate release. The imminent amnesty that was to see as many as a thousand detainees freed in time for the Easter holidays would hardly apply to a family with a name derived from *Ben Ari*, Hebrew for "Son of Ari."

Leo and Maria Benario now braced themselves for an extended detention that could well last through the spring. The weather reports for the upcoming weekend looked promising, but they knew Bavarian seasons to be temperamental, especially in the Dachau moorland. One of Maria's older brothers, Dr. Siegmund Bing, had frequented artistic circles in Dachau in his youth, and was familiar with the beauty as well as the rigors of the region.

Spring rains could be chilling and relentless. Late winter squalls could pelt the fields and moors with ice and snow. They packed Rudolf's winter coat as well as his insulated boots and decided to include his house slippers, along with three shirts, four changes of underwear, ten pair of socks, and twelve handkerchieves. Maria added a supply of Dicodid, Adalin, and Chinosol for Rudolf's bronchitis, as well as a fever thermometer so he could monitor his temperature.

TWO YEARS EARLIER, in the summer of 1931, when the Benarios moved from their elegant Erlenstegstrasse villa in a fashionable quarter of Nuremberg to the modest third-floor apartment on Moststrasse in Fürth, it seemed an ideal retreat for a beleaguered Jewish family. The quaint town, with its patchwork of cobblestone streets and timber-beam façades, had been providing solace and safe haven to Jews since 1528, when the margrave George the Pious, a German noble, accommodated two Jewish merchants for six years in exchange for a "protection tithe." By the seventeenth century, Fürth boasted a Talmud school, a synagogue, a Jewish cemetery, and the first Jewish hospital on German soil. Three centuries on, a Jewish family could worship in one of Fürth's six synagogues, and educate their children in the Israeli Elementary School and the Israeli High School. By then there were two Jewish cemeteries. In this north Bavarian province of Franconia, Fürth was known as "the Franconian Jerusalem."

The Benarios' move to Fürth had accompanied a dramatic turn in the fortunes of one of Nuremberg's leading industrial families. Maria was the daughter of Ignaz Bing, one of the two Bing brothers who in the late nineteenth century founded Bing Metal Works, a manufacturing firm that started out stamping tin plates but quickly emerged as one of Bavaria's leading manufacturing enterprises in kitchen utensils and metal toys. The legendary Bing Eisenbahn, a pioneer in the toy train market, overshadowed the Märklin brand in Germany, established the "00" gauge for toy trains in England, and for a time went head-to-head with Lionel trains for the vast American market. Ignaz Bing paid his employees generously and treated them well. In an era of frequent strikes and labor unrest, he boasted that he had never experienced a single strike among his three thousand workers. He enjoyed an equally amicable relationship with the city of Nuremberg, where he emerged as the city's leading philanthropist, funding shelters for the poor and hospitals and helping maintain local museums. He was made a privy counselor and, in 1891, awarded Nuremberg's silver medallion for service to the city. He was visited by the king of Bavaria. During World War I, Bing Metal Works stamped helmets, canteens, and other supplies for the soldiers at the front. By 1923, the factory, retooled for peace, occupied an entire city block, employing more than sixteen thousand workers, and laid proud claim to being "the largest toy manufacturer in the world."

Leo Benario married into the Bing family dynasty in 1907 but retained his position in Frankfurt as financial editor with the highly regarded newspaper *Frankfurter Zeitung,* the predecessor to the *Frankfurter Allgemeine Zeitung.* In 1913, Leo helped the French Nobel

Peace Prize laureate Baron d'Estournelles de Constant establish the German chapter of the International Conciliation Committee, a prominent prewar peace initiative. "This branch seems destined to have a great influence upon the leaders of Europe," an American publication, the *Advocate of Peace*, observed that summer, citing Leo as one of Germany's most influential peace advocates.

In 1918, when his father-in-law passed away, Leo moved his family from Frankfurt to Nuremberg, where he assumed the life of an academic. He taught courses in banking and investment at the Nuremberg Professional School of Business and Social Sciences. In 1924 he founded the Institute for Newspaper Research, and two years later published a history of the seventeenth-century newspaper business in northern Bavaria. A family photograph from those years shows Leo to be an elegant gentleman in his late fifties with a distinctly professorial bearing, sporting a three-piece tweed suit. Maria stands beside him, a woman of dark features and unassuming comportment, though some might say she looks like a worrier. Another photograph shows Rudolf casually seated in a wooden lounge chair in a tree-shaded garden. He is a well-groomed young man with pale skin and delicate features. A pair of wire-rimmed eyeglasses lend him a distinctively academic demeanor.

There is a keen intelligence in the gaze that Rudolf directs to the camera, but it is tipped with a hard-edged defiance that could be perceived as arrogance. He was by all accounts a difficult but bookish child possessed of a frail constitution. He was frequently ill. In 1927, when Rudolf enrolled at Friedrich Alexander University in Erlangen, it was already a bastion of political conservatism and radical nationalism.

The central square was dominated by an imposing statue of a muscle-bound German soldier with a naked torso, his wrists shackled to a cliff—a symbol of the restraints imposed by the 1919 Treaty of Versailles—his chiseled visage with its jutting chin and fierce eyes glaring west toward France, and atop his head a trench helmet of the type manufactured by Bing Metal Works during the war. Hitler addressed the students and faculty on several occasions. "When someone claims that all human beings are equal," the Nazi leader told a standing-room-only crowd of students and faculty in Erlangen's largest venue on February 26, 1928, "he is rejecting the entire future of our people." The "source of power in any person," Hitler insisted, lay in the "quality of his blood." He denounced pacifism, communism, and democracy in equal measure, and received a thunderous ovation.

When Rudolf arrived on campus in the spring of 1927 and found himself excluded from the myriad proof-of-blood student clubs, he cofounded with another student the Club of Republican Students—a nod to the democratic values of the Weimar Republic—and opened membership to "all those students belonging to the republican parties, whether the German Democratic Party, the Social Democratic Party of Germany, the German Centrist Party, or pacifist organizations, or those sharing similar values." The club organized public debates and provided information on university policies as well as networking opportunities with like-minded student clubs at other universities, including the Club of Independent Academics in Berlin and the Cartel of Republican Students for Germany and Austria. His leadership of a student club accorded him a seat on the student council, where he confronted the growing influence of the right-wing students, and on one occasion protested to the rector himself.

In November 1929, the National Socialists won a majority in student elections, securing fourteen of the council's twenty-five seats. On January 15, 1930, the newly elected body convened its first session of the year, where the National Socialist delegates voiced objection to Benario's presence. "Student Benario represents through his actions a destructive influence on the unity of the Erlangen student body," their spokesman claimed. They demanded he leave the assembly. When Benario stood his ground, the fourteen National Socialists rose and marched "in unity" from the room, dissolving the quorum and forcing the chairman to adjourn the session. The student council reconvened the next day without Benario. When one council member objected to Benario's exclusion, the matter was put to a vote. The delegates closed ranks. "Student Winterberg, speaking for the faction of the Youth Movement and Students at Work, declared that they fully endorsed the National Socialist faction's position after further inquiries about Student Benario," the *Erlanger Nachrichten* reported. Benario was declared a disruptive influence and banished from the council.

A day before the next round of student elections, Hitler returned to campus. "I do not think there is anything that speaks stronger for the victory of the National Socialist movement than the fact that ever more numbers of young Germans, especially the young people from the German intelligentsia, are finding their way to our beliefs," the Nazi leader observed. "There can be no liberation movement of a people that is not embraced at the universities, no triumph of a nation when it does not begin there." The following day, November 14, 1930, the National Socialists swept the university-wide elections, carrying 83 percent of the student vote. Friedrich Alexander was later hailed as the "first National Socialist university of the Third Reich."

By then, Benario's parents were living in diminished circumstances. The economic crash of 1929 had jolted the Bing family fortunes. Amid the deteriorating economy, the company tilted toward insolvency, and in November 1931, Bing Metal Works collapsed in bankruptcy. Leo and Maria left their villa in Nuremberg and moved to Moststrasse in Fürth, just off the main town square and a few streets from the apartment Chief Prosecutor Robert Jackson would occupy a decade and a half later. Rudolf lived with his sister and parents, working on his doctoral dissertation, on the legal framework of workers' councils between 1840 and 1849, the precursors to the modern-day labor unions, and quickly found his way onto the political scene.

Rudolf joined the Fürth Rowing Club, which was serving as a cover for the local political activists following the "Presidential Decree on Suppressing Street Violence," issued in November 1931, that banned public demonstrations amid increasingly violent clashes between the militant factions of the left- and right-wing parties. Rudolf worked to earn his place among the local proletariat, planting trees and hauling wheelbarrow loads of dirt to help shore up the riverbank in front of the clubhouse. He was referred to facetiously but affectionately as "Herr Doktor."

Rudolf soon took up with Ernst Goldmann. Goldmann was an unemployed high school dropout—he had attended Fürth's Israeli High School—who was estranged from his parents, Siegfried and Meta Goldmann, owners of a shoe shop on Schwabacherstrasse, just around the corner from the Benario residence. In addition, Ernst Goldmann was involved with the Communist Party.

In July, Rudolf was arrested during a street demonstration outside the Fürth employment office, where a belligerent crowd had been chanting, "Give us bread! Give us work!" He was charged, along with three other demonstrators, with violating the presidential decree against street violence.

At his trial, Rudolf readily admitted to his left-wing political affiliation, observing that the German Communist Party, of which he was not a member, was an officially registered organization that regularly participated in state and national elections, and was represented by delegates in both the state parliament in Munich and the Reichstag in Berlin. However, he denied any leadership responsibility in the demonstration. He insisted that he had been little more than a passive observer. The prosecutor asserted that Benario had been in proximity to the belligerent crowd and that following his arrest both the demonstration and the shouting subsided. He urged the judge to sentence the four men to three months in prison in accordance with Paragraph 2 of the presidential decree and, in addition, to fine Benario fifty marks for his leadership role. In the end, the judge dismissed the charges against the three other defendants but held Benario accountable, since he had not only expressed his "inner solidarity with the demonstrators" but also had "participated as long as possible" in the illegal gathering. The judge gave Benario the choice between eight days in prison or an eighty-mark fine.

Chastened by the experience, Rudolf appears to have withdrawn from political activism and devoted his attentions to completing his dissertation. Four months later, when the police intervened in another communist activity, Rudolf was notably absent. On that night, November, 23, 1931, the Fürth police raided the Golden Lamb restaurant and arrested thirty local communists, including Ernst Goldmann. At his trial, Goldmann, like Benario, reminded the judge of the legal status of the German Communist Party and argued that the gathering at the Golden Lamb had been nothing more than a meeting of party members, not a public demonstration, and thus was not in violation of the presidential decree. The judge acquitted Goldmann and the other twenty-nine defendants. But now both Goldmann and Benario were registered in police files.

The following autumn, Benario conducted the oral defense of his dissertation. On January 28, 1933, he was officially awarded a doctorate in political economy. Two days later, Adolf Hitler was appointed chancellor of Germany. On the evening of March 9, in the wake of elections the previous Sunday that saw the National Socialists claim nearly 44 percent of the vote nationally, a delegate to the Bavarian state parliament appeared on the balcony of the Fürth town hall and declared a "National Socialist revolution." "Also in Fürth, a city that was once Red and completely Jewified, we will make a clean and honest German city," he said. "As of today, the big cleanup of Bavaria begins!"

That night the streets echoed with the clatter of jackboots on cobblestones and the pounding of fists on doors as squads of local policemen, accompanied by storm troopers, moved through the town, arresting those they believed to be communists. Around 2:30 in the morning, they stormed the Benarios' second-floor apartment to take Rudolf Benario into protective custody. His parents objected, noting that their son was in bed with a 104-degree fever. The storm troopers ordered Rudolf out of bed, forced him to dress, then hurled him down the stairs. Neighbors heard screaming and shouting, then the dull thud of the young man tumbling down the stairwell. The next day, the *Fürther Anzeiger* reported that fifteen communists had been detained, among them "the all-too-well-known communist and Jew Benario." The brief news item was headlined "Peaceful Night in Fürth."

Two weeks after Rudolf was taken into custody, Leo learned that his teaching position had been terminated. "The retired editor and guest lecturer at the Nuremberg Professional School of Business and Social Sciences will be on leave for the Summer Semester 1933," the rector announced, "and his services will no longer be engaged after that point." There was no immediate explanation for the dismissal, but on Friday, April 7, the Law for the Restoration of the Professional Civil Service removed any potential administrative or judicial recourse. "To restore a national and professional civil service and to simplify administration, civil servants may be dismissed from office in accordance with the following regulations," the new law stipulated, "even when there would be no grounds for such action under the prevailing law." Civil servants who were not of Aryan descent were to be retired and those bearing honorary titles were to be "dismissed from their official status." The law provided an exception for non-Aryans "who fought at the Front for the German Reich or its Allies in the World War, or whose fathers or sons fell in the World War." As a peace advocate and a Jew who had spent the war years as an editor with the *Frankfurter Zeitung,* Leo had no grounds for appealing his dismissal. We do not know the exact sentiments that haunted the

Benario household from that day forward, but Victor Klemperer, a Jewish professor in Dresden who had fought in the war, certainly echoed representative apprehensions. "For the moment I am still safe, but as someone on the gallows, who has the rope around his neck, is safe," he noted in his diary in those days. "At any moment a new 'law' can kick away the steps on which I am standing and then I'm hanging."

On April 13, Leo sat at his desk drafting the letter to accompany the package of clothing and medications for his son. He knew Rudolf was strong-willed, opinionated, and occasionally aggressive, so he sought to strike a tone that might assuage any ire or irritation Rudolf's comportment might provoke among his keepers. As a former editor, Leo was sensitive to nuance in language, and he now sought to calibrate and measure his words in a letter that not only conveyed both respect for authority along with an understanding of rules and regulations, but also imparted a sense of paternal concern.

"To the Administration of the Dachau Concentration Camp," Leo wrote, "I kindly ask to give my son Rudolf Benario from the contents of this package those items that are permitted and perhaps to store for him the remaining items." Leo noted in particular his son's relatively frail health and expressed advanced appreciation for any "kindhearted updates" on his condition, "since with the exception of short intervals he has been suffering from bronchitis since November." He closed with a double courtesy, first with the traditional formality, "With high regard," followed by a subservient nod, "Most obediently yours," and sealed the missive with his two initials in an elegant and carefully rendered hand that suggested a man of refined manners and good order. For convenience, Leo appended a complete list of the package's contents.

That afternoon, the *Fürther Anzeiger* published a brief news item under the headline THREE COMMUNISTS SHOT TO DEATH DURING AN ATTEMPTED ESCAPE FROM THE DACHAU CONCENTRATION CAMP. The text read, "On Wednesday afternoon, according to a police report, four communists interned in Dachau attempted an escape. Since they did not respond to the guards' calls to halt, the guards fired on them, killing three of the communists and seriously wounding the fourth." The article did not mention names.

The *Amper-Bote* carried the story but included news of the anticipated Easter amnesty. "In these days, once again, several more detainees have been released from protective custody, including the Dachau workers Schwalbe, Schellkopf, and Zellner," the newspaper reported. It anticipated further releases in advance of the Easter holiday.

3

Wintersberger

THE NEXT MORNING, Good Friday, a day when many in Bavaria curtailed their work in observance of the solemn occasion, Josef Hartinger appeared in the office of Karl Wintersberger to report on the alleged failed escape attempts from the Dachau Concentration Camp. "I did not hesitate to give my opinion that the entire story of the escape was invented," Hartinger recalled. "I remember specifically that I said I was of the opinion that the three SS men had acted on instructions from the commandant."

After two years as the senior prosecutor for Munich II, Wintersberger had grown accustomed to Hartinger's instinctual reactions about investigations. But he knew that his deputy possessed "many years of experience in criminal legal practice and combines a quick mind, great intellectual agility and breadth with healthy judgment," as Hartinger's June 1931 performance evaluation noted. Hartinger's legal briefs were praised for their precision, clarity, and intelligence. His appearances both in departmental meetings as well as the courtroom were marked by "eloquence" with a generally "measured passion," except when confronted by injustice. Hartinger was known to slam files onto his desk, and colleagues recalled hearing his voice booming down the office corridors. Nevertheless, Hartinger was praised for the respect he showed toward superiors, colleagues, and subordinates, as well as the public at large. The black-and-white photograph stapled to Hartinger's personnel file shows a middle-aged man in suit and tie, slightly balding, with thick-framed spectacles and the onset of jowls. His jaw is set in a determined clench. There is something of a bulldog about him.

Wintersberger was older and more conservative than his deputy. He was twelve years away from retirement, widowed with one child, and in the final years of his career, looking ahead to the possibility of appointment as president of a district court and retirement in 1945 at age sixty-five. Wintersberger had begun his legal career under the monarchy and remained a royalist in spirit, obedient to and in the service of authority. Hartinger recalled that Wintersberger ran Munich II "in a mostly near-authoritarian manner." Wintersberger was exclusively responsible for the liaison with the state attorney general and the state justice minister, and retained signing authority for all Munich II memoranda and correspondence. "Rightfully so," Hartinger observed, "because he needed to have a complete overview, especially in political cases." Wintersberger had scored modestly on his law boards in 1907, compared with Hartinger's perfect score in 1926. Wintersberger, however, compensated for his academic limitations with hard work and "iron diligence." He and Hartinger enjoyed a "collegial" relationship.

As a deputy prosecutor for Munich I in the early 1920s, Wintersberger pursued his cases with resoluteness and a commitment to seeing justice rendered. It was a time when many in the Bavarian judiciary remained defiantly conservative and perilously antidemocratic, a point brought home by a controversial report, *Four Years of Political Murder,* published by Emil Gumbel in October 1922. In his study, this professor of statistics and former associate of Albert Einstein tracked the judicial proceedings for hundreds of murders per-petrated by right- and left-wing radicals between 1919 and 1922, and sought to hold individual judges and prosecutors accountable for lapses in judicial process. The Gumbel report, formally presented in a public session of the Reichstag, represented a devastating condemnation of the German judicial system in general, and the Munich I and Munich II jurisdictions in particular. "Of the thirty-five jurisdictions called to account, twenty-six did not respond, in particular in Munich, where most of the cases occurred," Gumbel reported. "Three hundred thirty political murders, of which four were perpetrated by the left and 326 by the right, were never pros-ecuted and remain unprosecuted today." Gumbel cautioned that such judicial negligence accompanied by the absence of individual accountability set a dangerous precedent that could lead to a spi-raling circle of public violence and undermine the foundations of democratic process and the future stability of the republic. "In another era, there was some political risk to committing murder, even a certain heroism," Gumbel asserted. "But with such leniency today, a person can kill without any risk of consequences."

Hitler underscored the Gumbel thesis a year later, on the night of November 8, 1923, when he fired a pistol into the ceiling of the Bürgerbräu beer hall in Munich and announced the overthrow of the Bavarian state government, with the goal of marching on Berlin, as Mussolini had marched on Rome the previous year, and establishing a fascist dictatorship in Germany. Hitler's plans came to an abrupt halt the following morning when a phalanx of state police and military fired on the right-wing rabble on Odeonsplatz, leaving eighteen dead and Hitler with a wrenched shoulder. The Bavarian judicial response confirmed Gumbel's worst expecta-tions. Since Hitler's stated goal was to topple the Weimar Republic, he could have been dispatched to the Reich Court in Leipzig, where a conviction for treason could have resulted in a death sentence. The botched beer hall enterprise, in fact, never made it beyond the Munich city limits, and so it was decided to try the defendants within the Munich I jurisdiction. Under the auspices of a sympathetic judge, Hitler transformed the monthlong trial into a media circus that concluded with a scandalously light sentence and an unrepentant defendant. "You may pronounce us guilty a thousand times over," Hitler proclaimed in his closing statement, "but the eternal goddess of the eternal court of history will smile and tear to shreds the brief of the state prosecutor and the sentence of this court, for she will acquit us." Hitler was given a sentence of only five years and was out of prison by Christmas.

A few weeks after Hitler's courtroom triumph, Karl Wintersberger and his Munich I colleagues were scheduled to prosecute the forty members of the *Stosstrupp Hitler* (Assault Troop Hitler, precursor to the SS) as co-conspirators for their role in the bungled putsch. This hard core of loyalists, who served as Hitler's beer hall protection squad, had spearheaded the failed putsch, blocking the entrances to the Bürgerbräu beer hall with machine guns, smashing the offices of the Social Democratic Party in downtown Munich, demolishing the printing press of the left-wing *Münchner Post,* and taking six Bavarian political leaders hostage. When the putsch collapsed, the Assault Troop members were arrested. Wintersberger was responsible for the investigation and preparation of the indictments.

Wintersberger made the same case for collective guilt against the Assault Troop that Warren Farr was to make two decades later in Nuremberg against the SS and its related entities. Like Farr, Wintersberger argued that the members knowingly and willingly participated in a joint criminal activity. "It is therefore not relevant in terms of the guilt of individual defendants," he argued, "whether and to what degree they were involved in individual actions."

On April 23, the opening day of the trial, the forty defendants paraded into the Munich Palace of Justice for what the media dubbed "the little Hitler trial." The Assault Troop members were in high spirits, catcalling and jeering at Wintersberger, then forty-three, as he entered the courtroom. Wintersberger was unmoved. He had prepared his indictments systematically and meticulously, defendant by defendant, fact by fact. While Hitler's trial had been marked by tirades, hyperbole, and repeated raucous interruptions by all parties, Wintersberger's prosecution was steady, measured, and precise in detailing hour by hour and man by man the defendants' complicity in the failed attempt "to eliminate through violence the Reich government and the Bavarian government, and to alter through violence the constitution of the German Reich and of the Free State of Bavaria."

Wintersberger knew that the forty Assault Troop members had met at the bowling alley of the Torbräu beer hall at six o'clock on the evening of November 8, 1923, boarded trucks in Balanstrasse a little while later, and arrived at the Bürgerbräu on Rosenheimerstrasse at 8:30. He also knew that Wilhelm Knörlein had positioned a machine gun on Rosenheimerstrasse, and Karl Fiehler and Emil Dannenberg each aimed a machine gun at the beer hall entrances. He knew that Josef Gerum led the assault into the hall. Wintersberger even noted the number of shattered windowpanes in the ransacked offices of the *Münchner Post*—380 by Wintersberger's count—and who was responsible for each action in descending order of culpability. He chronicled the Assault Troop's subsequent march the following day to Odeonsplatz, where they advanced with "the writer Adolf Hitler"—his legally registered profession—into the fusillade of police gunfire.

Wintersberger employed "all means of judicial rhetoric and sophistry," according to one defendant, to prove their culpability in the "collective crime of treason." Faced with the overwhelming, incontrovertible evidence, the judge, despite his evident sympathies for the defendants, was compelled to sentence all forty Assault Troop members to prison. The judge then exercised judicial prerogative and suspended the sentences, letting the unrepentant Nazis march triumphantly from the Palace of Justice.

Wintersberger remained undaunted. A week later, he returned

to court wielding an appellate decision overturning the verdict. According to the new ruling, the defendants had demonstrated "an exceptional measure of cruelty and brutality" and "absolutely no sign of regret." "It is necessary," Wintersberger argued, "to demonstrate to the defendants, who have not shown the slightest remorse, the seriousness of the legal system." Within a week, the entire Assault Troop was in Landsberg Prison to begin serving their sentences. The upended verdict inspired lasting admiration among many of Wintersberger's colleagues and the enduring enmity of the Munich-based National Socialists.

Now, a decade later, Wintersberger remarkably found many of these convicted beer hall putschists in government positions, with Hitler as chancellor and Hermann Göring, who had escaped prosecution in 1923 by fleeing across the border to Austria, as president of the Reichstag. Ironically, these men were now often forced to function within the constraints of governmental responsibility, ultimately accountable to President Hindenburg, who possessed the constitutional authority to appoint or dismiss the chancellor and his ministers at will. Two years earlier, Hindenburg had issued the presidential "Decree for Public Order" that criminalized the "terror against religious communities" or "language that was slanderous or malicious." In the face of a growing number of assaults on Jews, Hitler was compelled publicly to denounce storm trooper excesses and to call for them to cease and desist in their attacks. Himmler was also forced to rise to the Jews' defense. "For us, the citizen of the Jewish faith is as much a citizen as those not of the Jewish faith," he said during a March 12 press conference on protective custody, "and his life and his property are equally protected. We recognize no differences in this regard."

On April 13, 1933, the Nazi newspaper the *Völkischer Beobachter* underscored the seriousness of intent in a report on the murder of a Jewish lawyer earlier that week. "In Chemnitz the Jewish lawyer Dr. Wiener was seized in his apartment by three men in green uniforms with SA armbands and abducted in an automobile. On Tuesday his body was found in the Wiederauer Meadow with a gunshot wound to his head." The paper stated that it had clearly been an act of murder rather than a robbery, noting that "valuables and 440 reichsmarks in cash were found on his body." The local National Socialists had urged their members to cooperate with the police in identifying and apprehending the three killers, the article continued, noting that the party was reviewing its membership rosters from the previous six months, looking for potential suspects. They also assigned storm troopers to man roadblocks around Chemnitz inspecting cars and checking identity papers, and released detailed descriptions of the suspected perpetrators. Two of them were "tall, slender, and blond" and the third "heavyset with a narrow, somewhat pointed face and glasses." All three were in their twenties. The newspaper emphasized to its readers that nothing less than the reputation of the National Socialist German Workers' Party was at stake. "By all appearances, this is a case of provocateurs who could either be outside or within our ranks," it observed, "and are seeking to discredit our movement."

A day later, Wintersberger sat at his desk across from his deputy, Hartinger, who was insisting that Jews were being executed in a concentration camp that was being run under the auspices of Himmler. Despite their differing natures and investigative styles, Wintersberger and Hartinger in their two years together in Munich II had invariably arrived at the same conclusions, but on this occasion Wintersberger curtly dismissed his deputy's suspicions. Wintersberger knew firsthand the Nazi potential for violence. He also thought he knew their limitations. *"Das machen die nicht,"* he told Hartinger flatly. Not even Nazis would do that.

Hartinger knew when he had reached the limit with his superior. But he had looked into Wäckerle's cold blue eyes and fathomed his capacity for atrocity. He knew Wintersberger was wrong on the Dachau killings. He also knew that a criminal indictment, especially one involving chain-of-command responsibility and multiple murders, demanded hard and incontrovertible evidence. It needed to meet the Wintersberger standard. Meanwhile, the surviving victim of the shooting, thirty-two-year-old Munich salesman Erwin Kahn, lay in a hospital bed across town, fully conscious and talking.

4

Witness to Atrocity

A T 11:30 ON THE EVENING of April 12, a man was brought
into the emergency room of the Munich Surgical Clinic at
Nussbaumstrasse 35. His face was horrifically disfigured by two
gunshot wounds. One bullet had penetrated his skull just above his
cheekbone, bruising the surrounding tissue and blinding his left
eye, which showed heavy bleeding around the cornea. According
to the emergency room report, the ruined eye was "distended" as
a result of the injury. The other eye showed subcutaneous bleeding
but was fully intact. The man was lucid. He related an incident that
the attending physician appended to his medical record:

> The injured man stated: On April 12, the patient and three other
> Jews were called to an urgent work assignment. While the eve-
> ning meal was being distributed, someone suddenly called:
> "The four Jews should step forward." When they were being
> led away, suddenly shots were fired [at them] from [a distance
> of] 2–3 meters. The injured man fell to the ground but did not
> lose consciousness and shortly thereafter he was lifted up by
> the guards and since he was wounded in the head was taken for

medical treatment to Dr. Welsch in Dachau. There his wounds
were treated and he was taken to the hospital in Dachau and
from there to the Surgical Clinic.

Erwin Kahn could not have been delivered into more capable
hands. The Nussbaumstrasse clinic was Bavaria's leading hospital for reconstructive surgery and, indeed, one of the country's
foremost surgical centers for more than a century. It was here
that Joseph Lister pioneered the use of liquid antiseptic—until
then, medical tools were sterilized by open flame—reducing surgical mortality rates by as much as 70 percent and establishing a
medical standard for the entire profession. It was also here that
Dr. Erik Lexer, a student of Berlin's legendary surgeon Ernst von
Bergmann, compiled his two-volume landmark compendium *Comprehensive Reconstructive Surgery,* which served as the profession's
reference work around the world. The hospital treated as many
as two hundred ambulatory patients each day, most of whom had
suffered household and work-related accidents, though there were
occasional victims of street violence as well.

For Kahn, the late-night arrival in the Nussbaumstrasse clinic
marked the end of a monthlong ordeal that had begun early in the
afternoon of March 11. Kahn was a gentle-spirited man who had
never been particularly political, but the sight of brownshirted
Nazis hoisting a swastika flag over a state office compelled him to
act. He was joined by nearly fifty other fellow Bavarians and the
scuffle turned into a melee, as a result of which Kahn was taken
into protective custody along with the others. He spent the next
three days in the Ettstrasse police station and was then transferred
to Stadelheim Prison on the outskirts of Munich. He was living
apart from his wife, Eva, but she visited him there daily for the next
ten days, bringing him fresh clothing and updating him on their
young daughter.

On March 22, Kahn was among the first detainees to be transferred to the newly opened concentration camp outside Dachau. "You probably came to Stadelheim today and heard this time that I was forced to change to my current, and rather undesirable, domicile," he wrote Eva. "I am now in Dachau and specifically in a building in the former gunpowder factory." Kahn explained that he was still awaiting a formal interrogation to determine exactly why he was being held, but assured her that all was well. "There is no need for any fear since I am not a party member and never had any function, as you know," he wrote. His only real complaint was the cold floors in the barracks. He asked his wife to send "thick socks" along with shaving supplies and cigarettes. "I am only curious how long this thing will go on for, until we, or at least I am interrogated," he wrote. "I don't want to just eat and sleep and wait, but would like to get back to my job. In any event, please have no worries." He added a postscript. Eva should not have any concerns about their financial situation. He had been told by the camp officials that either the city or the state would provide a subsidy to the families of detainees for the duration of their incarceration.

About a week later, Kahn sent a second letter. He thanked his wife for the food she had sent and again expressed his desire to have the situation resolved as soon as possible. "I have but a single wish, to finally be interrogated so that things are clarified," he wrote. "I was not in any party and was not a capitalist. What do they want from me? I am trying to keep my head high." Eva knew her husband to be both patient and optimistic, but understood the situation was wearying if not worrying.

A few days later, Kahn wrote his parents. He thanked them for a food parcel, informing them that on April 1 he had officially requested an interrogation to clarify matters. He urged them not to worry. "I assure you once again that I don't know why I was arrested. In my entire life I was never in a party, and was just arrested on the street by an SA man. The main thing though is that I am still healthy, which helps me keep my head high. In general

I cannot complain. I ask you not to worry about me too much: I hope!! to be free before too long."

Five days later, authority for the concentration camp was transferred from the Bavarian state police to the SS. The following afternoon, Erwin Kahn mistakenly responded to Steinbrenner's call for "Kahn!" and was taken outside the compound with the three other Jews, and shot in the face. Erspenmüller sauntered over, his gun drawn, but someone screamed for him to stop. Erspenmüller hesitated, then relaxed his pistol. Kahn was lifted from the ground and carried back to the footbridge, then to the camp infirmary. An ambulance was called and Kahn was transported to the local hospital in Dachau, and from there to the Nussbaumstrasse clinic.

"Average-sized man with somewhat lowered blood pressure," the attending physician recorded on Kahn's arrival. He noted that the patient had suffered significant bruising and bleeding from multiple gunshots, observing, "A bullet wound over the left cheekbone has already been operated on." He recorded the damage to the left eye. Since his right eye was completely intact, Kahn could "clearly see those standing around him. There was no sign of unconsciousness on arrival."

Kahn was treated and placed in intensive care. He remained stable throughout the night. "Condition is basically unchanged," the physician recorded that Friday. "The patient remains fully conscious. Slight rise in temperature." On Saturday, the clinic informed Eva that her husband had been injured and wished to see her. She rushed to the hospital and found her husband lying in bed two in Hall 126, a sixteen-bed ward with bars on the windows and two storm troopers at the door. When they refused her entry, she summoned the attending physician, Dr. Hecker, who curtly dispatched the guards and led her to her husband's bed. She spent the next several hours at her husband's bedside. He described the shootings in detail. He said he watched as an SS guard raised his pistol, took aim at Benario, and fired. Benario collapsed, then Goldmann, and then suddenly he himself was struck by bullets, Kahn said. "My husband went on to explain that he then put his hands over his face and fell to the ground," Eva remembered. "He had no idea what happened next because he lost consciousness." Afterward, Eva consulted with Dr. Hecker. He informed her that her husband had managed well through the operation and would probably be fine, though he could well suffer from some paralysis as a result of the injuries. She departed, intending to return the next day.

"Fever rising. The patient is somewhat dazed, the injuries look good. In general no change in the clinical results," the medical record noted. "In the evening the patient is restless and no longer answers properly." Kahn's condition deteriorated with increasing rapidity as the night wore on. His breathing grew labored. His throat, clotted with blood, began to close. His sinus passages filled with pus from an infection. In the early hours of Easter Sunday, he began to fail, finally expiring at four o'clock in the morning.

AS PREDICTED, Easter proved to be a festive day, with clear skies and mild weather. Pageants, processions, and celebratory masses took place across this most Catholic corner of Germany. In the Dachau Concentration Camp, a barrack was outfitted as a chapel to make good on Gauleiter Wagner's promise that mass would be available for those detainees who could not be home in time to celebrate the occasion with their families. Since many of the detainees were communists, only twenty-eight of the camp's 539 detainees took advantage of the administrative beneficence. "Nevertheless, these twenty-eight as a 'small flock' received this moving hour of religious service with deepest gratitude," Father Friedrich Pfanzelt reported afterward, "and were so happy for every kind word that the priest was able to offer them, both collectively and individually."

News of the four dead men at Dachau came to their families in Munich, Nuremberg, and Fürth in small, painful doses. In Nuremberg, Bernhard Kolb, who was responsible for the city's Jewish affairs, first learned of Arthur Kahn's death when he received a request from the Dachau camp administration to retrieve Kahn's body. The corpse arrived by hearse in a sealed coffin. Suspicious, Kolb had the coffin opened and called in a local physician to perform an autopsy. The physician discovered a gruesome postmortem intrusion. The flesh around the bullet holes had been gouged and sliced away. "In my opinion and that of the doctor," Kolb later noted, "this was done because the camp administration wanted to conceal the fact that the bullets that killed Kahn had been shot at close range."

News of the shooting brought grief and dismay to the home of shopkeeper Levi Kahn and his wife Marta. Arthur was the oldest of their four children. He was an exceptionally bright and talented young man. He had been a state chess champion and had studied medicine at the University of Würzburg with the intent of entering the emerging field of cancer research. Like Benario, Kahn had been a political activist at the university, attempting to counter the rising tide of National Socialism among the students. Kahn was planning to attend the prestigious medical school at the University of Edinburgh in Scotland and had returned to Würzburg only briefly to retrieve his student records when he was recognized by a local Nazi. He was taken into protective custody and dispatched to Dachau on April 11, on the same transport as Benario and Goldmann. The manifest identifies Kahn incorrectly as a "communist functionary."

"When the news came that Arthur had been 'shot trying to escape,' my parents knew right away that he had been intentionally shot," Kahn's younger brother, Lothar, recalled. "I remember my father had to pay money before they would release his body." When word of Kahn's death reached the university in Würzburg, an administrator noted his passing on his student record: "According to newspaper reports, shot while escaping from the Dachau Concentration Camp."

Whatever rift life had torn between Ernst Goldmann and his parents was not healed in death. Siegfried and Meta Goldmann left it to Ernst's brother to travel from Denmark to identify the corpse and arrange for it to be interred in the New Cemetery in Fürth.

On the Tuesday after Easter, Leo Benario laid his son to rest. That day, he published a tribute to him in the *Fürther Tagblatt*. "With great sadness life was cut short for our dear son, brother, and fiancé, who was so filled with a thirst for knowledge and a life filled with such promise," he wrote.

That same day, Dr. Flamm conducted an autopsy on Erwin Kahn in the company of another physician, Dr. Müller. The cause of death was determined to be an acute infection of the bronchial passages and a high-grade inflammation of the larynx resulting from the two bullet wounds. The two physicians also determined there had been internal bleeding in the muscles around the larynx and on the left side of the chest. They underscored the fact that this internal bleeding was unrelated to the bullet wounds.* Kahn's corpse was interred in the Jewish Cemetery in Munich the following day.

That Thursday, a week after Hartinger received the call about the Dachau shootings, Eva Kahn appeared in his office to report Erwin's murder. She told Hartinger of her husband's ordeal at the Dachau Concentration Camp. "Hartinger was very nice to me and I came away with the definite impression that he was not a Nazi and had nothing in common with the perpetrators," she later recalled. She told Hartinger that while her husband had been unhappy with the situation at Dachau, he was willing to be patient until he was released. She had letters to prove it. More important, she told Hartinger what she had learned of the shooting incident from her husband in the hospital. The newspaper accounts of a failed escape

---

* Dr. Wolfgang Eisenmenger, professor emeritus of the Institute for Forensic Medicine at the University of Munich, has studied the Erwin Kahn autopsy and observes that by underscoring the absence of a connection between the multiple instances of internal bleeding, Dr. Flamm and Dr. Müller may have wanted to alert authorities to the possibility that the SA guards in the clinic were "not uninvolved" in Kahn's death.

attempt were untrue, she insisted. Her husband and the three other men had not attempted to escape. They had been led into the woods and gunned down in cold blood. She wanted Hartinger to press murder charges against the commandant and his men. She was willing to testify. "Nevertheless, [Hartinger] advised me, given the circumstances, to do nothing," she later recalled, "since there would be the risk that, if I pursued the matter further, I would also be arrested, and, as he said, might possibly end up on the same path as my husband."

Hartinger knew that without Wintersberger's support, he could not help Eva pursue justice, but he also knew that negligence was a frequent and common consort to arrogance. He was certain Wäckerle would kill again. He needed only to be patient and vigilant.

PART II

. . . UNTIL PROVEN . . .

5

The State of Bavaria

THE HEADLINE-MAKING NEWS for the *Völkischer Beobachter* on the day that Benario, Goldmann, and the two Kahns were shot was the appointment of the new state government in Bavaria. For the previous six weeks, since the arson attack on the Berlin Reichstag and the imposition of a presidential emergency decree, the Free State of Bavaria had been overseen by a caretaker government.

On the last Monday in February, fire was seen in the glass-domed and wood-paneled plenary hall of the Reichstag shortly after 9 p.m. The alarm was sounded immediately, but by the time the first fire-fighting units arrived, the flames had already consumed the plush red carpets and were churning across the delegates' velvet seats and scaling the oak-paneled walls, filling the chamber with heat and smoke. Shortly after 9:30, the vast dome collapsed. Shards of glass crashed into the inferno below. Flames leaped through the emptied steel frame into the night sky. Ten thousand Berliners gathered to watch a dozen fire engines battle the blaze in the winter chill, while two boats equipped with water cannons joined the desperate fray from the Spree. The conflagration had come a week in advance of national elections intended to break a gridlock in the Reichstag, which President Hindenburg had suspended, and to serve as a referendum on the Hitler government after it had been in office just over four weeks.

Suspicion and recrimination abounded. "That can only be an attack by the communists on our new government!" Hermann Göring, head of the Reichstag, claimed. The communists blamed the Nazis in return. "The burning of this symbol of free parliamentary government was so providential for the Nazis that it was believed they staged the fire themselves," Robert Jackson was to observe thirteen years later at Nuremberg. "Certainly when we contemplate their known crimes, we cannot believe they would shrink from mere arson." Some suspected Göring, whose residence was said to be connected to the Reichstag by a subterranean corridor. Others accused the Social Democrats, who were said (incorrectly) to have fled en masse to France. The next morning, during an emergency cabinet meeting, Göring cited a communist plot, allegedly discovered in a police raid, that provided for even greater disruption. "Based on the confiscated materials, it is clear that the communists wanted to create terror groups," the cabinet minutes record, "that they intended to burn down public buildings, poison public kitchens, even at the cost of sacrificing their own supporters." The terror plot, Göring said, also included provisions to sabotage power networks, rail systems, and industrial facilities, and to take hostage prominent persons as well as their wives and children.

Hindenburg called Hitler into his office and questioned him about rumors that the arson attack had been orchestrated by storm troopers as a pretext for arresting communists in advance of Sunday's elections. "Hitler said they were tendentious inventions by the foreign press," state secretary Otto Meissner recalled, "and referred to the investigation protocols of the police and prosecutors, which showed strong evidence of communist plans to overthrow the government through terrorist acts, armed uprisings, and strikes." Hitler urged the president to issue an emergency decree empowering the government to take security measures to avert a potentially wide-scale communist uprising.*

During the previous two years, Hindenburg had repeatedly exercised executive authority, guaranteed by Article 48 of the constitution, to issue presidential decrees. He had restricted the sale of firearms and suspended the right to public assembly. He banned the wearing of Nazi uniforms and the display of swastika banners in public. In March 1931, he responded to the desecration of synagogues and increasingly frequent attacks on Jews by mandating a minimum three-month prison sentence for anyone "who insults or desecrates establishments, customs, or objects relating to religious communities recognized by public law." Now, a day after the Reichstag had gone up in flames and with Hitler expressing alarm over even greater potential disruption, Hindenburg issued a "Presidential Decree for the Protection of the People and the State."

The emergency decree provided for the suspension of seven articles of the constitution protecting civil liberties, "including freedom of the press, freedom of assembly and association, as well as intervention in the mail, postal, and telegraphic and telephonic communications, orders of house searches and seizures."

While most people focused on the implications of the emergency decree on the civil liberties of the country's 65 million citizens, the state government of Bavaria was concerned by the less dramatic but more ominous implications of Article 2. "If adequate measures are not taken to reestablish public safety and order," the paragraph stated, "the Reich government can temporarily assume the responsibilities from the state authorities as necessary."

Bavaria's prime minister Heinrich Held assured Berlin there

---

* The attack on the Reichstag appears to have been a renegade act by the twenty-four-year-old Dutch communist Marinus van der Lubbe, but it remains unclear to this day whether he acted alone or was involved with a larger communist plot or possibly a National Socialist conspiracy. The alleged communist plan for massive disruptions presented in the cabinet meeting was a Nazi forgery.

was no need for a Reich governor in his state. The state could manage its own affairs without interference from Berlin. Held was a measured, conservative man, a trained lawyer and a founder of the Bavarian People's Party who had ruled the Free State of Bavaria with elegance and equanimity for nearly a decade. In a state legendary for its beer hall radicals, Held stood above the political fray in his top hat, tails, and walking stick. Many thought he should run for president. Held was also one of Germany's most outspoken advocates of local autonomy, who viewed with suspicion any dictate coming from Berlin. In 1919, when the newly minted Weimar constitution was being hailed for its accommodation of democratic values and structures, Held saw only peril. "Naturally, the conditions incorporated in the German national constitution are very flexible and unclear," he cautioned, "and open wide doors for skepticism about their legal nature and content, thus putting into question their possible impact on state law."

Held was particularly disquieted by Article 48 of the Weimar constitution, the "emergency decree article," that accorded the president the power to suspend the Reichstag and rule by decree. He saw in it the "seeds of dictatorship." Held had his apprehensions confirmed in 1931 when, amid growing political and economic crisis, Hindenburg exercised those powers by issuing forty-four presidential decrees, and when in the following year he dismissed three chancellors in quick succession. Adolf Hitler was his fourth chancellor in less than seven months. "The recent developments in public affairs in Germany are causing the Bavarian State Government great anxiety," Held wrote to Hindenburg. Held was especially disquieted by "rumors" about the imminent "abolition of state sovereignty." Held knew that the prime minister of Saxony had already written to Hindenburg expressing similar concerns, and wanted the president to know that anxieties ran equally high in the Free State of Bavaria. He appealed to Hindenburg as "guardian of constitutional law and justice" to stand as the bulwark for state sovereignty. Held's request was met with a disquieting silence. Two weeks later, the Reichstag erupted in flames.

While many viewed Hitler's panic as calculated histrionics masking a National Socialist appetite for power, Held saw it additionally as northern imperialism, an attempt to assert Prussian authority over a Bavarian dominion. It was a centuries-old story that had seen generations of Hohenzollerns and Wittelsbachs battling over power and territory so fiercely that in 1805 Bavaria sided with Napoleon against Prussia. After German unification in 1871, Bavaria retained its own railway system, its own postal service, its own monarchy, and its own military. In 1914, Bavarian soldiers marched to war in Bavarian regiments commanded by Bavarian generals under the authority of Bavaria's Royal Ministry of War. In November 1918, when the monarchy collapsed, Bavaria bolted from the Reich, declaring itself an independent country, and returned reluctantly the following year as part of the Weimar Republic with a special constitutional provision for reestablishing the Wittelsbach monarchy in times of emergency. When Hitler proposed installing Franz von Epp as Reich governor of Bavaria, Held threatened to invoke the monarchy clause and recall Prince Ruprecht to the Bavarian throne. There was serious concern among Hitler's ministers that the decrees could precipitate a Bavarian exit from the Reich.

Three days later, when the national elections delivered the National Socialists more than 40 percent of the electorate, Hitler moved to break the back of Bavarian independence. "We are masters of the Reich and of Prussia now, all others have withered to the ground in defeat," Hitler's future propaganda minister, Joseph Goebbels, crowed in his diary that evening. "Our success in these elections really hit new heights in southern Germany. This is especially gratifying because we now have the opportunity to crush the separatist federalism there." Hitler huddled with his key lieutenants to plan to eliminate this last bastion of state independence in the Reich. "In the evening we all met with the Führer and it is decided that we will now tackle Bavaria," Goebbels wrote in his diary three days later. "Although some squeamish souls who do not belong to the party continue to object, waffling about resistance of the Bavarian People's Party, etc., we are firmly convinced that Herr Held will not play the hero."* A plan was designed to destabilize the state through orchestrated public disorder as a means of invoking Paragraph 2 of the emergency decree and installing a Reich governor.

On the morning of March 9, Held was in his office in the Palais Montgelas when he heard a disturbance outside his window. Several hundred storm troopers had gathered on the square, shouting, chanting, and singing "The Horst Wessel Song." Shortly before noon, three top Hitler lieutenants, Munich gauleiter Adolf Wagner, the SA leader Ernst Röhm, and SS chief Himmler, marched into Held's office in jackboots and storm trooper uniforms. They pointed to the crowd outside the window. Röhm expressed concern about public safety, invoking Article 2 of the Hindenburg emergency decree. It was time, they told Held, to install Epp as Reich governor. Wagner slapped Held's desk with his whip. Held rose from the table. "I categorically reject this request," he said. "A decision like that cannot even be taken by me alone. I will convene a cabinet meeting for 2:30 this afternoon. I have nothing else to say, gentlemen!"

By then, however, storm troopers from across the state were thronging Munich. They arrived by train, bus, and automobile. Some reportedly came by bicycle. They moved through the streets, both celebrating and menacing, and converged on the square before Held's office. At 12:30, two Hitler Youth scrambled atop the old city gate on Karlsplatz and unfurled a swastika banner. By one o'clock, a second banner fluttered over the city hall. Röhm, Wagner, and Himmler returned to Held's office at four o'clock, this

---

* Goebbels was making wordplay with Held's name, which means "hero" in German. Goebbels had written, *"dass Herr Held kein Held sein wird."*

time with Epp. "The cabinet has decided not to follow your recommendation," Held informed them. "We will not be pressured by the SA." Two hours later, despite Held's decision, the Nazis proclaimed triumph. "General von Epp has just assumed complete power in Bavaria," Max Amann, the publisher of the *Völkischer Beobachter*, told a crowd from the balcony of the city hall. "Reichsführer SS Heinrich Himmler has assumed command of the police."

Held telegraphed Hindenburg requesting support from the Reichswehr Division VII garrisoned in Munich. Hindenburg wrote back suggesting that Held install a Reich governor. When Held dispatched a second request to Hindenburg, the response came from a Hitler associate, Interior Minister Hans Frick. "Since the restructuring of Germany's political situation has caused some disruptions within the population, public order and safety in Bavaria seem to be in jeopardy," Frick telegraphed Held at 8:15 that evening. "I shall therefore assume the responsibility of Senior Federal State Authority of Bavaria for the Reich's government, in accordance with §2 of the Public and State Protection Decree. Furthermore, I transfer the executive authority to General Ritter von Epp in Munich."

Two hours later, Epp appeared on Odeonsplatz before a sea of brownshirts and sympathizers that extended down Ludwigstrasse. The crowd was jubilant. "In order to prevent the spread of any potential rumors about Prussia or northern Germany forcing anything unfavorable upon Bavaria," the aging general said with awkward assurance, "I would like to remind you that the original path to our current liberation was led from Munich, that men like Hitler and Frick too come from southern Germany, and that nobody will ever dare to even consider restricting Bavaria's rights and that which it has historically, rightfully, and proudly earned."

Held ignored Frick's appointment of Epp. The Hindenburg decree explicitly stipulated that it was left to the individual state prime ministers to appoint Reich governors. But the next morning, when Held arrived at work, he found the Palais Montgelas swarming with brownshirts. An American journalist witnessed the "relentless march of the Nazi steamroller" that spring as brownshirts, "bristling with swastikas and other insignia, their revolvers dangling in plain sight from their hips," swarmed public offices across the country. "These rough characters contrasted ludicrously with the officials left over from the pre-Nazi era," he observed, "who were going about as if ashamed of their ceremonial toggery, looking—and doubtless feeling—like fish out of water." Held served out the week. On Saturday, he departed Munich to "visit" his brother in Switzerland. Shortly thereafter he resigned as prime minister.

On April 12, the day of the first murders at Dachau, Epp appeared amid the provincial baroque splendor of the Palais Montgelas to install his new state ministers. The aging general was a rough-hewn man who had earned his aristocratic title the old-fashioned way, through battlefield slaughter, and at age sixty still preferred the trench helmet to the top hat. In June 1916, as Colonel Franz Epp, a soldier of fortune and the son of a middling Bavarian landscape painter, he had led an assault with flamethrowers and hand grenades that brought him to the outskirts of Verdun. The French held, but Epp emerged from the battle with an Iron Cross First Class and the title "Ritter von Epp," or Knight of Epp. In the spring of 1919, having returned to Bavaria at war's end, he marched on Munich to crush a Bolshevik coup with bloody vigor, slaughtering hundreds of communists while his own soldiers suffered only minor losses. His appointment as Reich governor was hailed in the right-wing press as "Epp's Second March on Munich."

Now, standing in the Palais Montgelas, Epp mustered his new ministers into service. Adolf Wagner was to serve as minister of interior. The Nazi Party lawyer Dr. Hans Frank was the new minister of justice. The Nazi SA leader, Ernst Röhm, was made "minister without portfolio," as was an intimate Hitler associate, Hermann Esser, who was eventually placed in charge of tourism.

Hans Schemm, the founder of the National Socialist Teachers' League, was appointed minister of culture. Heinrich Held's former post of prime minister, which Epp had occupied for the past month, was filled by Ludwig Siebert, the Nazi mayor of Lindau, who was assigned double duty as minister of finance. The appointments offered no surprises, since the new ministers were all Nazis and most had been serving in caretaker roles for the past month. The only real news came at the end when Epp announced that the position of the state foreign minister would not be filled and that the ministry itself was being dissolved. The Palais Montgelas was to serve henceforth as the offices of the Reich governor. The Free State of Bavaria was no longer free. It was not even a state.

The following day, Epp hosted a reception for the ministers in his offices. On this occasion, he dispensed with formality. He was relaxed, even sentimental. "Everything that has been achieved in the past weeks would have been impossible if my colleagues had not been members of the 'movement' with the same soul and the same heartbeat, and had not been dedicated in complete harmony to the same ambitions and ideas," he told them. The elimination of Bavaria's ministry for foreign affairs, he said, would now permit the state to cooperate fully with the national government. "We are delighted to have been part of this development that sprang from the mind of our Führer and from the Reich president," he said, "and that has been recognized as the best and most fortunate solution for Germany." Epp envisioned "a thriving Bavaria in a strong Reich." The general closed his remarks with a heartfelt *"Sieg Heil!"* to the German people, to the Nazi movement, and, of course, to Adolf Hitler.

As always in Bavaria, the final word was reserved for the archbishop of Munich and Freising. "We owe the former Bavarian State Government our indelible, everlasting gratitude for protecting our homeland from the threats of communism and Bolshevism over the past decade," Cardinal Faulhaber wrote to Heinrich Held in those same days. "We equally owe our thanks to them for their efforts regarding our religion and customs, as well as the recovery of the socioeconomic situation of our people." Two days later, Faulhaber dispatched a "pastoral instruction" to his clergy reminding them of their obligations to respect the authority of the state, but underscoring the need to "to call a mistake a mistake, to call an injustice an injustice," and to reject those "cultural-political ideologies" that violate "the convictions of our conscience." He said violent transgressions should not be glossed "with a simple yes and an Amen."

FROM HIS SECOND-FLOOR OFFICE at Prielmayrstrasse 5, just across Karlsplatz from the Palace of Justice, Hartinger observed the political tumult of March and early April with dismay. He was a born-and-bred Bavarian and a card-carrying member of Heinrich Held's Bavarian People's Party, with an aversion to the National Socialist movement that dated back to his days as a student at Maximilian University. "Right after the putsch of November 11, 1923, I participated publicly against Hitler's followers in mass demonstrations in the Ludwigstrasse area in Munich," Hartinger recalled. In one confrontation on Odeonsplatz, Hartinger found himself surrounded by belligerents. "They called me a 'little Jew,' and twice I was nearly beaten to the ground," he said. He continued his opposition to the National Socialists with equal resolve as a junior prosecutor with Munich I, where he prosecuted infractions as Wintersberger had done a decade earlier.

On March 9, Hartinger had watched from his office window as throngs of storm troopers streamed down Prielmayrstrasse from the train station toward the Palais Montgelas and unfurled the giant swastika banner from the old town gate across the square. That same evening, elegant Theatinerstrasse, where Hartinger lived "nicely but inexpensively" in a fourth-floor apartment, was mobbed with storm troopers on their way to hear Epp's victory speech at Odeonsplatz. But for all Munich's street-level drama, the rising brown tide of National Socialism sweeping the country that spring caused barely a ripple in the offices and corridors at Prielmayrstrasse 5. By early April, there was but a single swastika lapel pin to be seen in Munich II. It belonged to Anton Heigl, an ambitious young deputy prosecutor who had been a fervent Social Democrat with a notable disdain for the National Socialist movement, especially the brutish storm troopers, but following Hitler's appointment as chancellor that January quickly changed political color, his sights set on promotion. The Heigl conversion chastened Hartinger and his two senior Munich II colleagues, Hans Hechtel and Josef Wintrich. "Whenever the three of us were having a conversation, as generally happens in any office, and Heigl would approach," Hartinger recalled, "we immediately changed our conversation if it was dealing with anything political, which in those days, of course, was usually the case."

Hartinger did not think that the new government was as bad as it could have been. Hitler had clearly kept the worst of his cronies at bay. The fanatical Julius Streicher remained in Nuremberg as editor of *Der Stürmer*. Even the choice of Epp as Reich governor was clearly a compromise. He was the only Reich governor in the country who was not also serving as a Gauleiter. More reassuring still, Epp, though certainly hard-bitten, ruthless, and antidemocratic, was more interested in public order than political ideology.

Hartinger was particularly heartened by the choice of Ludwig Siebert as Bavaria's prime minister and finance minister. Siebert, following his career as a judge, had already spent successful years as mayor of Lindau and Rothenburg ob der Tauber. Hartinger trusted in Siebert's sound judgment. Most important, Siebert was a latecomer to the National Socialist movement. Like Epp, he had previously been a member of the Bavarian People's Party. Siebert had joined Hitler's party just two years earlier as the National Socialists began making strides in elections. He was more a political opportunist than a Nazi ideologue, and again, like Epp, a devout Roman Catholic.

But two appointments troubled Hartinger deeply: Wagner as interior minister and Himmler as chief of police. Both men were cruel, arrogant, and ruthless, indifferent to laws or regulations. Hartinger was particularly troubled by Himmler's overlapping competencies. As chief of the Bavarian state police, Himmler controlled the state security forces. As Reichsführer of the SS, he controlled the Nazi Party's elite security forces. "It was naïve to think that anybody in his right mind who knew Himmler and the SS—even at the most superficial level—could ever trust him," Hartinger believed. Worse still, Himmler had installed his twenty-eight-year-old assistant, Reinhard Heydrich, as the new head of Department VI, the state police's security service. Heydrich suddenly had access to the secret police files for the entire Bavarian state, a dangerous intrusion by a private security force into the state structure. It was a model that Hitler ultimately expanded to a national level with perilous consequences, as Warren Farr was to observe twelve years later in Nuremberg: "Thus, through Himmler's dual capacity as Reichsführer SS, and as police chief, and through Heydrich's dual capacity as head of the Nazi intelligence unit and the state political police, a unified personal command of the SS and political police forces was achieved.* The working partnership between the Gestapo, the criminal police, and the Nazi Party intelligence unit under the direction of the Reichsführer SS resulted in the end in repressive and unrestrained police activity."

But in April 1933, Hartinger still retained his faith in the resilience of judicial structures. They had survived the collapse of the empire and endured the political and economic travails of twelve

---

* Hartinger made a similar observation but identified three overlapping capacities. "Himmler had authority over the SS as well as the political police in the Wittelsbach Palace in Briennerstrasse," he noted. "And not just these, but also, since he was police commander in Munich, all of the police in Munich as well, and thus had to be obeyed whenever he gave personal orders relating to police measures in the concentration camp."

years of the Weimar Republic. Certainly they would outlast the Hitler government. Somewhat reassuring for Hartinger was the appointment of Dr. Hans Frank as Bavaria's new minister of justice. Although clearly a member of the National Socialists, as a trained attorney Frank appeared to have an abiding commitment to the rule of law. "Tell me what the position of a judge is in a state structure and I will tell you its value," Frank was to tell the Nuremberg tribunal. "We are talking about one of the highest cultural achievements of Europe." In his most famous case as a defense attorney, the 1930 trial of three officers accused of conspiring in a pro-Nazi military coup, Frank brought Hitler to the witness stand and extracted a public commitment to respect legal processes. "I shall strive to come to power by legal means," Hitler swore in court, "and after the assumption of power I shall rule by legal means, so help me God." Frank saw this "oath of legality" (*Legalitätseid*) as a landmark moment in his client's political life.

Following his appointment as state minister of justice, Frank demonstrated similar respect for the Bavarian judiciary. "I assumed responsibility for a generally clean judicial administration in the traditional sense of the word," he recalled, "changing nothing in the ministry bureaucracy that was staffed with thoroughly qualified, first-rate experts." While offices and ministries across the country were restaffed with National Socialists, an estimated 200,000 across the country, Frank brought with him a single trusted colleague, Josef Bühler, and eventually hired two or three additional jurists, all of them with perfect scores in their law school examinations, none of them members of the Nazi Party.

Hartinger took comfort in knowing that men like Frank and Siebert, and even Epp, all Roman Catholic, all conservative, all loyal to Bavaria in blood or at least in spirit, were responsible for the state of Bavaria. "I considered all of them, even Frank, at least at that time and in that context, men of just and fair reason," Hartinger would later note. "From what we understood of Frank at the time, he too despised these murders in the concentration camp."

6

Rumors from the
Würm Mill Woods

HITLER HAD BEEN in power only a few weeks when rumors of Nazi atrocity began to proliferate. In the Baltic port city of Königsberg, a Jewish merchant named Max Neumann was said to have been set upon by local storm troopers and pummeled to the verge of death. Pepper was rubbed in his open wounds to heighten his agony. Not trusting the local doctors, his family drove him to a Berlin hospital where he was treated but died of blood poisoning three days later. There was the story of a young Jewish man in Berlin named Kindermann who was allegedly kidnapped, taken to a private residence in the north of the city, and beaten to death. His family only learned of the incident when they received a letter instructing them to retrieve his body from the local mortuary. Another young Jewish man named Krel was tortured to death and his corpse was hurled from a fourth-floor window to feign suicide. One Jewish survivor described an apartment at Friedrichstrasse 132 in central Berlin that had been converted into a makeshift torture chamber for use by local storm troopers. Its walls were spattered with blood. Even Nazi residents complained about the "daily and nightly screams and cries." The survivor, who wished to remain anonymous, recalled being flogged into delirium. "I could count only until the tenth stroke," he said. "After that, I no longer knew whether it was my own or someone else's body that was being beaten into pulp with india-rubber whips."

The German Foreign Office was rumored to have received more than 150 complaints from foreign consulates about incidents of "maltreatment and savage torture." The Polish embassy in Berlin had an "imposing list of affidavits" attesting to more than a hundred instances of Jews assaulted in their homes and businesses, robbed at gunpoint, or taken to "torture chambers where men 'in the uniforms of storm troopers' have beaten them with leaden balls." "The Reich minister of the Foreign Office reported that the French and American ambassadors had submitted complaints about SA excesses," the Reich Chancellery cabinet meeting minutes recorded on March 7. "The Reich chancellor asked whether the names of the SA men had been determined." He was of the "firm conviction that it was not SA men but instead probably communists wearing SA uniforms."

There were suspicions of atrocity stirring in Dachau within seconds of the shootings of the four young Jews. "The cracking sound hit us while we were sitting on planks between the barracks eating our soup," one detainee, Albert Andersch, remembered. "It silenced our conversation but we continued eating our soup to the end." Except, of course, the Jewish detainees sitting with them who stopped eating altogether. Josef Götz, a communist delegate to the Bavarian state parliament, incarcerated at Dachau, commented during his dinner, "That is fascism in its purest form." When Wäckerle learned of the comment, he ordered Götz to his office and threatened solitary confinement. "If something happens to me," Götz told a fellow detainee afterward, "you will know what it was about."

State police lieutenant Emil Schuler was in his quarters when he heard gunfire in the adjacent woods. He rushed toward the trees, only to be stopped by an SS guard at the Würm Mill Creek footbridge. The guard said he had instructions not to let anyone pass. Schuler pushed by him and rushed to the scene of the shooting, where Erspenmüller stood with his pistol drawn.

"I saw three men in front of me lying facedown on the ground, one of whom was screaming horribly and begging to be put out of his misery," Schuler remembered. Erspenmüller raised his gun to deliver the coup de grâce. Schuler screamed for him to desist. It would have been an act of "pure murder," he said. Erspenmüller halted. Schuler then ran to summon a police physican, a Dr. Meier, who happened to be at the camp, but as he reached the bridge, he heard renewed shooting. Schuler ordered the SS guard to find Dr. Meier, then rushed back to the clearing. Erspensmüller stood over the now motionless body of the supplicant, his pistol still smoking. When Schuler inquired about the fourth man, Erspenmüller led him into the woods and showed him a man lying facedown on the ground. He too was dead. They returned to the clearing to find that one of the detainees was still alive. Erspenmüller drew his pistol yet again. In that instant, Dr. Meier appeared. He ordered the wounded man carried back to the camp, where he was bandaged and, as we know, rushed by ambulance to a local hospital. Steinbrenner, who recalled that the man was delirious with pain and kept asking for his shoes, later heard that the detainee had related the entire incident of the shooting to the hospital staff.

The next morning, Anton Vogel, the *Lagerverwalter* (camp manager), assembled the detainees and informed them that the four Jews had been shot in a failed escape attempt. A detail of ten detainees was dispatched to the scene of the shooting. "I received the order from an SS guard, whom I did not know, to clear the things away, to cover over the blood, and to collect the bullet casings," detainee Matthias Grel recalled. "I collected a handful of bullet casings, probably about fifteen in all."

A message was smuggled out of the camp and found its way to England. "A few days ago we were going out as usual to work," an unnamed detainee wrote in the missive. "All of a sudden the Jewish prisoners—Goldmann a merchant, Benario a lawyer from Nuremberg, and the merchants Arthur and Erwin Kahn—were ordered to fall out of ranks. Without even a word, some storm trooper shot at them. They had not made any attempt to escape—all [*sic*] were killed on the spot and all had bullet wounds in their foreheads."

The myriad rumors of Nazi atrocity prompted journalists to investigate. The Nazis in turn orchestrated a public effort to dispel the alleged Jewish *Greuelpropaganda,* or horror propaganda. Near Berlin, a delegation of foreign correspondents was invited to tour a detention facility outside the town of Sonnenberg where they were permitted to speak with detainees, including Carl von Ossietzky, the renowned editor of the pacifist weekly *Die Weltbühne.* Louis Lochner of the Associated Press came away with the impression that many of the men "were indeed badly beaten up, but that apparently all cruel treatment has now stopped." Edgar Mowerer of the *Chicago Tribune,* one of the most relentless critics of the Hitler government, who had already interviewed a Jewish victim of Nazi abuse who showed Mowerer "his back beaten to a pulp," was hardly reassured by the facility and its camp commandant. "You know, Herr Mowerer, we were very angry at one moment," the commandant told him. "We even thought of sending a detachment of SA lads to beat reason into you. What would you have thought about that?"

"If there had been anything left of me, I suppose I should have staggered to a typewriter and written what I thought of it," Mowerer replied. When the commandant asked what that meant, Mowerer replied that it was "a typical Nazi victory."

"And what do you imply by that?" the commandant pressed.

"Fifteen armed men against one unarmed man," said Mowerer.

The *New York Times* does not appear to have participated in the Sonnenberg tour but did manage to arrange an exclusive tour of the Dachau Concentration Camp a week after reports of the shootings appeared in the press. On the afternoon of April 20—on Hitler's forty-fourth birthday—Wäckerle received a *Times* reporter personally and amicably.* "Permission to make the visit was very hard to obtain, but once it was granted," the reporter later observed, "everything was done by the prison commandant, a quiet-mannered, blond, blue-eyed young former officer named Wekerle [*sic*], to facilitate a thorough inspection."

For all the simmering brutality Hartinger had sensed in Hilmar Wäckerle, he failed to recognize, or at least appreciate, Wäckerle's capacity to blend mendacity with charm.

Wäckerle had shown such courtesy for the Easter holy days that Cardinal Faulhaber felt compelled to send a note of personal gratitude. "Today, I would like to thank you, Most Honorable Herr Commandant," Faulhaber wrote, "that you supported and announced the religious services for the Catholics in such an exceedingly friendly manner." Faulhaber urged Wäckerle to continue to provide such kind support and assured him that Father Pfanzelt would "in absolutely no way interfere in the penal processes of the state government." He observed that this "spiritual guidance" in the camp would "serve as testimony in the chronicles of this era for the humane treatment provided to the prisoners."

Wäckerle now showed similar accommodation toward America's most renowned newspaper. The *Times* reporter arrived at the camp entrance after the noon hour that Thursday and was given a white armband with a number, identifying him as a visitor, then led into the walled compound. It was a bleak but festive day. The fair weather that had blessed the Easter weekend had again given way to gray skies, chilling temperatures, and occasional rain show-

---

* The article appeared with an anonymous byline as a wireless dispatch to the *New York Times*, datelined Munich, April 22, 1933. The newspaper's chief correspondent, Frederick Birchall, who would receive the Pulitzer Prize for his reporting that year, was covering Hitler's birthday celebrations in Berlin.

ers that dampened the camp celebrations marking Hitler's birthday. Wäckerle told the reporter that there had been a parade with music that morning as well as speeches by Nazi leaders. To celebrate the occasion, he had excused most detainees from their work assignments and given each man extra rations and ten cigarettes. He observed that smoking was generally prohibited.

Wäckerle then took the reporter on a tour of his facility. They visited a guardhouse where one of several machine guns stood ready for use. They viewed the high perimeter wall that was patrolled by armed storm troopers. When the camp had first opened, local residents had stood near the gate to gawk at arriving detainees. Those days were over. That very morning, Wäckerle had issued a stern warning that curiosity seekers loitering near the entrance or attempting to peer into the camp would themselves be detained. Anyone attempting to scale the wall would be shot.

Wäckerle led the reporter into the "inner camp" with its double-rank of barbed-wire fencing strung with "high-voltage wiring" powerful enough to kill a man. The detainees stood about in listless groups with drab dungarees pulled over their civilian clothing, their heads shaved, while armed SS guards loomed with a menacing presence. Wäckerle explained that the 530 detainees consisted mostly of communist leaders, but that there were also medical doctors, lawyers, writers, and university students, as well as two members of the Bavarian state parliament. Each time Wäckerle and the reporter approached, SS guards and detainees alike snapped to attention.

"My guards consist of 120 storm troop men only, supervised by noncommissioned officers of the green police," Wäckerle explained. "They won't need to be increased even if the prisoners number 5,000." He noted that his men worked in rotations of twenty-four-hour shifts, thirty at a time. The prisoners' workday commenced at 6 with reveille and ended at 5:30 p.m., with a half-hour break for breakfast and two hours at midday. Dinner was served in the evening, with lights-out at 9:15.

Wäckerle led the reporter into several barracks. The quarters were clean and orderly but spare in the extreme. The fifty men assigned to each barrack lived like rabbits in a warren. They slept in wooden bunks stacked in tiers of three, from floor to ceiling, separated from each other by four-inch boards. Their bedding consisted of a bulky straw sack with a blanket. A bare lightbulb dangling from the ceiling provided the only illumination. The top-tier bunks had to be scaled with ladders. Each time the two men entered a barrack, the detainees jumped to attention; once, a man started playing a mandolin as if on cue.

Wäckerle also showed the reporter the SS quarters, equally spartan except that there were two instead of three tiers of beds, lending the space a somewhat lighter atmosphere.

Wäckerle explained that the detainees had access to books and newspapers, and received parcels from their families with food-stuffs. However, they were not allowed to see their wives, children, or friends, except in an extreme emergency. Nevertheless, shop-keepers were occasionally permitted to leave the camp to attend to business matters. Wäckerle said that seventy "well-conducted fathers" had been released in time for the Easter weekend so they could spend the holidays with their families. They now needed only to report to the police twice each week. Wäckerle said that many of the men, after years of unemployment, were happy finally to have something to do. In one barrack, Dr. Delwin Katz, a Jewish physi-cian from Nuremberg, was conducting examinations of inmates. In the kitchen, a burly man stood over giant cauldrons of sauerkraut with a thousand sausages. Wäckerle explained that he was a former communist who had gunned down a socialist deputy during the short-lived Soviet Republic. The only thing the men really missed, Wäckerle said, was "their Bavarian beer."

The reporter was permitted to interview a dozen detainees. When he asked one man what he thought of the food, the answer was crisp. It was "beautifully cooked" but the portions were too spare and there was not enough bread. Another, when asked if he had any complaints, was circumspect. He said he found no fault with the camp itself, but had no idea why he was being detained. He had never been involved in politics and had no connection with the Communist Party. He had once belonged to a socialist fraternity but nothing more.

"You all say you did nothing," Wäckerle snapped back. Wäckerle said if the man was indeed innocent, he would be released as soon as there was time to review his case in detail. The reporter noted the pervasive unease caused by the undefined and indefinite nature of "protective custody," as well as "the herding together of intellectuals and men of a low order." He discovered trained professionals and young students sharing close quarters with common criminals and social outcasts, many of whom looked "long-starved and crippled," all with shaved heads, all sullen, some brutish, some menacing, some depraved. "Many of the prisoners looked as if the community would not suffer from their seclusion," he wrote, "but there must be numbers who were made the victims of some private grudge in the wave of denunciations that followed the Nazi revolution."

Wäckerle and the reporter discussed the shootings of the previous week only once that afternoon. It was while they were observing the perimeter wall, just before they entered the wire compound. Wäckerle explained that martial law had been imposed on the camp; that he had ordered his guards to shoot anyone trying to escape. He said that the four men had been led outside the compound to "fell trees." When they bolted, they were shot. "They ignored a challenge and got about 100 yards into the woods before the bullets brought them down," Wäckerle said. "Three were killed." The reporter probed no further. He did not seem particularly attentive to the incident, but three days later, when his article appeared in the Sunday edition of the *New York Times,* the promise of atrocity billowed spectacularly in a boldfaced headline:

NAZIS SHOOT DOWN FLEEING PRISONERS

––––––––

Three Reds Are Slain Trying to Escape From
Dachau Internment Camp.

––––––––

A series of subtitles highlighted the imposition of martial law, the use of electrified fencing, and the fact that the *Times* had scored a journalistic coup as the first newspaper to be granted complete and seemingly unrestricted access to the Dachau Concentration Camp. The article retraced the reporter's tour of the facility step by step, from his arrival at the front gate, to his meeting with Wäckerle at the commandant's headquarters, to the visit to the guardhouse and viewing of the perimeter wall, to the the inspection of several barracks inside the electrified-wire compound. The article made only passing reference to the Dachau shootings and abided by Wäckerle's perfunctory explanation of the three deaths. The first insider account of the Dachau Concentration Camp gave the facility and its commandant a generally positive review. "Life at Dachau seems halfway between that of a severely disciplined regiment and that of a hard labor prison," the correspondent concluded. Wäckerle came across as a poster boy of the new Germany, a handsome but somewhat demure young man overseeing a complex mix of 530 detainees and 120 SS guards whom he was managing with a balance of sparring wit and martial discipline, without a wisp of atrocity.

THE SHRILL HEADLINE SUGGESTS that the *Times* editors gleaned as much drama and menace as they could from the 1,300-word wireless dispatch, leaving one to wonder how the headline might have read had the reporter realized that the four detainees had been "Jews" rather than "Reds." Or had he seized the sizzling lead Wäckerle handed him—that only three of the four men were dead—and traced the further fate of the surviving victim of the shooting, from the camp infirmary where Erwin Kahn was given triage, to the Dachau hospital where he was bandaged, to the Nussbaumstrasse surgical clinic where attending staff recorded his account of the shooting in his medical record, or ultimately to the Munich apartment of Eva Kahn to whom her husband had related the entire incident on the afternoon before his death? As it was, Wäckerle alone was left to provide an account of the first Dachau killings in America's leading newspaper of record. The day after the *Times* article appeared, on page twenty-two of the Sunday edition, Wäckerle received further validation for his version of the incident.

On Monday, April 24, Karl Wintersberger formally closed the Munich II investigation into the shooting deaths of the four Dachau detainees. In a three-page report to the attorney general's office, "Killing of Escaping Prisoners from the Collection Camp Dachau," the veteran prosecutor dismissed Hartinger's suspicions and officially confirmed Wäckerle's account of the incident. "Suddenly Arthur Kahn started running from his work and fled into the woods immediately adjacent to the open woods," Wintersberger said. "The three other prisoners immediately started running in different directions; two of them, Goldmann and Benario, gave the impression that they intended to flee, at which point the two guards, after repeatedly shouting 'Halt!,' repeatedly shot with their sidearms from a distance of approximately ten meters. Erspenmüller, who was in the vicinity and became aware of the incident, also fired several shots. Goldmann and Benario dropped dead not far from where they were working. Also Arthur Kahn was hit and fell between them dead." Wintersberger included the unflattering observation that the four men "were clearly somewhat lethargic and had to be warned repeatedly." He summarized the results of Dr. Flamm's forensic examination, but noted incorrectly that Kahn had not been able to provide an account of the shooting. "Due to his condition, it was not possible to conduct a legal deposition of Erwin Kahn before his death," Wintersberger wrote.

It was now official. Benario, Goldmann, and the two Kahns had been shot in a failed escape from the Dachau Concentration Camp. This was legal truth. The case was closed. In those same days, the detainee Ferdinand Wünsch, a trained gardener, was ordered to bury the victims' bloodstained clothing in the camp vegetable plot.

7

The Utility of Atrocity

W HEN HILMAR WÄCKERLE BOASTED to the *New York Times* reporter that 120 SS men could guard as many as five thousand detainees—there were five hundred at the time—he knew he was lying. For all his jaunty, fair-haired confidence, Wäckerle was in fact a beleaguered man. From his private quarters on the second floor of the commandant headquarters, he looked across a ruined industrial landscape overgrown with thickets of brush and weeds, and dense stands of trees. Wäckerle knew that the Dachau Concentration Camp, despite its official title, was little more than a makeshift barbed-wire outpost in an isolated moorland and lacked proper security.* The camp's alarm and communication system consisted of three telephones connected by field wire, two hand sirens—one for the guards and one at the commandant's headquarters—and an electrical system that dated from 1916.

An internal security assessment underscored the myriad perils.

---

* The camp's official title was the *Konzentrationslager Dachau,* or Concentration Camp Dachau, but the terms *Sammellager Dachau,* or Collecting Camp Dachau, as well as *Schutzhaftlager Dachau,* or Protective Custody Camp Dachau, were used interchangeably by the police, the courts, and the SS alike. The camp letterhead had *Konzentrationlager,* but Wäckerle referred to his facility as *Sammellager.*

"The following possibilities for enemy assault should be particularly noted," the report noted. "The woods between the Amper-
werk facility and the SS quarters; the woods northwest of the
'inner camp'; and those to the southeast of the foreign barracks."
The barracks and nearby villas were to serve as the main defense
line, though caution was urged to "cover the flanks and rear" as
well. The detainees posed the most immediate risk. "The first measure [in case of assault] is to prevent any connection between the
attackers and the prisoners," the plan noted. "The prisoners must
be locked in the barracks and machine-guns and rifles employed to
enforce security." Hand grenades were stockpiled. "In the case of
serious threat, they can be dispatched by the security officers."

Police lieutenant Schuler recalled Wäckerle's concern. "I noted
that at the time Wäckerle, who did not seem particularly confident,
was constantly afraid of an attack by communists," Schuler said.
"He repeatedly asked me for advice as to what was to be done in
such circumstances, since I had an armed police training unit while
his SS guards still did not know how to use guns."

The "concentration" of hundreds of communists heightened
the threat of armed assault by the underground "military political apparatus" of the Communist Party. Dachau itself was iconic
for German communists. In April 1919, when the Bolsheviks seized
power in Munich and established the short-lived Soviet Republic
of Bavaria, a unit of the Bavarian Red Army under the command
of the activist-playwright Ernst Toller scored a stinging victory
there. Toller had deployed his men along the Würm Canal near the
train station to counter an advance by regular army units. "As the
battle commences, all of the workers of the Dachauer munitions
plant—male and female—begin attacking the White Soldiers," the
playwright commander recounted in a brisk present-tense narrative highlighting the particular valor of the women workers who
swarmed the enemy. "They disarm the troops, round them up, and
drive them out of the town with blows and kicks." The government

troops retreated, leaving 150 prisoners, four pieces of artillery, and an untallied number of machine guns. The next day, Good Friday, the Bolsheviks proclaimed victory on posters in Munich—"Red Army Victory! Dachau has been conquered!" The Soviet republic was subsequently crushed, but the memory of the Bolshevik victory endured. Following Hitler's appointment as chancellor, the Bavarian communist leader Hans Beimler rallied twenty thousand followers in Munich's Circus Krone with the defiant battle cry, "We will meet again in Dachau!"

Along with the security threats, Wäckerle found on his arrival an atmosphere of accommodation, almost cameraderie, between the detainees and their keepers. For the previous three weeks, the facility had been under the command of the Bavarian state police, following an urgent request by the state government for "two police officers" and "forty to sixty police guards" to oversee a "collecting camp for political prisoners" outside Dachau. "A very energetic police captain is to be identified as their leader," the instruction stipulated. "He will also serve in the capacity of camp commandant until further notice." The order had been issued on March 20, 1933, with twenty-four hours' notice, and with the request that the police be at the facility by six o'clock the following evening "so that they can be assigned to their guard and patrol duties while there is still daylight." That same day, Himmler ordered the transfer of forty "protective custody" detainees from Landsberg Prison to Dachau, and held a press conference to announce the opening of Bavaria's first "concentration camp."

Amid the scramble, Company 2 of the Bavarian state police, under the command of Captain Schlemmer, arrived, and the first forty detainees were delivered on Wednesday. Schlemmer was appalled by what he found. The barracks were unheated. Food was served in a field kitchen. Unwilling to subject the detainees to such conditions, Schlemmer quartered the prisoners in a building next to his own headquarters. The detainees undertook joint foraging expeditions with the police in the abandoned buildings, and helped Reichswehr soldiers erect the barbed-wire fencing around the barracks. "The prisoners were treated decently," one state policeman, Johann Kugler, recalled. "They received the same food as we did, they used the same toilet and shower facilities, and played soccer with us." Detainee Martin Grünwiedl confirmed the cordial relations. "We worked with the soldiers like comrades and got along well," he recalled. "We broke off our conversations whenever an SS man approached."

Schlemmer called Adolf Wagner. Claus Bastian, the first detainee registered in Dachau, overheard Schlemmer's conversation. "He said he thought the imprisonment of the detainees was unlawful," Bastian recalled Schlemmer chastising Wagner. "On top of that, he accused the Gauleiter of misusing the state police for tasks for which there was no legal basis or official statement. There was not even a formal police order for such extensive use of so-called 'protective custody.' If such political measures were already being taken, then the most basic courtesy dictated that at least the financial means for provisions, etc., needed to be made available. It was impossible to make such demands on the state police."

Schlemmer and his officers were equally firm with the SS guards who had been assigned to the camp as "assistant police." They had been greeted on arrival by SS Standartenführer (Colonel) Johann-Erasmus Baron von Malsen-Ponickau, appointed by Himmler as their Munich-based head. "We have not come here to treat the swine in there humanely," the Nazi aristocrat instructed the men on arrival. "We no longer view them as human beings like us, rather as people of a second class." Malsen-Ponickau had helped Epp crush Bavaria's Soviet mini-state in 1919 and retained a hard-bitten memory of Bolsheviks. "If these swine had come to power, they would have cut off all our heads," he said. "Whoever cannot stand the sight of blood does not belong here and should step forward. The more of these swine that we knock off, the fewer we have to feed." A state police officer who overheard Malsen-Ponickau's remarks dismissed the fascist bluster. "Yes, that was horrible to hear, but as long as we are on guard here nothing will happen," the police officer told a detainee. "But if we leave, you are going to be in trouble."

For the first three weeks, the state police kept the SS at heel. "We always emphasized the fact that the guards were to strictly refrain from assaulting prisoners," one officer remembered, "and if anyone was found to behave in such an inadmissible manner, expulsion from the SS would occur. These threats had a certain weight because it would not only damage their honor, but would have also carried significant repercussions for their future." When SS lieutenant Robert Erspenmüller announced his intention "to knock off a few Jews," he was warned against touching "a single hair" of anyone in the camp. Erwin Kahn appreciated the police presence. "I was walking next to Kahn, who had a particularly prominent Jewish nose," fellow detainee Wilhelm Brink recalled. "Nearby there was a group of SS, including Steinbrenner and another SS man known as the boxer." These two SS men suddenly set upon Kahn. "Only the intervention of the green police prevented Kahn from being mistreated," Brink said.

On April 2, Himmler exercised his capacity as police chief and Reichsführer SS to transfer responsibility for the detainees from the state police to the SS. "The transfer is to take place as agreed between the head of the political assistant police and the commander of the state police," Himmler dictated, then scrawled a bold, runic-style "H. Himmler" beneath the instruction. Himmler's transfer order was an administrative fast shuffle that removed the detainees from police protection and placed them directly in SS hands, while the facility itself remained under police auspices. The formal transfer was set for eleven o'clock in the morning on Tuesday, April 11. "For security and training purposes, a police unit consisting of two officers and around sixteen state policemen will remain until the entire security and guard service is taken over by the assistant police," the minutes of an April 7 meeting record. Captain Max Winkler was placed in charge of the camp and Lieutenant Schuler in charge of training the SS guards.

That Tuesday morning, as scheduled, Wäckerle arrived as commandant and immediately struck an iconic pose. "The first time I saw Wäckerle at the camp, he was carrying a pizzle and had a big dog beside him," Hans Steinbrenner remembered. "After that, I never saw Wäckerle without his dog and pizzle." For Wäckerle, the assignment was a point of pride. "When Hitler took over power in 1933, I quit my job at the Reichsführer's personal request and was ordered to Dachau," he later boasted in his SS curriculum vitae. The job seemed tailor-made for the former cadet—he was enrolled in an elite military academy at age thirteen—and decorated frontline soldier who had been rushed to war as a seventeen-year-old corporal in the autumn of 1918. Wäckerle subsequently enlisted in the Freikorps Oberland that helped Freikorps Epp crush the Bavarian soviet mini-state. In 1922, Wäckerle joined the Nazi movement while studying farm management, along with young Heinrich Himmler, at Munich's Technical University. "I was with the party from the very beginning," Wäckerle observed, joining in "all its early struggles," including the 1923 Beer Hall Putsch. During the "years of illegality" when the party was banned, Wäckerle participated in assassination attempts in the French occupation zone. "In 1931, I rejoined the party in Kempten and helped establish the SS there," he noted. "Within the party I functioned as a senior agricultural adviser and served as a speaker at meetings." Wäckerle arrived in Dachau with sterling Nazi credentials and practical experience. Having managed farms in Thüringen, Upper Bavaria, and Allgäu for the previous eight years, he knew something about keeping living stock in barbed-wire enclosures.

Wäckerle made a quick tour of the "inner camp"; then he assembled the SS men and informed them that he expected iron discipline and blind obedience. Echoing Malsen-Ponickau, he insisted there was to be no accommodation with the detainees. He wanted the SS to be to Germany what the Cheka, the dreaded Soviet secret police, were to the Russians—men without mercy or conscience. Wäckerle explained that in former times when prisoners arrived at detention facilities, they were routinely given twenty-five lashes to instill fear and subservience. He was introducing a similar regimen for Dachau. He would be present for the arrival of detainees and would personally select those to be flogged. Wäckerle was joined by an additional seventy SS guards who replaced Captain Schlemmer and the departing state policemen of Company 2. Sixty more SS men arrived the next day. The camp now swarmed with SS. Meanwhile, transports continued to deliver detainees. The transport from Fürth and Nuremberg brought Benario, Goldmann, and Arthur Kahn, as we know. A second transport delivered another twenty-six men from Deggendorf, and a third from Miesbach added another twenty-eight. The next day fifty-six more detainees arrived from Kempten, Munich, and Sonthofen. Amid the tumult, state police captain Winkler and Lieutenant Schuler attempted to protect the arriving detainees from abuse but were ignored by the SS guards. "I should note in this context," Schuler later recalled, "that I did not enter the detainees' camp, which was separated from the rest of the camp by barbed wire, because I was not allowed in unless something happened or Commandant Wäckerle needed help."

The SS men exercised their newfound authority that evening with drink and gunfire. Steinbrenner marched into Barrack II at three o'clock in the morning, fired his pistol, and rousted the men from their bunks and into the night chill, where he assembled them for roll call. The next day, Benario, Goldmann, and the two Kahns were shot.

Wäckerle found a competent and like-minded deputy commandant in SS lieutenant Erspenmüller, who had been a police officer in

Rosenheim and had lost his job over his association with the Nazi movement. Josef Mutzbauer served as the office administrator with the pro bono assistance of a local lawyer, Otto Franck, who was rumored—incorrectly—to be related to the new state minister of justice, Dr. Hans Frank. Franck designed the camp registration system and for a time had shuttled police officers between Dachau and Munich in his private car. Dr. Delwin Katz, the Jewish physician whom the *Times* reporter saw, worked in the camp infirmary, along with part-time services from several Munich-based physicians, including Dr. Werner Nürnbergk, a graduate of the Ludwig Maximilian University medical school in Munich and SS lieutenant, who came to serve as the camp's first offical doctor.*

The guards were a mixed group. Hans Kantschuster had served in the French Foreign Legion and was said to be a heavy drinker, as was Karl Ehmann, who had terrorized the streets of Würzburg on a motorcycle emblazoned with a swastika. Karl Wicklmayr was studying philosophy in Munich. He had been a fervent communist in the 1920s but joined the Nazi movement after reading Nietzsche. He was known as "the student." Hans Steinbrenner was the son of a Munich gunsmith. He boasted of a personal connection to Ernst Röhm, who used to buy guns from his father.

The SS men were mostly young, untrained, and undisciplined. Many had been pressed into service in the camp and did not want to be there. Schuler recalled that over the Easter weekend "an entire shift of guards" did not even show up for duty. Detainees recalled pistols being shot randomly among the barracks. Bursts of machine-gun fire sent men scrambling for cover. A contingent of SS guards nearly massacred the entire kitchen staff. "They [the SS guards] did not know that at four o'clock in the morning the cook

* SS lieutenant Dr. Werner Nürnbergk (SS registration number 102278, born April 2, 1907) is listed as the camp doctor in June 1933, but was clearly present in the camp before this date as evidenced by documents bearing his signature from May. Werner Nürnbergk may well rank as the official SS camp physician of the Third Reich.

and kitchen helpers from Barrack VIII were the first to start working," detainee Walter Hornung recalled. "Fortunately, no one was hit. They threw themselves to the ground and fled back into the barrack."

IN HIS FIRST WEEKS as commandant, Wäckerle watched the arrival of diesel-driven buses carrying twenty-five to thirty detainees at a time, generally one transport per day, sometimes two, spewing exhaust and passengers onto the open square in front of his headquarters. He reviewed the arrival manifests that listed each detainee, his background and profession, and would identify those who would receive particular abuse. There were few men of real interest. Most of the high-value Bolsheviks were either still at large or had quietly slipped across the border to Brussels, Paris, Prague, or Moscow, beyond the reach of the government security forces. Some transports came from milk-run sweeps of Bavarian towns and villages, collecting clutches of detainees, five or six at a time. Others made single-stop deliveries from the larger cities like Bamberg, Würzburg, Augsburg, Rosenheim, and, of course, Munich. Mostly, they delivered second- and third-tier communist agitators, Social Democrats, a random professor or journalist or lawyer, and the occasional Jew, men who had glutted police stations, prisons, cellars, and warehouses across Bavaria for the past month, and were now being flushed out of the penal system and "collected" in the facility for which Wäckerle had responsibility.

On April 25, Wäckerle received a transport of high-value detainees gleaned from Munich security facilities: nine from the Ettstrasse police jail, thirteen from the Stadelheim penitentiary, and three from the prison attached to the Munich courts. He took particular note of the first half dozen names on the two-page typewritten transport manifest: Max Dankenreiter, Peter Distler, Rudolf Grohe, Herbert Hunglinger, Joseph Kraudel, and Sebastian Nefzger. These

were "people who, until November 9, 1933, served as spies within
the NSDAP," an appended annotation explained. "With the exception of Distler and Grohe the detainees have confessed their guilt.
Distler and Grohe did not deny the accusation."

Hitler had long suspected that state police agents had infiltrated
the party. As early as 1922, he had established his own "Security
Department," an internal spy unit within the National Socialist
Party, to gather intelligence not only on communists and Social
Democrats, but on those within his own ranks. This secret opera-
tion, essentially a one-man show, had been set up by Reinhard
Heydrich, then an exceedingly competent twenty-two-year-old SS
officer.

Of the six men singled out on the transport manifest—the first
harvest of Heydrich's gleaning eye—number four, "Hunglinger,
Herbert," was seen as perhaps the worst offender. The fifty-three-
year-old retired police major was among the earliest members of
the National Socialist movement, having joined in 1920. He had
played a central role in the *Führerschule,* the school for training
party leaders, and was said to have earned the rare honor of possessing "the trust of the Führer." An interrogation at the Ettstrasse
police jail had yielded his confession as a spy, and now he was being
delivered into the hands of Wäckerle.

The single most notable name on the manifest that morning was
that of Hans Beimler. "Beimler, number 7 on the list, is the leader of
the Communist Party Germany (KPD) of the district of Southern
Bavaria," an annotation noted. Wäckerle needed no instruction.
Beimler was the most publicly defiant, most fanatically unapologetic Bolshevik in all Bavaria, the founder of its Communist Party.
His tirades in parliament were legendary. He condemned National
Socialists, Catholic centrists, and Social Democrats in equal measure. He railed against the "financial bourgeoisie" and the "process
of fascistization" across the country. He considered the Nazis as little more than an "arm of the bourgeoisie." He called on the "work-

ing masses" to rise and crush the existing economic and political system. "Then the time will come to end all anguish," Beimler predicted in June 1932 during a seemingly endless rant before the Bavarian state parliament, "in a Red Bavaria, in a Soviet Germany." Six months later, Beimler publicly declared war on the Hitler government with his belligerent invitation to "meet again in Dachau."

Wäckerle believed Beimler to be not only a public provocateur but also a ruthless murderer. He recalled that in late April 1919, as the Freikorps rampaged their way through the streets of Munich and the communists battled for survival, Beimler had presided over the execution of ten hostages taken from the "bourgeoisie." On telegraphed instructions from Lenin in Moscow to take hostages, the communists held Count Gustav von Thurn und Taxis, the Countess von Westarp, and eight others as human barter in the unheated cellars of the Luitpold High School on Müllerstrasse. As the Bolshevik state tottered, the hostages were shunted up the stairs and into the high school courtyard and then summarily executed. "The corpses were plundered and mutilated to such an extent that even now, apart from three, we haven't been able to identify them," the *Münchner Neueste Nachrichten* reported. "Two of the corpses are missing the upper halves of their heads."

At the time, Wäckerle was an eighteen-year-old soldier fighting his way into Munich with the Freikorps Oberland, but the stories and images of the massacre followed him to Dachau. Steinbrenner recalled that Wäckerle had a collection of photographs of the butchery at the Luitpold High School that he showed his SS subordinates. He told them that Beimler was personally responsible for these atrocities. Wäckerle was mistaken, but it hardly mattered.

8

Steinbrenner Unleashed

IN HIS FIRST DAYS as commandant, Wäckerle came to appreciate Hans Steinbrenner. The twenty-eight-year-old SS man had only joined the party in February after Hitler's appointment as chancellor, like thousands of other opportunistic latecomers. However, Steinbrenner compensated for his lack of seniority in the movement with a near pathological hatred of Bolsheviks and a seemingly boundless capacity for sadistic violence against Jews. He made regular visits to the camp infirmary, across the hall from the SS changing room. Steinbrenner approached one man who was suffering from a toothache. Steinbrenner stroked the swollen cheek gently and inquired "with apparent concern" if the man was in pain. When the detainee said yes, Steinbrenner slugged him in the jaw, sending him to the floor. Steinbrenner asked if he was still in pain, then sent him on his way. He then drove his knee into the stomach of another man. The man collapsed, writhing in agony at Steinbrenner's feet. The remaining patients fled. Steinbrenner was said to have pressed burning cigarettes into men's flesh, kicked them in the genitals, and regularly lashed detainees to a bloody pulp. He would often demand that they race through mud and water until they collapsed. The abuse of Jewish detainees was dubbed *Juden-sport,* or Jew games.

Steinbrenner headed the *Schlägergruppe,* the camp whipping team. He was fascinated by the latent potential in those eighteen inches of turgid leather for inflicting pain. "After a few strokes I saw for the first time the effect of these lashings," he recalled. "The pizzle would begin to chafe the skin. The wound would then grow moist, but it never actually bled." Witnesses disagreed. Kasimir Dittenheber, who worked in a camp office, recalled that Steinbrenner was charged with "selecting" the Jews from the arriving transports and leading them into the Arrest Bunker, where, "as we could hear in the office, [they] were beaten in the most brutal manner." "Steinbrenner placed the greatest value on making certain that the head was not struck, so that the pain would last as long as possible," one detainee recalled. A physician was on hand with injections to revive those who had been beaten unconscious. One detainee described Steinbrenner as "the spiritual leader of all abuses." Many called him *Mordbrenner,* or "murder man," while to Wäckerle he was simply "Hans."

On April 26, a dank and drizzle-chilled day, Wäckerle watched casually, smoking a cigarette, while Steinbrenner and a team of SS guards awaited the arrival of the Munich transport, pizzles twitching expectantly in their hands. As soon as the bus carrying the new arrivals roared into the camp facility and came to an abrupt stop, the door flew open and the men tumbled out. Steinbrenner set his men upon the new arrivals, lashing, kicking, and cuffing them amid the screamed orders, "Into two rows!" The men were whipped and beaten into a double rank, then a guard barked the first seven names from the transport manifest with a crisp call and response, ordering each to step forward in turn.

"Dankenreiter!"

"Here!"

"Distler!"

"Here!"

"Grohe!"

"Here!"

"Hunglinger!"

"Here!"

"Kraudel!"

"Here!"

"Nefzger!"

"Here!" Nefzger, a veteran who had lost part of his left leg during the war, stepped forward on his prosthesis.

"Beimler!"

Hans Beimler, standing in the back rank, murmured a response. He was a low, dark, surly figure, with large, protruding ears. He was thick, hard, and defiant. Steinbrenner knew he would not break easily.

"Beimler!" a guard snapped a second time. Again there was barely a murmur. The guard repeated the name with the same measured force, each time drawing a heightened but still unsatisfactory response. The others grew restless. "We'll teach him how to do it," one detainee growled menacingly. "The Moscow hireling," another said. After eight, possibly ten calls, Beimler stepped forward. Andreas Irrgang was on the same transport and watched Beimler "beaten and kicked" by Steinbrenner. Beimler joined the six other detainees. "Are there any Jews here?" a young SS man shouted. "You, too, get over to the right side. Including baptized Jews!" Two young men, who might have been students, stepped forward. A guard then hung a cardboard sign around Beimler's neck with the hand-scrawled words *"Herzlich willkommen."*

Wäckerle had watched the selection process with cool detachment. Now he spoke. "These bastards are to be lashed right away," he said. "They are paid pigs and traitors—in addition, half rations for them." He pointed to the remaining detainees. "Those over there, I believe, are all proletariat who were misled by that one."

He pointed to Beimler. "We'll give them regular rations. In addition, each of them can keep five marks of the money he brought with him. Those other pigs don't get a cent."

The men were marched into the large processing hall and ordered to empty their pockets. Wäckerle stood to the side and observed while Steinbrenner ferreted among the men, looking for infractions. Steinbrenner stopped beside Beimler and reached into his coat pocket. *"Herr Kommandant! Herr Kommandant!"* he shouted. "This guy here ignored the order to put everything on the table!" Steinbrenner held up a small pencil. "He wanted to smuggle this."

Wäckerle looked at Beimler coolly, then ordered, "Fourteen days' strict confinement!"

Steinbrenner marched Beimler, along with Hunglinger, through the camp. They passed groups of workers along the road, who stared at Beimler. Others watched from rooftops where they were making repairs with buckets of tar. A mere two months earlier, Steinbrenner had been unemployed, with no education and little means of support. Now, on this dreary day, he found himself with command over one of the state's leading political personalities. Steinbrenner began lashing Beimler, whipping his shoulders and head and turning his large ears bright red. "Look over here," Steinbrenner called to the gawkers. "We have your beloved Beimler, who misled and corrupted your minds." Then he returned to Beimler and continued his lashing.

They entered the wire enclosure and proceeded past the double rank of ten barracks, to the back of the camp where the Arrest Bunker stood orphaned near the concrete perimeter wall. It was actually a half-barrack, a truncated, one-story structure, half the size of the others, and it housed the seven arrest cells, along with the SS changing rooms, a storage area for the bedding, and the camp infirmary. It was a convenient corner for atrocity. Detainees were lashed in the storage room, where the bedding could be used to muffle their screams. "If I wasn't wrapping a blanket around the head," Steinbrenner recalled, "then I was whipping, and another was holding the head." A doctor was always nearby to give an injection if a detainee fell unconscious during the lashing. The word *"Wache,"* or guardpost, was scrawled in chalk over the entrance.

The door was locked. While they waited for camp manager Vogel to bring the keys, Steinbrenner asked Beimler if he still "imagined" himself as a delegate to the Reichstag in Berlin. "Imagination," Beimler replied, "is a bourgeois concept that has no place in communism." Steinbrenner stared at Beimler, baffled, and decided to turn his attention to Hunglinger. "And you, traitor! You swine, you scoundrel, now we know that you spied on us and were in the pay of the police," he said. "And how you misled and deceived our SA men in the Führer school." As he reviewed Hunglinger's transgressions, he talked himself into a rage, cuffing Hunglinger across the face repeatedly. Unlike Beimler, who had remained belligerently defiant, Hunglinger, who had spent the previous five days in storm trooper hands at the Ettstrasse police station, accepted the blows with blunted lethargy.

When Vogel returned, he pulled a clattering set of keys from his pocket and unlocked the door. The arrest cells were little more than a row of converted toilet and shower stalls along the right side of a narrow hallway. The toilets had been ripped out and the windows blocked. The open sewage pipes breathed acrid moist air into the gloom. The cells were tight, narrow spaces equipped with a simple wooden bunk and a table with a plate, a knife, and a pitcher of water. A large sack filled with straw served as bedding. Hunglinger was placed in Cell 1 and Beimler down the hall in Cell 3. Josef Götz, who was still serving time for his dinner-table remark about the shooting of Benario, Goldmann, and the Kahns two weeks earlier, was between them in Cell 2.

The men had barely settled into their quarters when Steinbrenner appeared with two SS men. "Now we've got you, you traitor, you rebel," he barked as he flung open Beimler's door. "People are paying for your rabble-rousing." Then he commanded, "Get up!" As Beimler rose, Steinbrenner started whipping him, then shoved him into the corner of the cell. "Now will you admit that you betrayed the workers?" Beimler's response came low and glowering: "If I were to admit now to having betrayed the workers, out of fear of you hitting me," he told Steinbrenner, "then I would deserve to be beaten to death here and now." Steinbrenner slammed the door shut and moved to Hunglinger, who was beaten and pummeled and left lying on his bunk, moaning.

Vogel followed Steinbrenner a short while later, opening each door in turn and inquiring about his charges. Vogel possessed a sense of nuance and irony absent in the brutish Steinbrenner, preferring to administer torment in small, subtle doses. "Do you have any requests," he asked Beimler, "any wishes, any complaints?"

"None of the three," Beimler replied curtly.

Vogel handed Beimler a six-foot-long leather cord with a noose on the end and ordered him to stand on the bed and tie it to the shower fixture near the ceiling. "Yes, yes, just get onto the bed and hang the noose from the faucet," Vogel explained. When Beimler completed the task, Vogel instructed him in Arrest Bunker protocol. "In future, when someone enters the cell, you must strike a military pose and say: 'Detainee Beimler at your service.'" Vogel then explained that Steinbrenner's beatings would be a regular part of the Arrest Bunker routine. He spoke in a calm, reassuring tone, addressing Beimler with the more respectful "*Sie*" rather than "*du*," assuring him that Steinbrenner's excesses were not gratuitous, that these were brutalities with a purpose. The beatings would be painful, Vogel assured Beimler, then added, pointing to the noose, "And in case you begin to have any doubts, then you always have this option."

As Vogel walked down the hall back to the SS changing room, Hunglinger called to him, rapping on the inside of his cell door. Vogel unlocked the cell. Hunglinger explained that he needed to relieve himself. Vogel led him out. When Hunglinger returned, he asked Vogel for a favor. "Please just give me a revolver," he said. "I want to shoot myself. I can't bear the beatings any longer."

"We don't have any revolvers; besides, you're not worth the bullet," Vogel sniped. "You should have thought about the fact that you have a family earlier, and you should not have betrayed us." Vogel paused, then added, "Still, I want to be charitable with you." He handed Hunglinger a length of leather strip with a noose similar to the one he had just given Beimler.

That night, Steinbrenner returned, this time with five SS men. Vogel unlocked Hunglinger's door. Two men held the police major down and the other four set upon him. Hunglinger screamed. They whipped him until his cries faded to an exhausted moan, and then pummeled him until he issued little more than a half-conscious gurgling of pain. Vogel locked the door to Hunglinger's cell, then accompanied Steinbrenner's team down the hall to Götz's cell, where they repeated the same procedure.

By the time they came to Beimler, they were soaked with perspiration from the exertion. Their kepis were thrown back over their necks; their hair hung in their faces and was dripping with sweat. "Come on, lie down!" Steinbrenner screamed as the door flew open. "Come on, come on." The men swarmed Beimler, flogging him with their pizzles, two from the right and two from the left, while the other two offered a chorus of taunts: "Red Front! Heil Moscow! Hurray for the world revolution!" Beimler crumpled in pain, turning on his side, then rolling onto his stomach as they continued to whip him wildly, each delivering forty or fifty lashes. When they had finished, they grabbed each arm, opened Beimler's hands, whipped his palms ten times, then turned his hands over and lashed the backs until they swelled. "When they finally left the cell and I thought that there would be some peace and quiet, I soon realized that I had been wrong again," Beimler later recalled. "In the meantime they fetched a number of Jews from the camp and were beating them, one after the other, in an empty cell next to mine." By ten o'clock it was over. Peace descended on the barrack for the night. The doors were closed and locked and the lights turned out.

Steinbrenner and his whipping team returned the next morning at eleven o'clock and went straight to Cell 1, where they administered another round of beatings to Hunglinger. They again lashed and pummeled the fifty-three-year-old into near unconsciousness, at which point Steinbrenner pronounced with a knowing satisfaction, "That will do it." Later that morning, when they returned and opened the cell, Hunglinger was hanging from the leather cord. A suicide note lay on the table.

Hartinger arrived that afternoon and found Hunglinger's corpse still hanging by the cord. He seized the suicide note as evidence in a potential prosecution. He knew men could be held accountable as "accessories to unnatural death" under Paragraph 23 of the criminal code. He decided to show the note to Hunglinger's brother, who worked at the state court in the Palace of Justice. Hunglinger confirmed his dead sibling's handwriting and accompanied Hartinger to the morgue to view the body. "Only after Hunglinger's brother agreed," Hartinger said, "did I release the corpse for burial."

9

The Gumbel Report

I N 1922, Emil Gumbel published his landmark study *Four Years of Political Murder*, attempting to explain the unprecedented upsurge in violence and atrocity that had swept Germany in the immediate postwar years. Gumbel was distressed and baffled that a nation that for centuries had prided itself on its discipline and orderliness, that was called the land of "poets and thinkers"—*Dichter und Denker*—and had produced Bach and Beethoven and Brahms, not to mention Einstein (with whom Gumbel spent the war years in Berlin), possessed within itself the capacity for such bestiality and sadism. He was particularly troubled by the myriad brutalities that swept the Munich I and Munich II jurisdictions in the spring of 1919, when extremists from right and left battled for political power.

In the town of Perlach, twelve men had been rousted from bed at three o'clock in the morning, beaten and robbed, then packed into a truck, driven to the Hofbräuhaus in Munich, and leisurely shot in pairs between 11 a.m. and one o'clock in the afternoon. Their killers drank beer in between the rounds of execution. In a monastery near the town of Gerlach, fourteen young men were beaten, then butchered. "The soldiers, some of them drunk, trampled the prisoners," Gumbel quoted one witness. "They clubbed the men wildly with their guns and hit with such force that one sidearm barrel was bent and a brain splattered around." One victim had his nose kicked into his face. Others had the backs of their skulls smashed in. "Two soldiers who had slung their arms around each other," the witness recalled, "began an Indian warrior dance next to the corpses. They shouted and howled." Near Grosshadern, a hundred Russian prisoners of war who were awaiting return to their homeland were packed into trucks at five o'clock in the morning, driven to a gravel pit, and gunned down en masse. Twenty men were tortured and shot in Starnberg, four in Possenhofen, three in Grosshesselohe and neighboring Grünwald, three more in Grosshadern, and one each in Schleissheim, Harlaching, Schäftlarn, and Grossförn. In Tegernsee, a thirty-two-year-old woman and her six-year-old daughter were used for target practice.

By year's end, Gumbel had tallied nearly eight hundred murders across the state, and more than twelve hundred across the rest of the country. "How are such things possible in a country that was once so orderly," Gumbel wondered, "that once belonged to the leading cultural nations of our era and that, according to its constitution, is a free, democratic republic?"

Since Gumbel was a professor, the question was of course rhetorical, and he had the answers ready at hand. He held Prussia responsible for the imposition of militarism on the hodgepodge of otherwise peaceable principalities and independent city-states that had constituted the loosely configured nations of German-speaking peoples before Bismarck forged his Reich of "blood and iron" in the 1870s. He faulted the Hohenzollern monarchy in particular for its policies of intimidation during the Great War that had banned free speech and basic civil liberties. And Gumbel blamed the "psychological brutalization" of the war itself, which immersed an entire generation in unprecedented bloodshed. "The indifference with which one now regards political murders and the victims of turbulent street demonstrations in Germany can only be explained through the theory that war has hardened us to the value of a human life," Gumbel posited. He also blamed the press, which glorified the violence and published appeals for the assassination of public figures.

Gumbel also noted the unprecedented application of the law on "protective custody," which permitted the temporary detainment—usually for twenty-four hours—of an individual without due process. "Without any possibility of recourse, thousands sat in protective custody," Gumbel wrote. Hundreds of these detainees were shot allegedly attempting to escape. The term "shot while escaping" (*erschossen auf der Flucht*) became a public euphemism for extrajudicial execution, to which the courts appeared to turn a blind eye.

To make his point, Gumbel cited the case of Max Mauer, a socialist political activist who had been taken into protective custody by a military patrol and was shot allegedly attempting to flee. When the case was dismissed by a lower court, Mauer's wife appealed it to the Reich Court in Leipzig, the highest judicial venue in the country. As part of her evidence, she quoted one of the soldiers who tried to silence her protests as her husband was taken away. "Don't make such a scene," he said. "Your husband is not coming back." She also presented forensic evidence indicating that Mauer had been hit with several shots in the back with, according to the medical report, "one shot to the neck at the height of the larynx, about 2 cm left of the center." The three soldiers insisted that Mauer had attempted to flee across a field and that they had followed proper procedure. "The guard Kruppe had shouted 'Halt' three times," one witness testified, "and then, since Mauer continued running, began shooting at him until he collapsed."

The high court acquitted the defendants, citing a nineteenth-century law according soldiers the right to shoot prisoners attempting to escape. "According to the law of March 20, 1837, when someone is shot by a soldier, it should generally be assumed that the soldier acted rightfully," Gumbel summarized the decision. "The soldiers do not need to prove this. It is up to the survivors to provide evidence that the soldier transgressed their limits of authority and that there was no attempt at escape by the victim. This is, of course, practically impossible." When the trial was over, the court required the wife to cover all its costs. "Although we are used to murderers not being tried justly in Germany," Gumbel commented drily, "up until now at least some civil courts had the objectivity to give the victim's relatives a compensation for the court costs. After the decision of the Reich Court, even this option has been practically obliterated."

Gumbel's point was simple: A responsible judiciary was necessary in order to uphold the rule of law. He argued that the generation of judges responsible for the judicial system in the early years of the Weimar Republic had been born and educated in the monarchy with limited notions of freedom, but even more so—and here Gumbel revealed his leftist political inclinations—as part of the conservative middle class, with little interest or taste for broad popular democracy.* "Countless social bonds connect the murderer-officer with the judge who will acquit him, who will close the case, who will believe the witness who described the 'attempt at escape' in detail," Gumbel asserted. "They are of the same flesh and blood. The judge understands their language, their tactics, their thoughts. Subtly his soul sways along with the murderers, covered by a mask of pretense to proper procedure. The murderer goes free."

Gumbel argued that judicial collusion was a "prerequisite for political murder." To make his point, he tabulated the comparative murder rates in individual states. Between 1919 and 1921, Bavaria

---

* Gumbel commented on the impact of political ideology on the nature of political murder, noting that the right-wing belief in strong leaders—as opposed to the communist embrace of the masses—resulted in the targeted assassination of left-wing and centrist political leaders. "The effectiveness of this technique for the moment is indisputable," Gumbel wrote. "The left no longer has any signiifcant leaders, no one for whom the masses can have the feeling: he has suffered so much for us, he has risked so much for us, that we can blindly trust him." Right-wing leaders survived and thrived—foremost among them, Adolf Hitler.

registered the largest number of political murders, followed by Prussia, but with a dramatic decline (more than 70 percent) in the Rhineland, which was still occupied by the Allies and where judges were accountable to the independent Rhineland Commission. Gumbel's conclusion: You could not rely on a constitution or open elections or a free press as a gauge or guarantee for a stable and functioning democracy. "If we are to find a satisfactory answer," he asserted, "we must instead take into consideration the implementation of regulations, the adherence to laws, the actions of the police, the spirit of the administration, and most of all, the attitude of the state." Gumbel made a point of reminding judges and prosecutors alike that it ultimately was in their own interest to adhere to due process and legal norms. He concluded, "They must simply realize that through their actions," by abusing the system or twisting the laws, "they are making themselves culpable."

JOSEF HARTINGER WAS twenty-nine years old and completing his third year as a student in the law faculty of Ludwig Maximilian University when Gumbel published his report. In many ways, Hartinger was the perfect candidate for collusion in the conservative undercurrent that Gumbel saw undermining judicial process, and with it the very foundations of democratic process. Hartinger was born in rural Bavaria in the age of monarchy and into a devout Roman Catholic family rooted in martial tradition. His mother was the daughter of a military officer. His father had served the Wittelsbach monarchy as a *sous-brigadier*—a junior officer—in the "Body Guard of Archers," the personal protectors of the Bavarian kings. In August 1914, Hartinger, then twenty years old, abandoned university studies to go to war in the first fevered wave of nationalism, enlisting in the 10th Bavarian Field Artillery Regiment. "Cannonier Josef Hartinger," as he described himself, trained for two years before being sent to the Western Front as a junior officer, where he was thrown into some of the fiercest fighting of the war, first in the Vosges highlands along the French-German border, then in the trenches around Verdun, and eventually with the offensives in Flanders in the summer and autumn of 1917, where Hartinger earned an Iron Cross.

That September, Hartinger was transferred to the 6th Field Artillery Regiment, and in February 1918 he was promoted to junior sergeant. His reviewing officer praised Hartinger's "technical abilities" and his battlefield capacities. "He has full command of the maneuvers and movements of his unit," the officer observed. "His personal comportment here is impeccable."

In early March, the 6th Field Artillery Regiment advanced to the front in preparation for an all-out offensive intended to force an end to the war. By then, poison gas belonged to the standard arsenal of artillery units, in particular "green cross" gas—named for the green marking on the ignition caps—a lethal tincture of 95 percent chlorine with phosgene that scorched eyes, lacerated lungs, and left victims heaving blood. Between March 11 and March 20, munitions were transported forward to the regiment: 2,500 high-explosive shells and 1,000 projectiles with poison gas for each position. Initially, the prospects for gas were poor, with rain and fog, but on the evening before the offensive was scheduled to begin, the weather cleared.

At 4:40 a.m., on March 21, the horizon erupted in massive artillery barrage, followed by an infantry assault supported by tanks. As the British front collapsed, the 6th Field Artillery Regiment advanced, capturing men, military dispatches, and supplies, including a phonograph with a recording of "It's a Long Way to Tipperary."

Six days later, Hartinger crossed the Somme with his regiment at Chipilly and the following day joined the assault near Hamel, just east of Amiens. Again the weather cooperated. They cleared a second British position with a massive gas attack and advanced yet again with orders to suppress British artillery fire in preparation for a major assault on Villers-Bretonneux. Hartinger and his men spent the night burrowing in amid the ruins of a nearby village as munitions were brought forward. The German artillery barrage commenced at dawn. The British guns responded only sporadically. Then suddenly the front flared with an enemy barrage that virtually obliterated Hartinger's unit. "The bursting of shells was accompanied by the crash of collapsing houses," the regimental history recorded. "Rubble covered teams, artillery, and ammunition. Rafters, bricks, and gravel whirled through the air." After four days, the regiment had lost its commander, 2 battery chiefs, 4 lieutenants, 40 junior officers, 11 officers, and 323 regular soldiers along with 379 horses and 1 veterinarian. Hartinger emerged from the slaughter unscathed and ready for more. He was awarded Bavaria's Military Service Medal and was subsequently promoted to lieutenant, committing himself to three more years of military service.

Following the armistice in November 1918, Hartinger returned home to Amberg to find Bavaria in a state of political chaos. After the Red Army victory at Dachau, he joined ten thousand other demobilized veterans in enlisting in the state militia, the Freikorps, where he found common cause with future adversaries in crushing the Soviet Republic of Bavaria. Hilmar Wäckerle, as noted, enlisted in the Freikorps Oberland, while Hans Frank, Adolf Wagner, and the Baron von Malsen-Ponickau all rallied to the Freikorps Epp, as did Heinrich Himmler, who had been a few months too young to make it to the front. Hans Steinbrenner was just thirteen at the time, and in a fevered delirium from an abscessed leg, but he never forgot the sounds of artillery and gunfire in the streets, and, of course, the sight of the Bolsheviks raiding his father's gun shop.

On May 1, the Freikorps Epp spearheaded the drive into Munich along with the Freikorps Oberland. The battle-hardened Epp pressed as mercilessly through the streets of Munich as he had two years earlier outside of Verdun, massacring the haphazard elements of the Bavarian Red Army. By Gumbel's calculation, nearly five hundred Red Army soldiers died in the fighting, were executed, or were "accidentally killed." Another estimate placed the number at one thousand. Epp lost fewer than forty men.

Hartinger had enlisted in the Freikorps Hilger that March, but he had also registered as a student and was living in a first-floor apartment at Blütenstrasse 14 in Munich, where he was a firsthand witness to the butchery. Despite possessing all the qualifications of a right-wing radical, as defined by Gumbel, Hartinger appeared to undergo a transformation in that blood-spattered spring of 1919. He resigned from his Freikorps, relinquished his officer's commission in the Reichswehr (abandoning secure monthly pay), and enrolled as a student in the department of law at the Ludwig Maximilian University, joining the first class of German law students to be educated in a multiparty democratic republic.

The legal profession, as Gumbel observed, was steeped in monarchist values and notoriously conservative. When the Criminal Procedure Code was first introduced in the late nineteenth century, it was decried by many in the judiciary for its imposition of foreign concepts such as habeas corpus and the right to self-defense. "I also believe that the ethics in demanding of the accused to explain his guilt or innocence are superior to the Anglo-American method, in which the defendant has a right to defend himself," one eminent jurist had loftily asserted at the time. "It is fundamental to the German character that one answers directly and honestly when faced with a charge." A legal authority of the day, Adolf Dochow, wrote a handbook for judges providing instructions for subverting the Criminal Procedure Code. "The accused is not obliged to give an explanation," Dochow observed; "however, the judge does not have to alert him to this right."

Two generations later, things had begun to change. By the time Hartinger enrolled in the law faculty in the spring "emergency semester"—foreshortened as a result of the postwar turmoil and the Bolshevik revolution—the law faculty offered five different courses on the Criminal Procedure Code alone. Kurt Tucholsky, the wry observer of German fancies and foibles, marveled at the handbooks on civil rights that proliferated in the Weimar Republic, noting that the "book in Germany most frequently cited after the Bible" was the Criminal Procedure Code.

The decision to abandon his military career and devote himself to legal studies plunged Hartinger into poverty. His father had been ruined by the postwar financial crisis and could provide no means of support, a point Hartinger underscored in an application for student aid on May 25, 1919. "I have no personal resources and it is impossible to find work at the moment," he wrote. Two years later, he was still in school but still without support. A financial request form he submitted to the Office of the Indigent on May 14, 1921, summarized his continued financial desperation: Military Income: 0. Civilian Income: 0. Support for Reserve Officers: 0. A welfare administrator visited Hartinger in his single-room quarters at Blütenstrasse 4 and found him living in "dire need." It was determined that "Hartinger's critical financial situation is probably directly related to his service at war." Finally, that May, Hartinger secured a 500-mark student subsidy.

Despite the hardships, Hartinger was an excellent student. He completed his final round of examinations in June 1924 with top-level scores. Shortly thereafter he secured an entry-level position in the Bavarian civil service and was assigned for three months as prison assessor in Amberg, where he was introduced into "a number of responsibilities of the State Prosecutor," including "implementation of penal procedures and prison affairs."

Hartinger impressed his superiors with his capacities from the outset. "His gift for sharp analysis, combined with an extensive and well-rounded education, allows him to quickly grasp the criminal cases and recognize the key elements of each case," a supervisor observed. He went on to serve as an assistant deputy prosecutor in Passau, then as a civil court judge with Munich I, where he remained for the next six years, establishing a reputation as a man of impressive capacity and an unrelenting opponent to the rising Nazi movement. "In my position as a prosecutor with Munich I, I was ruthless in prosecuting National Socialist excesses," Hartinger recalled. "Through my determination I was able to convict Rib- bentropp [*sic*], the editor of a Nazi newspaper, for press violations after he was repeatedly acquitted in the matter."* In March 1931, Hartinger was promoted from assistant prosecutor in Munich I to deputy prosecutor in Munich II.

By then, the once struggling student was now a state civil ser- vant with a salary ranked in the "special class." Thanks to his wife's relatives, he was living "comfortably" in an elegant street lined with fine clothing and jewelry shops, just around the corner from the stately Munich State Opera House and the Palais Montgelas, and just down the street from Odeonsplatz, which abutted the Wittelsbach Palace Gardens, open to the public for strolls. From his apartment, it was a brief tram ride to his office, or a pleasant twenty-minute stroll.

Hartinger referred to Munich affectionately as "my second home" after Amberg. At the age of thirty-nine, he was well situated and happily married, with a five-year-old daughter and the promise of a bright career in the Bavarian civil service. If all went according to plan, Hartinger would spend several more years with Munich II, and could anticipate eventually being appointed as a chief prosecu- tor, then a district attorney general, and possibly even a president of a district court, with the prospect of a full pension when he reached retirement age in the late 1950s.

---

* Hartinger appears to be thinking of Alfred Rosenberg rather than Joachim von Rib- bentrop. Rosenberg served as the editor of the Nazi daily newspaper *Völkischer Beobachter* from 1923 to 1938, and was repeatedly charged with press violations. Ribbentrop had no involvement with the National Socialist movement until 1932, when he met Hitler and joined the Nazi Party, serving as Hitler's foreign minister from 1938 to 1945. Since significant portions of the Munich I court records have been destroyed, there is no way of confirming the particular trial to which Hartinger is referring.

But then came that phone call from the Dachau camp. What he had heard and would subsequently see and learn reminded him of the troubled spring of 1919. The legal system had failed to respond back then, as Emil Gumbel made clear, and the consequences had been horrific. What happened in Germany in the spring of 1919 would not be allowed to recur in the spring of 1933. It was Hartinger's firm conviction that the past would not repeat itself, at least not in the Munich II jurisdiction.

10

Law and Disorder

B Y MONDAY, May 8, all hell seemed to be breaking loose in the Dachau Concentration Camp. In less than thirty-six hours, one detainee had committed suicide, another had died in a failed assault on a guard, and a third had vanished into thin air. For all the order and discipline on which Wäckerle prided himself, he appeared to have lost control of his camp. Word of the chaos spread quickly. That Wednesday, the Dachau newspaper reported on the dramatic developments in the nearby detention facility:

> During the night from May 8 to 9, the mechanic and well-known communist leader Johann Beimler of Augsburg escaped from the Dachau Concentration Camp. . . . A 100-mark reward was set by the camp administration for any information leading to the capture of the fugitive. . . . The former chairman of the communist faction in the former Bavarian parliament, Fritz Dressel, of Deggendorf, who was arrested only a few days ago in Munich and taken into protective custody, committed suicide in Dachau during the night of last Monday. The reason for his suicide is unknown. He probably killed himself because of depression.

> Yesterday, Tuesday afternoon, the detainee Götz, former communist member of parliament, was shot while violently assaulting one of the guards. A judicial commission immediately started an inquiry.

News of the Beimler escape went national, then international. The escape was trumpeted in the left-wing press from London to Prague to Moscow. One of the most wanted men in Germany, a prize catch of the Hitler government, had simply vanished from one of the most heavily guarded and secure detention facilities in the country. The Beimler escape represented a massive security failure for the facility and a public embarrassment for Wäckerle. Two weeks after his star turn in the pages of the *New York Times,* the "quiet-mannered, blond, blue-eyed" former officer was humiliated.

The worst part for Wäckerle was that he had seen it coming. The week before, Beimler had complained about a serious pain in his lower abdomen. The symptoms suggested appendicitis. Wäckerle checked with his superiors. Instructions came that Beimler was to be taken to a hospital. He was entrusted to Captain Schlemmer, who accompanied him to the Nussbaumstrasse clinic for observation. The attending physician determined immediately that there was nothing wrong; Beimler was "feigning illness." "After consultation with the officials in the penitentiary in Stadelheim," where Beimler had been before his transfer to Dachau, an internal memo records, "it was decided that he will not be kept in the sick bay but rather in a solitary security cell." Beimler was transported back to Stadelheim. The prison was put on high alert. The area surrounding the prison was searched for suspicious activity, but "absolutely nothing abnormal was observed." Three days later, when Beimler was returned to Dachau, Wäckerle was waiting.

It was another wet, miserable spring day, the air dank and chilled, the ground muddy and covered in puddles. Surveying the transport list, Wäckerle saw among the twenty-nine prisoners not only Beimler, but a number of other notable communists. Willy Wirthgen was the leading communist activist in Allgäu, where Wäckerle had run a farm several years before. Back then Wirthgen was considered "a particularly dangerous communist," as was Hans Rogen, who had "allegedly shot SA man Kiefer on the Giesinger mountain." There was also Josef Hirsch, a communist on the Munich city council notorious for anti-Nazi tirades, and Fritz Dressel, yet another delegate to the state legislature. "That one is an especially dangerous communist," an annotation on the transport list noted. Word also had it that Dressel had spit in the face of an SS man at the Ettstrasse police station. There was Max Holy, who, despite his involvement with the Red Assistance, the Communist Party's international liaison unit, was said to "count among the decent communists." Finally, there was Joseph Rahm, who had reportedly kicked an SS man while being beaten at the Ettstrasse police station.

The arrival of these men came amid heightened concern on Wäckerle's part. "On that day, when three buses of detainees arrived from Kempten, Wäckerle was particularly agitated," police trainer Emil Schuler recalled. "He apparently came from Kempten and it seems that among the newly arrived prisoners he had spotted some of his political enemies. Thus I assume that in his rage and also fear of a communist revolt, Wäckerle gave orders to Erspenmüller to shoot some prisoners that evening."

Wäckerle wanted the men sorted and identified immediately. As the transport arrived and the men tumbled from the truck, Wäckerle's men set to work with flailing pizzles and curses. "Where is Dressel? That swine spit in my face." "Just don't forget Rahm. That bastard hit an SS man." Rahm, a young man of twenty-one, was pulled from the ranks and set upon by SS men who beat and cuffed him to the ground, then pummeled him with their boots as he writhed in the mud, bleeding from his mouth and nose. Wäckerle watched the scene with cool detachment, as usual smoking a cigarette, then pronounced his sentences for the Arrest Bunker. "Beimler, my friend, fourteen days of strict detention," he said. "Dressel gets five days so that he doesn't spit on any other SS men. Hirsch, give him some time to think about his actions against the nationalist factions in the city council—three days. Rahm, five days."

The men were marched to the Arrest Bunker, where Vogel was waiting for them. Vogel placed Hirsch in Cell 1, where Hunglinger had hanged himself the previous week, and, since Götz was still in Cell 2, he assigned Dressel and Beimler together in Cell 3, with Rahm in Cell 4. Steinbrenner arrived a short while later and flung open the door to Cell 3. "What, you bastard, you spit on an SS man?" he screamed at Dressel, commanding him to strip and lie on the bunk. Steinbrenner then ordered his men to set upon Dressel with their pizzles, starting with the soles of his feet and gradually working their way up his legs, across his buttocks, back, and shoulders to the top of his head. Beimler was next. "And you, you coward, you swine, it's your turn now," he said. "We're going to beat your feigned illnesses out of you all right. Strip!" Steinbrenner watched Beimler undress, ordered him onto the bunk, then put his whipping team to work again. When they finished, Steinbrenner slammed the door and moved on to Rahm, who stood in his cell bleeding and terrified.

"Why is that young guy there?" Vogel queried Steinbrenner, who explained that Rahm had reportedly kicked an SS man at the Ett Street police station. Rahm said that while he was being beaten he had flinched and accidentally struck an SS man. There was no defiance in the battered young man, only fear. "Yes, that seems more logical to me, than that this young kid could have hit an SS man," Vogel mused. "We can't really consider that hitting. I would defend myself the same way if I were being beaten." Vogel and Steinbrenner reflected for a moment, then released Rahm, dispatching him to the regular barracks. Dressel was now moved into the empty cell.

Hirsch was selected for particular abuse. "He was one of the real bosses out there," Wäckerle had told Steinbrenner, and signaled with his hand to let Hirsch really have it. "Hard, really hard," he had said. In the cell, Steinbrenner ordered Hirsch to strip. When Hirsch did not respond quickly enough, Steinbrenner tore the clothes into shreds himself, then set his men on Hirsch. They broke Hirsch's nose, smashed out his front teeth, and kicked him in the genitals, then began lashing him bloody with their pizzles. Hirsch blacked out. "So, you dog, you dead dog, you're awake again," Steinbrenner said when Hirsch regained consciousness. The other SS men told Steinbrenner to leave Hirsch alone. He had had enough. But Steinbrenner went after him again, giving him another four or five lashes.

Steinbrenner and his team returned later in the day for another round of flogging. They started with Hirsch, then Götz, then Beimler, then Dressel, each time the same routine—the clack of boots, the jangling of keys, the order to strip, the thrashing from heel to head, with an occasional cuff or kick as seemed appropriate, the slamming of the door, the jangling of keys, and the lock bolted down.

The next day, Steinbrenner returned in the company of Wäckerle, who stood in the narrow, dank hallway amid the swarm of accompanying SS men, with Steinbrenner in the lead. "Götz, the troublemaker, is in there," Steinbrenner explained, opening the door, then adding, "A first-class criminal." Beimler was next. "In here we have a particularly special example of a Bolshevik pig," Steinbrenner said. Wäckerle studied the battered, glowering man with the protruding ears, made a few comments, then turned. Steinbrenner slammed the door. Vogel turned the lock. They proceeded to Dressel for a similar routine. During a separate interrogation, Hirsch had the toes on his right foot twisted out, and his right thumb broken.

Steinbrenner returned the next day for another tour, this time with the SS man who had scuffled with Dressel. He gave the man an opportunity to view Dressel and ask, "Are you going to spit at me again?" The guard was then given free rein with Dressel. Steinbrenner trooped down to Beimler's cell. When Beimler leaped to attention as Vogel had instructed, Steinbrenner kicked him in the stomach and hurled him into the corner, pointing his pistol at him. Beimler stared coldly into the barrel, unflinching. "Turn around!" Steinbrenner ordered. Beimler turned to the wall. Steinbrenner placed the barrel against the back of his head, then said, "You pig, you are not worth a single bullet. But you will be hanged tomorrow morning at seven. You can still pray and write a letter." Steinbrenner returned that evening for another round of beatings. "He has five days and should get twenty-five [lashes] every day," Steinbrenner instructed a guard outside Dressel's door. The men had to break at some point. They had managed with Hunglinger; they would manage with these.

Wäckerle arrived at the Arrest Bunker on the morning of the fifth day in the company of Steinbrenner. He let his attack dog loose on Dressel. The Arrest Bunker was shrill with Dressel's screams as the dog set upon him. "An hour later Dressel was brought into the sick bay, covered in blood and unconscious," Friedrich Schaper, a detainee in the sick bay, recalled. "Dressel was laid on a straw sack about five meters from my cot. Dr. Katz bandaged his lower arm. Steinbrenner entered and explained: 'He cut open his arm with a knife.'" Katz wanted to give him an injection for his heart. "In that same moment Steinbrenner came back into the sick bay and said, 'He's not getting any treatment, let him die straightaway, he spit at an SS man in Ettstrasse.'"

Steinbrenner had Dressel returned to his cell later that day in the company of two SS orderlies who were instructed to "take care of" the wounded man. Around two o'clock the next afternoon, Wäckerle appeared in the Arrest Bunker in the company of Steinbrenner. "Hey, Beimler, how long are you thinking of continuing to pester mankind with your existence?" Wäckerle asked casually as he entered the cell. "I already told you once before that you need to realize that you are superfluous in today's society, in National Socialist Germany." Wäckerle pointed to the knife on the table. "We didn't give you that knife to cut bread," he said. "That's for something else." Beimler replied that he had been a member of the German Communist Party for fourteen years and was not about to give up now. He told Wäckerle that if he thought he was "superfluous" he should simply give the order to have him shot.

"Will you look at that! Now the swine is getting cheeky," Wäckerle said, smiling. "Shoot you? No, you swine, you aren't worth a bullet. We're going to just let you starve." Beimler said he had been incarcerated for four weeks and was three-quarters starved and would survive the final quarter. Steinbrenner then punched him in the chest with full force. Beimler lurched back against the wall so hard, he cried out in pain. "Look at that," Wäckerle said. "He can still scream." Leaning against the door, he turned to Steinbrenner. "Screaming doesn't help much." He smiled knowingly. "Around here things are quick and silent." The door was slammed shut.

Two minutes later, Wäckerle was back to fetch Beimler. He led him down the corridor to Cell 4. Dressel lay dead on the cold, bare floor, his bandage ripped off, a puddle of blood beneath his opened wounds. "So! Now you see how to do it," Wäckerle told Beimler, back in his cell. "No need to think that we took you in there to see your friend one last time in order to say goodbye to him. You are just supposed to see how to do it, and that he wasn't as much of a coward as you. He had much more character than you, you spineless pig."

Wäckerle and Steinbrenner then went to Götz and repeated the same procedure. When they were finished, Wäckerle returned yet again to Beimler's cell. He asked him whether he had thought it through. Beimler said he had not changed his opinion. "Let me tell you something," Wäckerle said. "I'll give you until five o'clock. It's three now, and if you haven't done it by five, then we'll finish you."

That afternoon an investigation team accompanied by Emil

Schuler entered the camp. "Both [Dressel's] arteries were opened," Schuler recalled, "and it occurred to me at the time that the arteries had not been opened in a way that one normally finds in suicides." The slashes did not run across the wrist but instead followed the artery up the arm. "It was said that such wounds could only be made by a doctor or someone with training," Schuler observed. Despite suspicions of foul play, the SS account could not be refuted.

Steinbrenner returned to Beimler's cell sometime later. "I've heard you want to hang yourself," he said. "I don't care how you do it, if you're too much of a coward to use the knife. Do you know how to do it?" Steinbrenner tore a strip from Beimler's sheets and fashioned it into a noose. He put his head into it to demonstrate. "So now I've done everything that I can to help you, I can't do any more," he said. "So, all you need to do now is stick your head inside it, and hang the other end onto the window, and it's all done. In two minutes it's all over. There is nothing to it. And in any event you're not getting out of this cell alive anymore." Steinbrenner paused, then barked, "The commandant's orders are to be obeyed!"

Beimler looked at Steinbrenner and said he would prefer to wait. He explained that it was his son's birthday and that the twelve-year-old was celebrating the event with his grandparents, since both his parents were in prison. He asked for a one-day reprieve. "I don't want my son always to be reminded on his birthday that it was the day on which his father committed suicide," he said. Steinbrenner mused for a moment, then told Beimler that his was a "plausible reason" for a delay. He would discuss the matter. He was certain that Wäckerle would grant a "grace period" under the circumstances, but asked Beimler to give him his word of honor. Beimler looked at Steinbrenner and reminded him that for the last four weeks he had been denounced as a traitor to his country, to the workers, a traitor plain and simple. "I wouldn't ask a man, if I am convinced he is a traitor," he said, "to give his word of honor." Steinbrenner paused. "All right then," he said. "Then just give me your word!"

Steinbrenner departed to consult with Wäckerle and returned a short while later. "So I told the commandant about it," he reported. "And he is giving you, because of your son, for his birthday, until tomorrow morning. But I'm telling you now, don't you dare greet me alive tomorrow morning when I unlock the door." That night Beimler alerted Hirsch of his intentions. "Beimler was in the cell next to me and I knew of his plan to escape that night," Hirsch recalled, "since I had been communicating with him through tapping signals."

The next morning, Steinbrenner entered the barrack with his usual command when making the rounds, "Get the hell out here!" Hirsch responded instantly, rushing outside to relieve himself, knowing full well what would follow. He was returning as Götz was just emerging from his cell, when Steinbrenner discovered Beimler was missing. When Hirsch and Götz feigned ignorance, Steinbrenner flew into a rage, lashing and kicking them. "Just wait, you are dead dogs," he said as he locked them in their cells. "You'll talk soon enough." A short while later, the camp siren sounded and the detainees began assembling outside the barracks. Steinbrenner returned with Erspenmüller, who ordered Hirsch to bring his straw mattress into the corridor. Erspenmüller had his pistol drawn. Hirsch recognized the danger immediately. The SS could use the excuse of shooting a detainee "trying to escape," Hirsch knew, but would not risk shooting a man in his cell. Hirsch refused to leave it. Steinbrenner lashed him, then kicked him with his jackboots, but Hirsch would not budge. Erspenmüller walked down the corridor to Götz, where he was joined by Steinbrenner and Karl Wicklmayr. Hirsch recalled that after four weeks of relentless beating, Götz was "no longer mentally normal." "Sometimes he would simply not respond to questions or would give confusing answers," Hirsch remembered. He had grown "slow and clumsy." Another detainee, Rudolf Wiblishauser, recalled seeing Steinbrenner with two other SS men force Götz into the toilet stall, where they beat him bloody.

"Afterward I had to clean the stall," Wiblishauser recalled. "There were large patches of blood on the walls as well as scraps of skin and flesh and tufts of hair." Wiblishauser was certain the hair was from Götz because it was blond, the same color as Götz's. Steinbrenner later gave Götz strips of the *Völkischer Beobachter* to use as bandages to stop the bleeding. Battered and listless, Götz lifted his straw mattress into his arms as instructed and stepped into the hallway. An instant later, a gunshot was fired.

In the meantime, Wäckerle, convinced Beimler still had to be in the camp, had the barracks cleared. SS guards marched through the quarters with bayonets, slashing and piercing everything in sight. Crawl spaces were searched. The detainees were assembled outside and forced to conduct repeated roll calls. "Gradually, those in the front rank realized what had happened, and a hot thrill ran through the assembled ranks like a wildfire," a detainee recalled. "One of those who had been tortured, Hans Beimler from Munich, had escaped his executioners from the Arrest Bunker that night." When it was clear that Beimler was no longer in the camp, Wäckerle ordered men and dogs into the surrounding woods and fields. But Beimler was nowhere to be found. "As we later learned, he was able to stay in Munich for several weeks while his wounds healed," the detainee remembered, "and then he escaped abroad as the first crown witness of Dachau."*

Accounts of the Beimler escape abounded. One held that he had worn thick socks to scale the electrified fence. Another claimed he had used a blanket to scuttle beneath the wire. Someone said he had strangled a guard, slipped into his uniform, and sauntered through the gate. Max Holy, the "decent communist," was thought to have engineered the escape. Josef Hirsch claimed it was two SS men

---

* Beimler escaped across the German-Czechoslovak border to Prague, then to Moscow, where he completed an account of his time in Dachau. The book was published that August under the title *Im Mörderlager Dachau*, and in English translation as *Four Weeks in the Hands of Hitler's Hell-Hounds: The Nazi Murder Camp of Dachau*, providing the first detailed account of atrocity inside a Nazi concentration camp.

who owed Beimler a favor. Beimler later gave his own dramatic account. "I was able to take advantage of a series of lucky breaks," he recounted. "I succeeded, despite a high risk of death—a risk I had taken into account in preparing my escape—not only to break through the triple layers of barbed wire (the middle one was electrified) but also to climb over the two-meter-high wall." He claimed to have tottered on the top of the concrete wall for an instant, wondering whether he had been seen, then when miraculously no guard appeared to have noticed him, he leaped to freedom.

Wäckerle's humiliation by Beimler and revenge on Götz was compounded by the removal of Hirsch from his custody. "Shortly thereafter, the captain of the state police came and ordered my transfer to Munich," Hirsch later recalled. "As I was led away, I had to step over Götz's corpse." Hirsch later observed that the state police had literally saved his life.

Wicklmayr took responsibility for the shooting. He told the police that Götz had been passing him in the hall with his pillow and straw mat when suddenly Götz set upon him. Wicklmayr pushed him away, but when Götz lunged a second time, he was forced to shoot. Götz died instantly. Steinbrenner said that he had been in the SS changing room when he heard the scuffle and gunshot. "I opened the door and saw Wicklmayr standing there with a smoking gun in his hand," he recalled. "Götz was lying on the ground, shot through the head." The pistol had been fired at such short range that the bullet penetrated Götz's skull and then went straight through the door of the adjacent cell where a new arrival, Franz Stenzer, was being held. Steinbrenner entered the cell to recover the spent projectile. "You are lucky," he told Stenzer. "It could have hit you." Götz's straw sack was soaked with blood and the walls were splattered. "It looks like a slaughterhouse in here," Vogel observed. Detainee Friedrich Schaper was ordered to clean the hallway. "I used a rag to wipe up the blood, which was still warm, and wrung it out in a bucket," he said.

Kasimir Dittenheber worked with Wicklmayr in the camp office and did not believe the story. Dittenheber knew Wicklmayr was considered a *Sonderling,* an outsider, among the other SS guards, but he did not believe "the student" was capable of killing a man. Other detainees shared the same opinion. Wicklmayr was a quiet, thoughtful young man who was not assigned to any particular commando and spent most of his time filling out detainee registration cards in the camp office. He liked to chat with the detainees, especially a writer named Arthur Müller with whom he discussed literature. Wicklmayr aspired to be an editor. Dittenheber wondered why such a person had ever joined the SS. "Whenever an SS man like Steinbrenner came and demanded the keys for the arrest bunker," Dittenheber recalled, the camp manager Vogel gave them a hard time. "These SS men invariably went to the cells and, as we could hear in the office, abused the detainees." Dittenheber never heard a sound when Wicklmayr asked for the keys.

The problem for Hartinger, of course, was the absence of credible eyewitness testimony. The SS guards closed ranks and kept their stories straight. The detainees were afraid to speak. Hartinger's only hope lay in forensics. The following morning, Dr. Flamm arrived to examine Götz's corpse. He confirmed the cause of death from a bullet wound, but noticed a blood-crusted wound on the left frontal lobe just behind the hairline. Flamm reported this to Hartinger, who decided to keep the investigation open until the cause of the wound had been determined.

11

A Realm unto Itself

M Y FATHER IS on the city council!" Wilhelm Aron screamed. "I will have you reported!" But Hans Steinbrenner did not care. He gripped Aron's head in an armlock and smothered his protests with camp bedding. The twenty-five-year-old Bamberg junior attorney was in the camp storage room, his lean, athletic body stretched naked on a table, while Johann Kantschuster and Johann Unterhuber lashed him again and again. The two SS guards worked their way from Aron's calves up his legs toward his buttocks while Aron screamed his muffled threats into the blue-and-white-striped camp bedding.

But Willy Aron was serious about the recourse. His father, Judicial Counsel Albert Aron, was not only a municipal legal adviser, he was also a member of the Bamberg city council, and one of the district's most prominent attorneys, one of three Bamberg attorneys with an office on Luitpoldstrasse in the center of town.

As a junior attorney, Willy was already able to represent clients in court and preparing for his final bar examination, which would elevate him to the full privileges of an attorney-at-law. Were the circumstances different, he could bring these SS brutes to justice on his own. It would not be the first time he had brought a National Socialist into a courtroom.

Despite his youth, junior attorney Wilhelm Aron had already made headlines in the Bamberg press for three high-profile trials. Aron was a tall, handsome young man, with chiseled features accented by his fair reddish-blond hair, light skin, and penetrating blue eyes, which traced back to his father's Prussian provenance. He was an active member in a local fencing and private social club, the Wirceburgia. On occasion, he sported monocles in a good-natured gibe at his more conservative club members. He inscribed his name twice in the club registry—once in the distinct Teutonic script of the era called *"Stechlin,"* and again in Hebrew letters, a nod to his Jewish origins. Aron was proud of his Jewish heritage, confident of his legal capacities, defiantly anti–National Socialist, and a fervent Social Democrat. He had belonged to the socialist youth movement and had flirted with communism, joining torchlight parades and rallies for the poor and indigent. According to a local newspaper account, he had led a socialist song evening that included a German rendition of the Soviet anthem "Tomorrow We and the Sun Will Rise."

In January 1932, a year after the first of his two legal examinations, Aron represented five defendants in a "sensational trial" against a Bamberg criminal ring that included twenty-four men involved in a series of illegal activities. In one incident, four defendants broke into a local warehouse and made off with eight bottles of Prosecco, eight bottles of beer, several jars of preserved fruit, and fifteen bottles of schnapps, all of which they consumed that same night. The conservative *Bamberger Volksblatt* spoke of "serious crimes against property committed in a gangland manner." The *Freistaat,* a local socialist newspaper, struck a more sympathetic tone, describing despairing men "who were led onto the criminal track because of long unemployment." Aron represented five of the defendants—a worker, two laborers, a plasterer, and a woodworker—and decided to appeal to the court's sympathies by focusing on the plight of the unemployed men. The strategy worked. While the Bamberg prosecutor argued for a seven-year prison sentence for one of Aron's defendants, Aron succeeded in having the term reduced to eighteen months.

That same year, Aron appeared in another high-profile case, this time representing a local saddlemaker accused of providing abortions for local girls. Bamberg was the seat of one of Bavaria's six bishops, and conservative Catholic sentiments ran strong within the town. Few lawyers risked taking on such a case. Initially, Albert Aron agreed to take the case; in October he transferred it to his son. The case involved a young woman from Nuremberg who had gotten pregnant by a visiting medical student from Egypt. When the man abandoned the girl and returned home, a friend of the pregnant girl recommended the Bamberg saddlemaker as an abortionist. When the police were alerted of the matter through an "anonymous report," the local prosecutor brought charges against the friend, the girl, and the saddlemaker.

Aron had planned for his client, the saddlemaker, to plead not guilty, since he had not yet admitted to the crime, but when it became evident that the other defendants had already identified him, Aron changed strategy, arguing that rising public opinion was calling for the lifting of the national ban on abortion. "It is only a matter of time until §218 will succumb to the long-standing call for change being demanded by millions of women and men," he said, securing a reduction of his client's sentence from eighteen months to one year. The *Bamberger Volksblatt* denounced Aron's courtroom defense in an article warning of an "Epidemic of Abortions."

That December, Aron was back in court and in the headlines again, this time as the lead defense attorney for a group of Social Democratic activists following a violent clash with local Nazis. The incident had occurred on election night in July when the National Socialists secured a landslide victory in national elections. The

Social Democrats were gathered that evening in the Nöth Restaurant on Schillerplatz to follow the election returns and deliberate on the results. Suddenly, a group of Nazis, celebrating the victory, approached the restaurant looking for a fight. "The attackers approached with rubber truncheons, leather straps, and steel rings," one of Aron's defendants observed. "We defended ourselves with garden chairs, broken chair legs, and logs that were stacked in the courtyard." It took the police a full hour to quell the melee. More than a dozen of those injured were rushed to the hospital. Nazis and Social Democrats alike were arrested. The incident was dubbed "Slaughter on Schillerplatz."

During the trial, Aron took an aggressive stance against the National Socialists, insisting they had been the aggressors and countering the false claim that they had summoned the police when in fact they had rushed to find reinforcements. Most notably, Aron put not only the National Socialists but also the prosecution on the defensive. Why, Aron wanted to know, did the prosecution issue an indictment against Josef Dennstädt, head of the Social Democratic Party, but not against Lorenz Zahneisen, his National Socialist counterpart, even though Zahneisen had not only been present but had been seen "holding a nail-studded club"? The prosecutor provided an extended and evasive retort but eventually conceded before the court, "Because of new and concrete evidence found in the main trial, Zahneisen will have to undergo a criminal investigation as well." The *Freistaat* hailed Aron as a town hero. A local pro-Nazi newspaper denounced him as a *"Saujude,"* or Jewish pig.

Three months later, on the morning of March 10, Aron was taken into protective custody in the same sweep that caught Benario, Goldmann, and hundreds of others across Bavaria. Like Benario, Aron was held in local detention, where he passed his time studying for his upcoming law boards, unaware that instructions had already been given by the president of the examining board to cancel his participation in the exam because of his detention. "Should he be released from protective custody and try to continue his legal training," the president ruled, "then he will be notified that he is until further notice on leave and will not be allowed to continue his preparatory work." Two weeks later, Aron found himself in a world beyond the law.

To put an end to Hartinger's repeated intrusions, Himmler instructed Wäckerle to place the camp under martial law and to draft regulations under which detainees could be shot. The eighteen-paragraph set of "Special Regulations" outlined the rights and obligations of the concentration camp's residents, including both detainees and SS personnel. Paragraph 1 was simple, declarative, and explicit: "The Collecting Camp Dachau falls under the rule of martial law." The second paragraph established the inviolability of its borders: "In the case of a detainee's attempt at escape, the guards and escort troops have the right to make use of their firearms without warning." Here, the local regulations drew on the 1837 Prussian law that, much to Emil Gumbel's dismay, had permitted soldiers to execute more than a thousand detainees with impunity. Infractions for which detainees could be punished included "intentionally lying," "defying the camp regulations," "offending or slandering," "collecting signatures for a collective complaint," and "being in any way in contact with or trying to contact someone outside of the camp without permission." Paragraph 8 outlined four offenses for which a detainee could be executed:

1. Anyone who tries to defend himself physically or resists the guard troops or members of the camp commando physically.
2. Anyone who compels or tries to compel another prisoner to disobey the members of the camp administration or guard troops.
3. Anyone who incites or tries to incite behavior mentioned under number 1 and 2.
4. Anyone who participates in collective disobedience or a physical attack mentioned in number 1.

From a juridical perspective, paragraph 18 was the most consequential. It bore the heading "Jurisdiction" and accorded the commandant his own legal jurisdiction within the camp perimeter and established a judicial process that was clear, simple, and comprehensive. "The jurisdiction within the camp and regarding the prisoners is exercised without exception by the commandant of the camp," the regulation stipulated. "All cases that fall under paragraph 18 undergo trial in the camp court, which consists of the administration of the camp, one or two of the officers in charge, and one of the SS guards." The prosecutors were to be selected by the commandant from among the SS. In case a decision could not be reached, the commandant was to cast the deciding vote. In the absence of the commandant, the powers devolved to his deputy. In six brief pages, the Dachau Concentration Camp was transformed into the smallest jurisdiction in the country.

On May 15, a bright spring day with warming temperatures, three transports arrived in Dachau, two from Nuremberg and one from Bamberg, adding ninety-five detainees to the camp population. As usual, the trucks roared through the gate and stopped on the square in front of the commandant's office. A clutch of SS guards stood waiting, pizzles twitching expectantly in their hands, but this time the camp legal counsel Otto Franck was there to oversee the arrivals. As the men tumbled out of the transport, an SS guard identified a short, balding man in his late fifties. "Here we have the Jewish pig Schloss," he called out. "Do with him whatever you want." Louis Schloss was a shopkeeper from Nuremberg who had been featured repeatedly in *Der Stürmer* as a "typical Jewish pig." Franck commanded Schloss to step forward and strip. Schloss was a stocky man with a thickish, flabby belly and buttocks. He undressed awkwardly before the assembled men, and was then ordered to lie facedown on the large curved fender of the bus. The SS men, with sleeves rolled up and kepis thrown back, set upon him, flailing him mercilessly into unconsciousness. The other detainees watched in silence.

When the SS guards had finished with Schloss, Franck ordered Willy Aron to step forward. "I still see our dear Willy, tall, reddish-blond hair, blue-eyed, freckled and in shorts, a breadbag dangling from his belt, the former emblem of the hiking and friends-of-nature youth," a fellow detainee recalled. "He looked at us optimistically, the way he always was." Emil Schuler, the police trainer who had intervened in the shooting of Benario, Goldmann, and the Kahns, was also witness to Aron's arrival. "He had barely gotten off the truck when an SS man lunged at him, beat him to the ground and stomped on his body with his feet," he remembered. "I immediately intervened and yelled at the SS man for his behavior. He said it was none of my business, I was just a police officer. Thereupon I issued a complaint to the commandant and shortly thereafter I was sent back to Munich."

When the new arrivals had been assembled into a double rank, Aron was ordered to identify himself.

"Aron, Wilhelm," he yelled out. "Junior attorney."

"Not anymore," Franck shot back. He had already been informed of the decision to revoke Aron's legal privileges.

Besides Aron and Schloss, four other Jewish detainees were pulled from the ranks that morning—Max Bronner, Bertoldt Langstädter, Hans Neumann, and Hans Oppenheimer—and handed over to Steinbrenner, who took them to the isolated storage room in Barrack II. "We were called in there one by one and had to undress upon command," Oppenheimer recalled. "We were laid down onto the table, held by SS men, and whipped by the others with pizzles from our thighs to our necks until we fell unconscious."

Whether it was Aron's defiance and threats or his striking appearance, he appeared to have provoked a particularly impassioned ferocity. While four SS men held Aron in place, Steinbrenner and Johann Unterhuber stood on either side and began the routine lashing, first across his calves, then along the back of his thighs, then across his buttocks, and up across his back to his neck, only to repeat the process in the other direction. The lashes cut into the skin. They began to draw blood. The men whipped Aron into unconsciousness, then threw him into the toilet stall and hurled his clothes and pouch after him.

After some time Aron managed to get dressed and stagger out of the barracks and into line with the other Jewish detainees, who were now ordered to assemble in front of the barrack. Oppenheimer, who stood beside Aron, remembers the blood streaming down his legs from the open wounds in his buttocks. Suddenly Aron collapsed. An SS man saw him fall and ordered, "Get up, you Jewish swine!" Aron struggled to get to his feet but he could not find the strength. He held up his hand to Oppenheimer for help. When the SS man saw Oppenheimer reach down, he lunged forward and drove his boot with a deep powerful kick into Aron's lower back. The blow knocked Aron unconscious. The other detainees were ordered to march to the barrack, leaving Aron a broken heap on the ground.

Aron was dragged back to his barrack and dumped onto his bunk. Defying a camp rule against detainees entering barracks other than their own, one of Aron's friends sought him out. "When I came into the room, people were sprawled on the beds as if they were already half-dead," he recalled. "I found Aron, who was lying crumpled on a straw sack. I rearranged him and asked what was wrong. Aron groaned incessantly and indicated that he had internal injuries." "His buttocks had been lashed such that the flesh was torn off and the bones lay bare," another detainee recalled. When he asked Aron if he could do anything to help, Aron weakly asked for water.

Aron was taken to the sick bay, where he was attended to by Dr. Katz, and "visited" regularly by Steinbrenner, Unterhuber, Erspenmüller, and, once or twice a day, Wäckerle. "During the morning visit around about 9–10, Steinbrenner as well as the second in command Erspenmüller fetched Aron from his hay sack, to continue his beating," a fellow barrack mate recalled. "The procedure took place in a room next to the guard's changing room, where they beat the Jew Aron's naked body and infected wounds yet again." Aron grew delirious. He began to thrash so violently that he had to be tied to the bed. The following morning, Steinbrenner appeared again. He stood over Aron and commanded, "Get up!" Aron did not move. Steinbrenner kicked him with his boot. Aron remained still. When Steinbrenner went to the table to write a notice of infraction for Aron's disobedience, Dr. Katz called to him, "He's dead you know." Steinbrenner marched out.

Later that day, Aron's corpse was placed in a shed with several other corpses. "Rumors had it that on arrival of a new transport, four Jews were immediately taken aside and were beaten in the cellar under the prisoners' kitchen," Steinbrenner recalled. "It was said that salt water was poured onto their open wounds to heighten their agony." Steinbrenner noted further that Wäckerle was concerned about a repeat intrusion by Hartinger—despite the new camp regulations—and ordered the corpses burned.

That night, around ten o'clock, the shed burst into flames. The camp alarm sounded. Chaos followed. The Dachau fire department responded to the alarm but the firefighters were halted at the main gate and refused entry. Inside the walls, Anton Schöberl, a detainee responsible for the camp fire brigade, assembled his men, but their firefighting equipment had been moved. Schöberl eventually located the gear and rushed his men to the scene. Flames were already cutting through the roof. The firefighters attached their fire hose to a nearby hydrant but discovered it was not operable. They located a second hydrant and attached the hose. An SS man, however, refused them access to the shed, insisting he had orders to keep it locked. Schöberl clambered onto the roof of the shed and started breaking the roof tiles to clear an opening for the fire hose. "I could still recognize Aron but not the others," he said later. "Aron was a noticeably slim man and because of the light from the flames I could distinctly recognize him." The fire hose was passed onto the roof and the flames eventually extinguished. Schöberl and his crew were then ordered to leave the equipment and proceed to the canteen, where they were all given a round of beer. Afterward they returned to their barracks in the wire enclosure. The next morning, they were dispatched back to the shed to retrieve the firefighting equipment. The door was still locked.

"It was rumored that the structure had been intentionally torched and all the delays preplanned," Steinbrenner was to say years later, "to prevent the real cause of [Aron's] death from being clarified." The official cause of death was given as pulmonary edema, allowing Aron's abused and charred body to slip unobtrusively through Paragraph 159 of the Criminal Procedure Code and beyond the reach of Josef Hartinger. Aron's body was placed in a sealed metal coffin and shipped to Bamberg, where word had it that the twenty-eight-year-old had died of "heart failure."

The *Bamberger Volksblatt* reported Willy's death in respectful but notably circumspect terms. "The corpse of junior attorney Willy Aron who passed away in the Dachau Concentration Camp was transferred to Bamberg yesterday," the newspaper noted on May 13, "and interred in the Israelite Cemetery at seven-thirty in the evening." The funeral was attended by an exceptionally large number of mourners, not only from the Jewish community, but also from Willy's broader circle of friends, including members of the Wirceburgia fencing club. Rabbi Katten gave a eulogy in front of the sealed coffin. He spoke of the pain felt by the parents for the loss of their only son. He said that Willy's fate, which had shaken so many so deeply, had been "the fate of the Jews for centuries." He noted that Willy was now in a better place and closed the ceremony by again offering words of comfort to his parents. A friend of Willy's offered further remarks as Willy was lowered into his grave. The funeral was observed by local SS men, who maintained watch for several days afterward to make certain the coffin was not disinterred and opened. One rumor held that it contained only lead plates in place of Willy's abused and charred corpse.

In those same days, the *Völkischer Beobachter* reported on the Hitler government's efforts to curb animal cruelty. The newspaper reminded readers of the Field and Forest Police Law that provided "a fine of 150 marks or up to a week in prison" for anyone caught disturbing eggs or nesting birds. In addition, the minister of transport, Paul von Eltz-Rübenach, had publicly condemned the mistreatment of animals, especially horses, being transported across German territory. "In response to repeated complaints about the intolerable conditions on trains transporting foreign horses on the German railway system, the Reich transport minister in cooperation with the management of the German Reich Railway Company and the respective Reich and Prussian offices, have taken measures," the minister said. "A special procedure will be introduced on a test basis to prevent too many animals being placed in individual railcars." He also observed that a watchman would accompany each transport in order to assure "orderly treatment" of the animals. The May 11 article bore the headline REICH TRANSPORT MINISTER AGAINST ANIMAL CRUELTY.

ON MAY 13, a day after the Dressel investigation was closed and Willy Aron was laid to rest, Dr. Moritz Flamm declared himself a full-blooded Aryan. With his tight, elegant signature, Flamm confirmed three generations of pure Aryan lineage, and declared that he had never been a member of the *Reichsbanner*, the militant wing of the Social Democratic Party; the German Communist party's Iron Front; the Human Rights League; or the republican Union of Judges or Civil Servants.

Flamm was responding to a directive from the president of the Munich II court requesting compliance with the April 7 Law for the Restoration of the Professional Civil Service. This was the same law that had cost Leo Benario his teaching position at the Nuremberg Professional School of Business and Social Sciences, and deprived Emil Gumbel of his professorship at the University of Heidelberg. The law had come amid a cascade of spring legislation—the March 23 Enabling Act that invested Hitler with near dictatorial powers, followed a week later by the first *Gleichschaltungsgesetz* (synchronization law) of March 31, and the second synchronization law of April 7—that strangled the surviving vestiges of state sovereignty. In mid-April, a police officer could still push an SS guard to the side on the Würm Mill Creek footbridge, or order him to fetch assistance to help a wounded Jewish man. A surgeon could still scare off a storm trooper in front of the door to the room of a patient in the Nussbaum Street surgical clinic. The archbishop of Munich and Freising could still order the state minister of the interior to release prisoners in time for the Easter holiday. By early May, this was no longer the case. Individuals grew increasingly cautious. The SS was growing ever bolder. A swastika flag fluttered permanently over the Dachau Concentration Camp.

The National Socialists were no longer intruders in the system, they were becoming the system. The judicial foundation on which Hartinger relied began to crumble. Pro-Nazi sentiments proliferated. "What is usually very simple in the administration of the prosecutor's office proved exceedingly difficult and complicated under the conditions of that time," Hartinger recalled. "The director of administration for the prosecutor's office was a Nazi, and was bearer of the golden party pin, which he always wore. The security guard, who was responsible for transferring the files, was of the same persuasion. The entire bureaucracy was filled with Nazi sympathizers." People hesitated to report transgressions by members of the Nazi Party. Witnesses grew reticent. Files were misplaced. Evidence disappeared. The investigation materials regarding the shooting of Benario, Goldmann, and the two Kahns, along with the police sketches, could no longer be found.

IN THE QUIET HOURS of the evening when his colleagues had left for the day, Hartinger stayed behind, and with a single trusted colleague, whose name he never revealed, he began to register the crimes of this strange and troubled spring that had such disturbing resonances with that similarly troubled spring of 1919 when the judicial system had faltered, and with it the entire country, plunging Germany into a national bloodbath that left its citizens, as Emil Gumbel had noted, barely able to recognize themselves amid the atrocity and bloodshed. Hartinger believed that a system as abusive as the Nazi regime could not long endure. As evidence vanished, he was determined to register the criminal events in the conviction that the perpetrators would ultimately be brought to justice.

With characteristic clarity and precision, Hartinger began chronicling the Dachau Concentration Camp killings. "On April 12, 1933, the student Arthur Kahn from Nuremberg, the political economist Dr. Rudolf Benario from Fürth, and the salesman Ernst Goldmann from Fürth were killed by pistol shots from the guards, SS man Hans Bürner, SS man Max Schmidt, and SS lieutenant Robert Erspenmüller," Hartinger dictated as his assistant typed. "In addition, the salesman Erwin Kahn from Munich was so severely wounded from pistol shots that he died on April 16, 1933." Hartinger went on to note that Benario, Goldmann, and Erwin Kahn "lay dead or seriously wounded in the immediate vicinity of their work area." Arthur Kahn was found lying "ca. eighty meters from the work area in the woods." Hartinger noted that the three SS men testified that they had shot because three of the men were "attempting to escape," and that the fourth man, Erwin Kahn, "ran into the line of fire."

In recording the observations by the three guards, Hartinger employed a German grammatical device known as indirect discourse, which attributes statements to a particular person while distancing the author from the veracity of the statements. Hartinger offered neither opinion nor analysis. He stated the evidence as it stood. He made no reference to the fact that the four victims were Jewish.

Hartinger was equally clinical in recording the Dressel suicide.

He observed that Dressel was found in his cell "dead with wrists slashed" with "intrusions in [the] skin" on his back, thighs, and buttocks "that could be traced back to beatings."

Hartinger did the same with Josef Götz, recounting not only SS man Wicklmayr's testimony, once again in indirect discourse, but also including the file numbers of the testimony, G 766/33, and citing the Flamm forensic examination—BLR.41—along with an observation of ancillary abuse. "Aside from the fatal bullet wound, a gash-like wound, 5 by 1 cm. wide, running horizontally across the left frontal lobe and covered by a scab, was discovered just behind the hairline," he observed. "The cause of the wound could not be determined as of yet."

Hartinger may have been losing faith in the potential of the current judicial system, but he retained confidence in the strength of hard forensic evidence as well as in the enduring and transcendent power of justice. He did not realize, however, that Wäckerle himself was about to deliver the incontrovertible and incriminating evidence he was seeking.

12

Evidence of Evil

A WEEK AFTER Willy Aron's death, Hartinger received a report forwarded to Munich II by Hilmar Wäckerle describing the suicide of a fifty-three-year-old detainee named Louis Schloss, who apparently had hanged himself the previous afternoon in his cell in the Arrest Bunker. In compliance with Paragraph 159 of the Criminal Procedure Code, Wäckerle had reported the incident to the local gendarmerie, which in turn had informed the Munich II prosecutor's office. The local police chief, Captain Schelskorn, had inspected the scene of the death and written a formal report. Wäckerle was now forwarding the report to Munich II. The report of the incident, typed on concentration camp letterhead and including technical details such as the victim's profession and date of birth, was brief and to the point:

Schloss was a detainee in the concentration camp Dachau. Because he was unwilling to work, he was placed in solitary detention. On the 16th of May 1933 at 13h, SS officer Unterhuber checked on Schloss for the last time in his cell. The camp administrator, Vogl [*sic*], entered Schloss's cell on the same day at 14h30, and found him hanged and already dead. Schloss had tied his suspenders around his neck, attached the noose to a hook on the wall, and thus ended his life. The judiciary was notified by an officer at the Police Station Dachau.

It was noted that Schloss was "of Israeli religion." The report was signed by Captain Schelskorn, and accompanied by a brief note signed by Wäckerle.

The previous evening, when news of the incident arrived, Hartinger had dispatched Dr. Flamm along with Judge Meyer and Secretary Brücklmeier to investigate the matter. They had departed Munich at 6:30 sharp and arrived at the entrance to the camp in the falling light of early evening sometime around seven o'clock. The three men were taken to the Arrest Bunker, where they were met by Vogel, who took them to Cell 4. As Vogel opened the cell door, they were witness to a horrific scene. A middle-aged man with short dark blond hair was dangling by a pair of suspenders a few inches over a bench in the corner. He was wearing a white flannel shirt, a gray-and-black-striped pair of cloth trousers, and gray-and-green-striped socks with brown slippers. Schloss was half sitting on the bench, a noose around his neck. It was an odd, awkward posture, even in death. He was still wearing his eyeglasses.

Wäckerle was present and provided the identical account he affirmed in the brief report to Munich II. Camp physician Dr. Nürnbergk was there as well. He explained to Flamm that he had administered "camphor and a cardial injection" in an attempt to revive Schloss but that it had been in vain. Considering the circumstances, however, it seemed curious that Dr. Nürnbergk would not have removed the noose from around a man's neck before attempting to revive him.

Flamm had Schloss removed from his suspenders. "I was the one who cut the Jew Schloss loose," Karl Kübler recalled. "His neck was in a noose so tight that I could not open it and had to cut it off."

Flamm had the corpse stripped, then laid out on the bunk for a forensic examination. Schloss's skin was cool but his body was still pliable; rigor mortis had yet to set in. Flamm noticed a few bruises over the eyes and some dried blood in the nostrils, and a bit of blood on the lips. Schloss's neck bore a single two-centimeter-wide track from the hanging. Flamm also found a seven-centimeter-long slash across his chest, and several bruises. "On the glans of the penis a scab the size of one penny," Flamm noted. The corpse was rolled onto its stomach. "The skin of his entire back from the shoulders to the buttocks is dark purple with a tint of red with numerous dried-up dark blue lashing streaks," Flamm recorded in his notes, "in particular across the right shoulder blade, the right loin, and the right buttock." The skin in the lower part between the shoulder blades was "dark purple" from lashing. The backs of both arms bore similar signs of abuse. It was as if the man had been subjected to torture. It was a horrific sight.

After filing his report, which included a sketch of Schloss hanging in his cell, Flamm went to see Hartinger. "Whether the cause of death was hanging or whether the corpse was hanged later cannot be determined by examining the corpse," Flamm explained to him. "Due to the extensive bruising, death by a fat embolism seems plausible."

Flamm had decided to conduct an autopsy, but Dr. Nürnbergk objected. The circumstances made it clear the man had hanged himself, he said. Flamm disregarded the objection. He ordered that Schloss's corpse be removed to the viewing hall at the Dachau town cemetery for an autopsy. He had also requested photographs.

That afternoon, May 17, Flamm, Meyer, and Brücklmeier drove to the cemetery, where Schloss's corpse was waiting for them on a table in the viewing hall. Two attendants stood nearby. Frontal photographs were taken. He was rolled over and his lacerated back was also photographed. Dr. Flamm then set to work. It was exactly three o'clock. For the next three hours, he worked his way through

Schloss's body, cutting through the skin and deep into his tissue and organs, working patiently, systematically, through the still, stiff corpse. He removed samples from Schloss's neck, vital organs, part of his brain, his liver, his spleen, and his kidneys, as well as a portion of skin with the "marks from hanging on the neck," to send to a laboratory for microscopic analysis.

Just as Flamm finished, word came that there had been yet another death in Dachau. Ten minutes later, Flamm, Meyer, and Brücklmeier were back at the concentration camp.

The three men were met by Max Winkler, of the state police, and Karl Ehmann, the guard who said he had shot a detainee during a failed escape attempt earlier that day. The victim was Leonhard Hausmann, a thirty-one-year-old communist town council member from Augsburg, who had clashed the previous August with Ehmann. Ehmann was notorious for his excessive drinking and violent behavior. When Ehmann shot the wife of a local communist through a bedroom window, Hausmann distributed Ehmann's picture to local communists. Nine months later, Hausmann was in Ehmann's hands.

Ehmann explained that Hausmann had left the wire enclosure with a work detail of fifty detainees that morning at about 7:15, accompanied by four SS guards. "Guards were standing around the area where they were working," Ehmann said. "I personally was moving around among the detainees, instructing them on their various duties." Ehmann had instructed Hausmann and another detainee to dig up saplings and carry them to another area. Around 10:30, Ehmann said he noticed that Hausmann was no longer there. Suddenly he saw a man wearing prison garb in a ducking posture running through the trees toward the gravel pit. Ehmann ran after him and started shouting for him to stop. The man kept going. Ehmann said, "He just glanced back at me once while running. That is when I, as is stated in the camp rules, drew my .8 pistol and, without aiming, fired at the fleeing man." Hausmann collapsed instantly "without making a sound. When I got to him, he gave one short, deep gasp," Ehmann noted. "I thought he was dead." Ehmann told the guards to get the other detainees back into the camp and rushed to report to police captain Winkler.

Ehmann could not recall the exact position from which he had shot Hausmann. He estimated it to have been at a distance of ten to twelve meters but it did not surprise him that the bullet found its mark. "In the war I was with the 2. Uhlan cavalry regiment and a sharpshooter in my unit," Ehmann explained. "I am the son of a huntsman and thus I know how to handle a gun like that. That is also why it didn't take long for me to take aim before I shot the fugitive in the back."

Winkler confirmed Ehmann's account. He knew Ehmann to be a calm and responsible man. Winkler recalled that Ehmann had arrived at his office at around 11 a.m. to report that he had shot an escaping detainee. Winkler had Ehmann describe the circumstances. Winkler informed Wäckerle of the incident, then accompanied Ehmann to the scene of the shooting. "The corpse had obviously not been touched," Winkler noted. "I held the dead man's hand. It was still warm." Winkler ordered a guard to stand watch over the body until the police arrived. "The guards follow specific regulations for the use of their weapons," Winkler reminded the investigation team. "Within these regulations, the guard must take action in the case of an escape attempt and use his firearm," he said. "The guards as well as the prisoners are familiar with these regulations." Captain Winkler was certain that SS guard Ehmann was just doing his duty.

Another SS man, twenty-seven-year-old Ludwig Wieland, was witness to the shooting and confirmed Ehmann's account as well. Wieland was forty or fifty meters away from Ehmann, watching his detainees, when the incident occurred. He heard Ehmann shouting, then he heard the shooting of a pistol. Then Ehmann came to him and told him to get his prisoners back into the camp immediately.

"The terrain on which Hausmann was working is very difficult to oversee due to shrubs, undergrowth, and a stand of young firs," Wieland said. He knew the terrain well. "This is what must have inspired Hausmann to believe his escape would be successful. If the head guard Ehmann had not been so diligent and attentive, Hausmann would surely have succeeded in fleeing." Wäckerle, too, confirmed Ehmann's account. He noted the particular circumstances around the gravel pit that made it especially vulnerable to escape.

"Prosecutor Hartinger ordered that a sketch of the scene of the shooting had to be made," Johann Bielmeier, chief of the Dachau police, recorded in his memorandum of the incident. "It is noted that a detailed report of the shooting of Hausmann was prepared by the department of the political police and submitted to the district court in Dachau." The appended pencil map included Wäckerle's headquarters and two adjacent buildings, with the dense forest and gravel pit beyond. "Since the forest has been left untouched for fifteen years and has overgrown completely, it would have been exceedingly easy for Hausmann to escape into the brush," Bielmeier observed. "If Hausmann had reached the gravel pit that is indicated on the sketch, or if he had been able to reach the forest opposite to him, his escape would surely have been successful." Bielmeier went on to note that the woods led down to the Amper River, and the only thing stopping Hausmann at that point would have been "some very faulty old barbed wire" that was left over from the time of the munitions factory.

According to the forensic examination conducted by Flamm, Hausmann was wearing a blue shirt that was saturated with blood from a chest wound. A puddle of blood "the size of a plate" was "still moist on the ground." Hausmann's eyes were half open. His right side and neck were smeared with "partly dry and partially still liquid blood," Flamm noted. On the back was a "jagged opening of 12 mm. in diameter with very ragged edges." And on the front of the chest "a circular opening of 6 mm. in diameter surrounded by a bluish-black edge." He found no other "injuries on the body." There was no need for an autopsy. The cause of death was clear: "a shot through the left chest cavity. The bullet entered the back at the height of the tenth vertebra and exited in the front at the height of the sixth rib," Flamm concluded. "Based on the trajectory of the bullet, it can be assumed that the heart was damaged, leading to internal bleeding in the left chest cavity." The examination confirmed Ehmann's account except, as Flamm observed in a handwritten note, "Based on the nature of the bullet hole in the overalls, the shot must have been fired at less than one meter distance." Flamm took tissue samples for evaluation.

Dr. Merkel in the forensics laboratory confirmed Flamm's findings of a close-range shooting, but with greater precision. The tissue samples indicated that Ehmann had fired his gun from a distance of less than three inches. Hausmann had not been shot fleeing; he had been executed.

In those same days, Flamm also delivered the forensic evidence Hartinger had been seeking in the case of Louis Schloss. "The autopsy has shown that the cause of death could not have been through hanging," Flamm reported, noting the extensive contusions and the destruction of the fatty tissue. "This is consistent with death by an embolism." In brief, Schloss had been beaten to death, then placed in a noose fashioned from his own suspenders and hanged from a nail on the wall of his cell. Hartinger now had incontrovertible forensic proof of homicide in two cases. After six weeks of frustrated efforts, he had criminal evidence that met the Wintersberger standard.

Under Article 234 of the German criminal code, Hartinger was now in a position to prosecute Ehmann for homicide. More important still, Hartinger also possessed evidence implicating Wäckerle and Nürnbergk. The two men had violated their Paragraph 161 obligations of the Criminal Procedure Code requiring them to cooperate "fully with the prosecutor" and "not obscure any facts relating to an investigation." He knew it would be difficult to con-vince Wintersberger to issue murder indictments against unidenti-fied perpetrators, but if Hartinger could implicate Wäckerle and the senior SS staff, he could perhaps demonstrate a pattern of abuse within the facility, which he felt could stand as a collective indict-ment of the concentration camp's entire SS administration. Given Munich II's growing visibility because of the presence of the con-centration camp in its jurisdiction, a Paragraph 159 death in Dachau possessed potential for strong interest by the press, including the international press. "I had one hope in particular, namely, that the Nazi officials would have been forced by Hindenburg and Ritter von Epp, and Gürtner [the former Bavarian minister of justice and the Reich justice minister at that time], as well as a few of the less rabid Nazis, to have the SS removed from the camp and replaced by regular police or a military unit."

Hartinger's timing could not have been more opportune. Hitler had just suffered a diplomatic fiasco in London. He was in the midst of highly sensitive negotiations with Rome. The Reich's banker, Hjalmar Schacht, was helping turn the tide of public opinion in America. "Basically, I was intent on making the public aware of what was going on in the camp, especially abroad," Hartinger later said. He knew the Nazis still had "a certain degree of respect" for foreign opinion, if for no other reason than economic necessity.

PART III

GUILTY

The assistant trial counsel Warren Farr making a case for the collective guilt of the Nazi SS before the Nuremberg tribunal on the afternoon of Wednesday, December 19, 1945. Farr presented some of the earliest forensic evidence of the Holocaust.

The February 27, 1933, arson attack in Berlin on the Reichstag, seat of German representative democracy, came a month after Adolf Hitler's appointment as chancellor. The next day, President Hindenburg issued an emergency decree, at Hitler's urging, that suspended personal liberty in the name of national security.

Storm troopers in Berlin taking communists into "protective custody" on March 6, 1933. Since "protective custody" was extrajudicial, there were no indictments or arrest warrants, and thus no legal recourse.

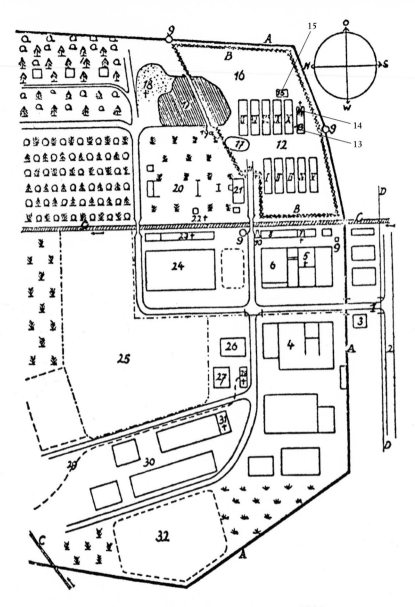

DACHAU CONCENTRATION CAMP, 1933

This drawing with the accompanying legend indicates the structures in the camp at the end of 1933. The drawing first appeared in 1934 in the monograph "Konzentrationslager," part of Sozialdemokratische Schriftenreihe (Social Democratic Publication Series), published in Karlsbad [Karlovy Vary], Czechoslovakia. The "inner camp" with barracks is in the upper right quadrant.

A. The wall around the camp, nearly three meters [ten feet] high and fortified with barbed-wire barriers*

B. Barbed wire and high-voltage wire around the prisoner barracks. In front of the wire is a low fence.*

C. Canal [Würm Mill Creek]*

D. Fence

1. Main entrance to camp*

2. Road to Dachau, constructed by the prisoners*

3. Guard house*

4. SS facility with kitchen, mess hall, and dining area for the SS

5. Prisoner kitchen with cellar [where four Jewish detainees were allegedly beaten to death]*

6. Prisoner arrival hall, registration room*

7. Prisoner dining area*

8. Lavatories

9. Machine gun tower with searchlight* [constructed after Beimler's escape]

10. Monument

11. Entrance to the prisoner barracks*

12. Prisoner barracks; the Roman numerals correspond to the accommodations of the ten companies of prisoners [Barrack II was known as the *Judenbaracke,* or "Jew Barrack"]*

13. Revier, infirmary for prisoners [Aron]*

14. Arrest Bunker [Hunglinger, Dressel, Götz, Lehrburger, Schloss, Nefzger]*

15. Washhouse

16. Roll call area for prisoners*

17. The Rondell

18. Gravel pit* [Strauss]

19. Old gravel pit with pond* [Hausmann]

19a. Footbridge over the pond

20. Shooting range for the SS* [Benario, Goldmann, A. Kahn, E. Kahn]

21. SS camp guards

22. Torture chamber "Schlageter House"

23. Newly built detention cells, bunker, and lavatories

24. Workshops for the craftsmen

25. Training ground for the SS with obstacle course, climbing wall, foxholes, trenches, etc.

26. Commandant's headquarters*

27. Revier for SS

28. Facility housing generators and weapons depot

29. Main power line

30. SS quarters

31. SS lavatories

32. Sports grounds for SS

+ Cross marks indicate key locations in the camp where prisoners were abused.

* The author has added asterisks beside locations relating to incidents in the spring and summer of 1933 (primarily in the upper right quadrant). The names of murder victims have been added in brackets.

The barracks of the abandoned Royal Munitions and Powder Factory near the town of Dachau, just north of Munich, served as a concentration camp to relieve Bavaria's penal system of overcrowding.

The detainees were accommodated in barracks in a wire enclosure known as the "inner camp." High-voltage wiring strong enough to kill a man provided additional security.

The ten barracks of the "inner camp" initially housed approximately fifty detainees each. The barbed-wire fencing is clearly visible in this photograph, as are additional wire entanglements.

Initially, detainees were transported to the *Konzentrationslager Dachau* by bus and in open-backed trucks, thirty at a time. In this photograph from spring 1933, a bus arrives at the main entrance of the facility.

In this May 1933 photograph, arrivals in Dachau wait near two SS men (far right). "As long as we are on guard here, nothing will happen to you," one state police officer had told detainees the previous month, "but if we leave, you will be in trouble."

A state police captain objected to the use of his men for a form of detention he considered illegal. As Munich police chief and Reichsführer SS, Heinrich Himmler simply shifted power from the state police to the Nazis' private security forces, the SS, in April 1933.

Hilmar Wäckerle was handpicked by Himmler to be Dachau's first camp commandant. As a trained farm manager, the thirty-three-year-old SS captain was familiar with managing livestock in barbed-wire enclosures. A day after Wäckerle arrived in Dachau, four Jewish detainees were shot in an alleged escape attempt.

A week after the Dachau shootings, a reporter from the *New York Times* toured the concentration camp and interviewed Wäckerle. On April 23, 1933, the *Times* mistakenly reported that the shooting victims were communists, and failed to mention that all four were Jewish.

NAZIS SHOOT DOWN FLEEING PRISONERS

Three Reds Are Slain Trying to Escape From Dachau Internment Camp.

MARTIAL LAW PREVAILS

High Voltage Wiring Surrounds Site—Life of Men Described by First Reporter Allowed In.

The "inner camp" as it looked in spring 1933 at the time of the visit by the *Times* reporter. By then, the commandant was having Jewish prisoners selected from arriving transports and placed in Barrack II, known as the *Judenbaracke* ("Jew Barrack").

Josef Hartinger was considered a rising star in the state civil service. As a prosecutor in Munich, he was responsible for criminal investigations in Dachau. His anti-Nazi sentiments earned him the epithet *Jüdling,* or "little Jew."

Hartinger was praised for his mastery of the criminal code (*Strafprozessordnung*), which outlined the duties of public officials, as well as the legal rights of citizens. Paragraph 160 obligated Hartinger to investigate any death by "unnatural cause." This updated version of the code appeared in May 1933 at the time of Hartinger's Dachau murder investigations.

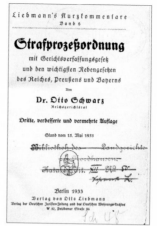

Rudolf Benario was killed along with his friend Ernst Goldmann in the alleged April 12 escape attempt. Both men had been taken into protective custody in early March for their political opposition to the Nazis. This photograph shows Benario in 1931 or 1932.

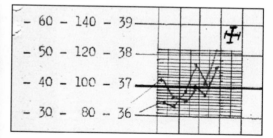

Arthur Kahn, a medical student at the university in Würzburg, was taken into protective custody in March. He died the same day as Benario and Goldmann.

Erwin Kahn was critically wounded after being shot repeatedly on April 12. He was rushed to a Munich hospital, where he related the shooting incident to the attending physician. Kahn died four days later. This excerpt from Kahn's medical record charts his deteriorating condition.

Karl Wintersberger was Hartinger's direct superior and was well known for his vigorous prosecution of Nazis in the 1920s. When Hartinger told Wintersberger he believed the SS were executing Jews in Dachau, Wintersberger responded, "Not even they would do that."

The Nazi newspaper *Völkischer Beobachter* announces the appointment of German war hero General Franz von Epp as Reich governor of Bavaria. Reich governors monitored state compliance with national security measures following the Reichstag fire and were part of Hitler's strategy of centralizing power in Berlin.

As Bavaria's state minister of justice, Dr. Hans Frank clashed repeatedly with police chief Himmler over the treatment of concentration camp detainees. In 1933, Hartinger saw in Frank a bulwark against Nazi excess. Ironically, Frank would later be hanged at Nuremberg for his central role in the Holocaust.

Many camp guards were Nazi street ruffians recruited into service as SS guards. "My guards consist of 120 storm troop men," Wäckerle told the *Times*. The guards worked in twenty-four-hour rotations, with thirty men to a shift.

The Dachau detainees were subjected to a grueling schedule. Their workday began with reveille at 6:00 a.m. and ended at 5:30 p.m. Here detainees pull a grading drum for leveling road surfaces.

Most of the construction work in the camp was undertaken by the detainees. The photograph shows some of them constructing a watchtower along the camp perimeter.

One detainee recalled that Benario, Goldmann, and the two Kahns were lounging between Barracks II and III when they were summoned by SS guard Hans Steinbrenner and led away to their executions.

This barrack interior shows detainees before striped uniforms were introduced. One Jewish detainee, Karl Lehrburger, attempted to hide himself on a top-tier bunk to avoid detection but was discovered and later executed by Steinbrenner on Wäckerle's orders.

Detainees transport straw sleeping sacks to their barracks. Josef Götz was shot in the forehead while carrying his sack down the hall of the Arrest Bunker. SS guard Karl Wicklmayr claimed Götz had assaulted him.

Meals were taken in a large hall equipped with wooden benches and tables. It was Götz's remark over dinner that the shooting of Benario, Goldmann, and the two Kahns was "fascism in its purest form" that resulted in his execution three weeks later.

Hans Beimler, a communist Reichstag delegate, was the commandant's prize catch. His dramatic nighttime escape from Dachau made international headlines and was a public humiliation for Wäckerle.

Beimler published his firsthand account of Dachau atrocities under the German title *Im Mörderlager Dachau* within months of his escape. He described in detail the deaths of several detainees and focused particular attention on Steinbrenner.

Hans Steinbrenner was Dachau's most notorious SS guard. He led the camp "whipping team" and personally selected Benario, Goldmann, and the two Kahns for execution. He was nicknamed *Mordbrenner,* or "murder man."

Wilhelm "Willy" Aron was a twenty-five-year-old junior attorney from Bamberg who was beaten to death by Steinbrenner and his whipping team. His corpse was burned in a shed in order to obscure the traces of the beating. This photograph is taken from Aron's university file.

Aron's university record noting his residence in Bamberg; his state citizenship, first as a Prussian then as a Bavarian (as of April 9, 1929); his religion, "Israelite"; and the universities he attended in Erlangen, Würzburg, and Munich.

Aron's death notice in the *Bamberger Volksblatt*: "Our only child, Junior Attorney Wilhelm Aron, was unexpectedly taken from us by death. The funeral was conducted in stillness. Bamberg, May 22, 1933. Attorney and Judicial Counsel Aron and Wife."

Unser einziges Kind

Referendar Wilh. Aron

wurde uns plötzlich durch den Tod entrissen.
Die Beerdigung hat in aller Stille stattgefunden.
BAMBERG, den 22. Mai 1933.

Rechtsanwalt Justizrat Aron und Frau

The physician Dr. Werner Nürnbergk issued fraudulent death certificates to avoid proper legal investigations. He later became increasingly concerned about his criminal culpability.

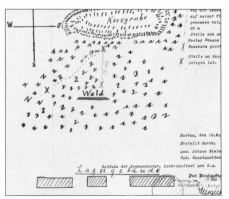

Dr. Moritz Flamm, a state medical examiner, delivered the hard evidence Hartinger needed for his murder indictments. There is no extant photograph of Flamm, but his signature reflects the precision and clarity for which he was admired by Hartinger and others. The SS tried repeatedly to murder Flamm, and most likely eventually succeeded.

Thirty-one-year-old detainee Leonhard Hausmann was shot while allegedly trying to escape. The SS guard claimed he fired from a distance of ten to twelve meters; forensic evidence, including this drawing, showed the distance to be less than thirty centimeters.

The first six names on this transport list, dated April 24, 1933, were state police agents caught spying on the Nazi Party. Herbert Hunglinger (4) committed suicide in the Arrest Bunker. Sebastian Nefzger (6), an amputee and veteran of the Great War, was beaten, strangled, hanged, then had his wrists slit to feign suicide. Beimler (7) was tortured and instructed to hang himself, but of course escaped.

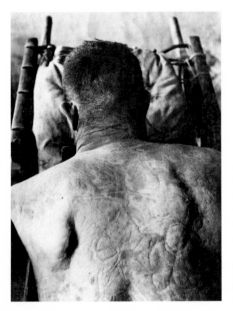

A forensic photograph of Sebastian Nefzger's corpse with evidence of torture from Steinbrenner's whipping team. Dr. Flamm's detailed autopsies for Dachau victims, as long as thirty pages, were eventually presented at the Nuremberg tribunal.

In the face of mounting foreign criticism of Nazi practices, Himmler transferred Wäckerle in July 1933. "Of course, I could not have known that his successor would be even worse," Hartinger later wrote. The new commandant, Theodor Eicke (left), had been a patient in a psychiatric clinic before assuming responsibility for Dachau.

Eicke is seen here releasing detainees as part of a 1933 Christmas amnesty. Dachau became the "model camp" for Nazi atrocity, with the first crematory oven and the first gas chamber.

Hans Frank testifying at Nuremberg. He recalled that the Hartinger indictments were so divisive among the Nazi leadership that Hitler intervened and ordered the state investigations terminated.

The Dachau Concentration Camp Memorial Site gate today with the words *"Arbeit macht frei"* ("Work shall set you free"). It is less than a hundred meters from the place where Benario, Goldmann, and the two Kahns were shot. "The trail of blood that began in Dachau," one Holocaust survivor claimed, "ended in Auschwitz."

13

Presidential Powers

A PLEASANT WEEK at the end of May with summerlike temperatures brought Dachau residents the cheering news that their town was considered the "most famous place in Germany."

"Dachau has been known and talked about for many reasons," the *Dachauer Zeitung* reported on May 23. "Dachau residents are simple peasant people who fiercely hold to their traditions; the distinctive farmer's garb and the women's embroidered dresses are well known." And then, of course, there were "all the luminaries in the firmament of art." The Dachauer counted among their number the German impressionist Max Liebermann, the early expressionist Lovis Corinth, and the pioneering modernist Emil Nolde. Most famous was Carl Spitzweg, the legendary nineteenth-century master of the quaint and cozy. Copies of his painting *The Bookworm*, depicting a befuddled old man on a wooden stepladder in the Dachau palace library, graced the walls of bibliophiles the world over. And then there was the munitions factory that in its day was "one of the largest enterprises" in Bavaria.

The front-page article heralded Dachau's sudden and dramatic rise to both national and international prominence through the conversion of its abandoned munitions factory. "Dachau has recently received a new distinction in that it now has become a center for the concentration of political prisoners," the *Dachauer Zeitung* wrote. "Representatives from the foreign press have already visited the camp and will be reporting on this to the entire world. It is there that communists and other enemies of the people are made to do useful work."

The newspaper went on to note that for a time Dachau registered some of the highest unemployment figures in Germany. The camp proved to be a boon to the local economy. Off-duty SS men flocked to Café Bestler for its jazz and supply of local girls. Initially there had been scuffles with Bestler regulars, but the SS ultimately prevailed. The Teufelhart Bakery, which had been providing bread to generations of Dachau residents, secured a contract with the new facility. The butcher Wülfert delivered not only meat but also dried ox penises that were used as pizzles. The eighteen-inch-long strips were soaked in a large cauldron of water in the camp kitchen to keep them pliant and were fetched by the SS guards as needed. "These pizzles were always brought along with the meat deliveries by car to the camp," Paul Hans Barfuss, a detainee assigned to the kitchen, recalled. "The shop owner himself was said to have delivered them in person."

The *Dachauer Zeitung* credited Heinrich Himmler in particular for the town's revived fortunes. "Dachau has attained its most recent fame through an action by the police headquarters in Munich, and that pleases us greatly," the paper noted. More than a hundred "dangerous" shopkeepers had been taken into protective custody, their establishments shuttered and affixed with a warning pasted across the door: "Business closed under police orders. Store owner in protective custody in Dachau. The political police commander of Bavaria. Himmler." The newspaper trumpeted its gratitude: "Bravo, Herr Police Commander!"

———

TWO DAYS BEFORE the *Dachauer Zeitung* published the heartening report of the town's revived fortunes, Adolf Hitler met with three cabinet ministers and two personal advisers to discuss the urgent matter of Germany's deteriorating reputation abroad and its impact on the national economy. The week had brought multiple warnings of concern for the German economy. A report on declining German exports, due in part to a foreign boycott, warned of potentially grave domestic consequences. "The situation is threatening because the negative effects on German industrial production cannot be avoided," a May 24 report cautioned. The minister of transport, Eltz-Rübenach, who had sought to improve conditions on the German rail system a few weeks earlier, now worried about the very survival of the German shipping fleet. He spoke confidentially of an impending catastrophe in an industry that already had seen a 30 percent decline since the 1929 Wall Street crash. "Recently the situation has been exacerbated, on the one hand through the boycott of German goods and shipping that is beginning to pose a serious threat, and on the other hand through the decrease of the dollar by about one-tenth," Eltz-Rübenach reported. "The situation is so serious that the very existence of the German maritime shipping industry is endangered." He saw the "desperate" need for remedy. In Hamburg and Bremen, the country's two major ports, the municipal economies had collapsed. Local governments were demanding millions from the national treasury. Among these historically "Red" electorates, there was growing talk of labor strikes.

Hitler understood the importance of foreign relations, as demonstrated in a ministerial meeting on trade tariffs a few weeks earlier. "The Reich chancellor pointed out that the foreign policy interests take priority over the domestic economy," the April 7 meeting notes record. "If Germany was to be isolated in international affairs, then the domestic economic interests would suffer."

Hitler also knew that the president was watching. Hindenberg had left Hitler with a relatively free hand during his first months in office. He had issued, at Hitler's urging, presidential decrees banning the communist press, suppressing civil liberties, curtailing state autonomy, and permitting the swastika banner to be hoisted beside the national flag as a sign of national unity, gradually strangling the democracy he had taken a solemn oath to protect.

Some saw signs of senility in the aging president's acquiescence to his forty-four-year-old chancellor. In Dresden, the quiet, despairing Jewish chronicler of that troubled era, Victor Klemperer, lost all hope after seeing Hindenburg in newsreel footage at a commemoration ceremony that March. "When I saw him filmed about a year ago," Klemperer wrote in his diary, "the president walked somewhat stiffly, his hand on the wrist of his escort, but quite firmly and not at all slowly down the Reichstag steps; an old but vigorous man." Now, a year later, the president moved with the "tiny laborious steps of a cripple." Hindenburg reminded Klemperer of his own father during the last two months of his life following a stroke at Christmas 1911. "During that time, he was no longer in his right mind," Klemperer remembered. "I am now completely certain that Hindenburg is no more than a puppet, that his hand was already being guided on January 30 [when Hitler was appointed chancellor]." Klemperer saw little hope in Germany being "rescued from the grip of its new government."

In fact, Hindenburg knew exactly what he was doing. He had long harbored intentions to return Germany to monarchical rule but had wanted to wait for an economically and politically stable time to effect an orderly transition. Otto Meissner, his chief of staff, later insisted that upholding the constitution "was his first priority." A less respectful observer noted that Hindenburg adhered to his constitutional oath "like a corporal following military regulations." By 1931, Hindenburg had visibly wearied of the Weimar Republic. The 1929 stock market crash, coupled with the rising radicalism on the right and left, compelled him to resort increasingly to the Article 48 powers that had so troubled Heinrich

Held back in 1919.* The Reichstag passed thirty-four laws in 1931, compared with forty-four decrees issued by the president. "Field-Marshal Paul von Hindenburg, President of the German Republic," one foreign observer noted in 1931, "has entered upon the eighty-fifth year of his life with the upright carriage of an oak, and upon the seventh year of his presidential term with the resolute mien of a dictator."

In May 1932, Hindenburg was elected to a second term with a solid 52 percent, handily defeating Hitler, who polled 38 percent, and Ernst Thälmann, who trailed with 10 percent but nevertheless retained the support of six million loyal communists. After serving as president of the Weimar Republic for eight tumultuous years, Hindenburg was convinced that democracy, imposed on Germany "in its hour of great despair and inner weakness," did not really "align with the true needs and characteristics of our people." The key objective for this second-term president was to place his country firmly back on the road to monarchical rule.

But when Hitler approached Hindenburg about appointing him as chancellor that August, the old man dismissed the idea out of hand. "The Reich president in reply said firmly that he must answer this demand with a clear unyielding 'No,'" the meeting minutes recorded. "He could not justify before God, before his conscience, or before the Fatherland the transfer of the whole authority of government to a single party, especially to a party that was biased against people who had different views from their own." Hindenburg pointed out that this would cause unrest in the country and could also raise concerns abroad that could complicate Germany's fragile international situation.

Hitler repeated that he wanted complete control or none.

---

* Hindenburg applied a "25-48-53 formula" of constitutional articles empowering the president with near dictatorial power. He could invoke Article 53 to appoint and dismiss government at will; Article 48 to issue emergency decrees; and Article 25 to suspend the Reichstag, eliminating its capacity to rescind the Article 48 emergency decrees. In addition, Article 23 invested him as commander in chief, with the capacity to enforce that authority.

"So this means you will join the opposition?" Hindenburg asked.

"You're not leaving me any other choice," Hitler replied.

"Then let me warn you: Lead the opposition with dignity and remain completely conscious of the responsibilities and duties you hold toward your homeland," Hindenburg said. He also warned Hitler about the consequences if he did not. "I will intervene without mercy against any acts of terror or violence, even if they have been committed by members of the SA."

That autumn, there was talk of "civil war" between the militarized wing of the German Communist Party and the million-strong army of SA storm troopers. In early December, Eugen Ott, a lieutenant colonel in the Reichswehr, tabulated the potentially devastating consequences of domestic turmoil that included mass strikes in the harbor city of Hamburg and the collapse of heavy industry in the Ruhr, as well as a potential Polish incursion on disputed territory in the east. The Reichswehr, with a mere 100,000 soldiers under arms, would be incapable of maintaining order.

In January, Hindenburg agreed to appoint Hitler as chancellor, with Papen as vice chancellor. Hitler would crush the political left and appease the political right. Papen would hold the center. The president acquiesced. "I really don't know what could still go wrong," Hindenburg told Papen the night before Hitler's appointment. "You are vice chancellor as well as Prussian minister-president. With the exception of two minister positions, all posts are occupied by our people. And in any event you will attend every meeting I will have with Hitler." Hindenburg could not stand the thought of being alone with his new chancellor, whom he viewed as little more than a fascist means to a monarchical end. The president and chancellor found common cause in dismantling the democratic structures of the Weimar Republic, but Hindenburg retained his presidential powers. He had dismissed three chancellors in quick succession, and retained the constitutional authority to do the same with Hitler. "Hitler was smart enough [. . .] not to provoke opposition from the conservative ministers and risk having the cabinet split," Papen observed. "In the case of serious contention he would close the discussion and seek to achieve his aims through individual meetings with the respective ministers."

Hindenburg kept Hitler on a short leash. He called him into his office after the Reichstag fire. He repeatedly took Hitler to task for his anti-Semitic policies. That spring, Hindenburg received a distressed letter from Prince Carl of Sweden. The increasing reports of anti-Semitic excesses, the national boycott against Jewish shops, and the new law banning Jews from the civil service were cause for grave concern for the Swedish prince. He urged Hindenburg to spare Germany "from the nightmarish spectacle of racial persecution" in a country where the people were "rightfully admired for their great culture."

Hindenburg turned to Hitler, demanding an explanation. Hitler assured Hindenburg that the situation was not as bad as it was being depicted. He blamed the foreign press. Hindenburg wrote to the Swedish prince, informing him that he had raised the matter with the chancellor, that the civil service law was directed not so much against non-Aryan Germans as against those "Jews and non-Germans from Eastern Europe" who had immigrated to Germany after 1918—he blamed in particular the lax immigration policies of the Weimar Republic—and that the stories of atrocity had been greatly exaggerated. "Such infringements, which are by the way not nearly as widespread as they are depicted in the foreign press," Hindenburg wrote, "have been countered successfully and stridently by the Reich government." The Swedish prince could rest assured "that the German people have on the whole maintained an exemplary discipline, recognized even abroad," though, in a line he struck from his missive, he confessed to sharing the prince's concern about the treatment of the Jews, "that I equally deplore and regret." Hindenburg was not covering for Hitler. He was protecting the good name of his country.

Hindenburg watched developments with cool detachment, generally tolerating the excesses, but not hesitating to intervene when it seemed necessary. In early April, Captain Leo Löwenstein, president of the Reich Association of Jewish Frontline Soldiers, wrote to Hitler protesting the imminent civil service law banning Jews from public service. Löwenstein recalled that of the half million Jews in Germany, ninety-six thousand had fought in the war and twelve thousand had given their lives for the fatherland. "After the blood sacrifices and services made to the homeland, we firmly believe that the German Jews are entitled to equal rights as citizens," Löwenstein wrote the Nazi leader on April 4. "However, it is with deep pain that we see how we are being dishonored and how wide circles of Jews are being deprived of the base of their economic existence."

Hindenburg was also pressed on the matter. "I pleaded successfully with Hindenburg that soldiers who had taken part in the war should under no circumstances be affected by this law," Papen would later tell the Nuremberg tribunal, "for I always held the view that a German, no matter of what race, who had done his duty to his country should not be restricted in his rights."

Hindenburg dispatched a stern missive to Hitler. "Dear Herr Reich Chancellor," he wrote on April 4. "In the past few days a number of cases have been reported to me in which veteran judges, lawyers, and judicial officers who had been performing their duties flawlessly were put on leave and will soon be dismissed completely, merely because they are of Jewish descent." Hindenburg said he found "such treatment" of long-serving Jewish professionals "completely intolerable." The president assumed Hitler shared the same sentiment and demanded immediate remedial action. "In my opinion," the former field marshal dictated, "all officials, judges, teachers, and lawyers who have been injured in war, were soldiers at the front, are sons of soldiers who fell at the front, or even who have lost their own sons in combat, should, as far as they give no particular reason to be treated differently, be left in office." Hindenburg wanted Hitler to understand that "if they had enough merit to fight and to bleed for Germany, then they should also be seen as worthy of further serving the homeland in their profession."

The civil service law was redrafted. At a stroke, Hindenburg saved the careers of nearly half the Jewish civil servants. A similar intervention on behalf of Jewish doctors and lawyers secured the livelihoods—at least for the time being—of thousands more. "Thus far Prussia has a total of 11,814 licensed lawyers, 8,299 of which are Aryans and 3,515 are Jews," Prussia's ministry of justice reported that spring. "Of the latter, 735 fought at the front and 1,383 were long-standing lawyers. There are 923 Jews in office who have lost their rights to represent clients. Currently, the total of licensed Jewish lawyers numbers 2,158."

Hindenburg received another distressed missive in early May from Carl Melchior, a veteran German diplomat and contemporary of Hindenburg, who had played a central role in reestablishing Germany's postwar reputation. Like Sweden's Prince Carl, Melchior had grave concerns about the new chancellor. "For more than seventeen years the German government has trusted me, as a delegate and as an expert, to conduct negotiations mainly of an economic nature with foreign countries," Melchior wrote Hindenburg on May 6. "Recent developments in the situation of foreign policy have filled me with grave concern. Just a few months ago the leading statesmen of England, France, and Italy recognized the German right to parity in armament." This had been achieved through "the tenacious work of various statesmen and diplomats." Now Germany was being treated with belligerence and suspicion. Melchior also observed, like so many others, the "great shock" arising from the new government's treatment of "entire groups" of citizens "whose ancestors have inhabited Germany for centuries." "If Germany treats its own citizens in such a manner," Melchior wrote, they were asking themselves "how would it have treated us if the outcome of the war had not been in our favor? What dangers do this new Germany and its government have in store?"

With his pointed missive, Melchior was reminding Hinden-burg of his constitutional obligations and capacities as the ultimate authority in the country. He was also outlining much of the agenda that Hitler himself had set for the Nazi Party, and had been bellow-ing in beer halls for more than a decade. Hitler was merely making good on his rhetoric. The Nazi Party program, as framed in 1920, promised, in point 2, to abrogate the Treaty of Versailles, and, in point 4, to make citizenship contingent on race. "Consequently," it stated, "no Jew can be a citizen." The program also promised to establish "a strong central power in the Reich," and committed the party leadership to a blood oath. "The leaders of the party promise to support the implementation of the points outlined in this pro-gram," it concluded, "by sacrificing their own lives if necessary." Hitler had reiterated most of these points in *Mein Kampf*, and now set out to implement them as head of government. To this end, he added Joseph Goebbels to his cabinet in the newly created post of minister of propaganda and public enlightenment.

"In the long years of party struggle I have learned how to influ-ence the masses in order to win them over to certain ideas," Goeb-bels explained at his first cabinet meeting. "You, gentlemen, will have to do exactly the same if you want the entire German peo-ple to accept without protest the political and economic measures taken by the government." Amid the deteriorating international situation, Goebbels intended to apply the same skills abroad. "The world will learn to see that it does no good to have itself enlight-ened about Germany by Jewish emigrants," he observed a day after the April 1 boycott of Jewish shops that outraged the international community. "We need to launch a campaign of spiritual conquest, one which we must spread throughout the world, just as we did in Germany itself. In the end, the world will learn to understand us."

That spring, Hitler launched a private foreign policy initia-tive either skirting or sidelining traditional diplomatic channels targeting Rome, Washington, D.C., and London. From informal exchanges, Hitler knew of potential interest on the part of the Vatican in signing a concordat with Germany. It would not only be a major foreign policy coup, healing a rift opened four hundred years earlier by Martin Luther, but also an effective domestic ploy in forcing the alignment of Germany's Roman Catholics with the Hitler government. Pope Pius XI and his close adviser, Cardinal Pacelli, had been papal representatives in Warsaw and Berlin respectively, and had experienced firsthand the communist potential for violence, especially in Poland where a Red Army incursion in 1919 had seen Bolsheviks burn churches and slaughter clergy wholesale. Hitler had the perfect emissary in his vice chancellor, Papen, who was a devout Roman Catholic and longtime associate of Pacelli.

On the morning of Wednesday, April 12, just after eleven o'clock, as Hans Steinbrenner flogged Benario, Goldmann, and the two Kahns through their final hours, Papen sat in the gilded chambers of the Vatican with Pope Pius XI and Cardinal Pacelli. "His Holiness greeted my wife and me with much paternal kindness," Papen recalled, "and he said how delighted he was to see a person like Hitler at the head of the German government, someone who was finally willing to declare an uncompromising battle against communism and nihilism." The warm welcome extended to Hitler's emissary by the pope and Pacelli was fueled not only by a common concern over communism but by a fear of the fragility of the Hitler government. The pope wanted to close the deal before Hindenburg threw his latest chancellor out of office.

In those same weeks, Hitler sent the recently appointed Reichsbank president Hjalmar Schacht to Washington, D.C., to court President Franklin Roosevelt. Schacht was a respected, old-school banker, famous for his top hat and cigars, who was smooth and sophisticated, with an instinct for identifying common interests. "Roosevelt and Hitler both entered office nearly at the same time," Schacht observed. "Both owed their election to the preceding economic depression. They both had the task of firing up the economy through state intervention."

Hitler also dispatched Alfred Rosenberg, his chief ideologue and editor of the *Völkischer Beobachter,* to London, as part of the Goebbels offensive. Rosenberg had aspired to the position of foreign minister in the Hitler cabinet, but Hindenburg had made it clear to Hitler that Konstantin von Neurath would continue to represent Germany in its foreign affairs. Neurath was an elegant and experienced diplomat with the personal credentials Hindenburg desired in representing the country abroad. "My grandfather, my great-grandfather, and my great-great-grandfather were ministers of justice and foreign affairs in Württemberg," the baron told the Nuremberg tribunal. "On my mother's side I come from a noble Swabian family whose ancestors were mostly officers in the Imperial Austrian Army." The "pin-striped diplomats" at Wilhelmstrasse 7 represented a bastion of aristocratic lineage and privilege that proved resilient to Nazi intrusions. In March, Hindenburg signed a presidential decree, after some hesitation, that permitted the Nazi Party's swastika banner to be flown alongside the traditional Reich flag as a sign of national unity, but the directive was ignored by German embassies on the grounds that it violated diplomatic protocol "requiring that abroad, flags can only be displayed that have been registered with the foreign governments."

Hitler, frustrated with the arrogance and obstructionist attitude at Wilhelmstrasse 7, established the Foreign Political Office (*Aussenpolitisches Amt,* or APA) within the Nazi Party, and installed Rosenberg as its head. "With the creation of the APA, the particular desires and the unique aspirations of National Socialism will find expression within the area of foreign policy," Rosenberg told the *Völkischer Beobachter* on April 3, 1933. Rosenberg set London as his first diplomatic mission. He proved to be singularly unprepared.

Unlike Papen and Schacht, who traveled as emissaries of the Reich chancellor, Rosenberg arrived in London as a representative of the Nazi Party. He spoke no English and received a notably cool reception. "We in this country," the British foreign secretary, Sir John Simon, told Rosenberg, "do not care to see the press suppressed, persons deprived of their living on account of their race, and minorities, including elected representatives of the people, shut up in concentration camps because of their political opinions." Simon said to Rosenberg that "in two months Germany had lost the sympathy which she had gained in this country in ten years, and especially in those quarters which had hitherto been sympathetic to her."

Rosenberg's situation worsened when, without consulting the German embassy, he placed a wreath emblazoned with a swastika at the Cenotaph, Britain's national war memorial, then offered a stiff-armed Nazi salute "in honor of the fallen British and in honor of Chancellor Hitler and the German people." A British veteran removed the wreath and hurled it into the Thames. "I've removed it as a deliberate protest against desecration of the Cenotaph by Hitler's hireling," he told the police upon his arrest. "It is also a protest against the brutal barbarism which at present exists in Germany."

That afternoon, the British foreign secretary was summoned before the House of Commons to account for the Rosenberg visit. In what capacity had Rosenberg come to London? As a representative of the German government? As a representative of the Nazi Party? As a personal emissary of Adolf Hitler? The foreign secretary fumbled for an answer. He confessed that the status of the Rosenberg visit was not "exactly clear." That evening, Rosenberg held a press conference at Claridge's hotel, where he was staying, and sought to explain Hitler's policies, in German, to a crowd of journalists. It did not help that the Nazis staged their first book burnings that same day.

The next day, London "raged" at the Hitler aide. At Madame Tussauds wax museum, a protester dumped a bucket of red paint over a likeness of Hitler and hung a sign around his neck with the words "Mass Murderer." During a lunch at Claridge's a well-dressed couple rose to their feet. The woman began distributing leaflets while the man railed against Rosenberg. "The government

of this representative of Hitler is stained with the blood of German workers," the protestor shouted as Rosenberg watched in
silence. "It has suppressed trade unions, the Socialist and communist parties. Jewish people are being persecuted." A melee ensued.
Tables were overturned. The incidents made headlines around the
world. "Rosenberg Has Another Sad Day," the *Chicago Daily Tribune*
reported in a headline story. Thirteen years later, during his trial
at Nuremberg, Rosenberg offered a similar assessment. "A number
of incidents occurred which showed that the sentiment was very
repellent," he recalled.

The catastrophic state of Germany's foreign relations was not
lost on Hitler. Five days after the Rosenberg debacle, Hitler took
matters into his own hands. On May 17, he addressed the Reichstag
with a message intended for the world. He talked about the Bolshevik threat. He talked about his country's desperate economic
conditions. He talked about the need for revision of the Treaty of
Versailles and Germany's vulnerability to attack. He recalled Roosevelt's proposal for American intervention in European affairs.
"Germany would welcome the generous suggestion of the American president that the powerful United States of America would
serve in Europe as a guarantor of peace and would provide a great
comfort for all those who are truly interested in peace," he said.
Only America, he said, possessed the necessary capacities.

The next day, Hitler addressed the American people in an
exclusive interview with the American journalist Thomas Russell
Ybarra for the popular American magazine *Collier's Weekly*.* "In
observing the American attitude toward Germany, some things
have been beyond my understanding," Hitler told Ybarra. "Cer-

* Thomas Russell Ybarra appears to have secured his Hitler interview through a combination of professional credibility and personal connections. He had met Papen in 1932 and
published a biography, *Hindenburg: The Man with Three Lives,* that same year. A note in the foreign ministry files says, "He is basically the rare type of respectable American journalist who
makes an effort to write objectively and seriously." ("Aufzeichnung des Oberregierungsrats
Thomsen über eine Unterredung des Reichskanzlers mit dem Sonderkorrespondenten von
Collier's Weekly, Ybarra," May 18, 1933, *Akten zur deutschen auswärtigen Politik,* 461.)

tainly Americans are interested in the maintenance of peace in
Europe, aren't they? Certainly they don't want to see Europe go up
in flames. Certainly they have economic interests which they want
to see consolidated."

Ybarra found Hitler courteous, measured, even statesmanlike.
The Nazi leader wore a dark suit and tie. "His face was solemn—
but it always is," Ybarra observed. "And he didn't smile—but he
rarely does." The two men sat across from each other in armchairs
close enough that Hitler could drive home his points by tapping
Ybarra's knee. Hitler talked about unemployment, about the immigration of "Jews from eastern Europe," about the "reign of terror"
that was being touted in the international press.

"Whatever violence there was is now past," Hitler said. "Perfect calm reigns in Germany. Not a street has been destroyed,
not a house. Where is this terror they talk about?" Hitler wanted
Americans to know that he had not torched the Reichstag even if
he thought it might have been a good idea. "The accusation was
made that the Reichstag fire was set by members of my party," he
said. "Do Americans really believe I needed to do such a thing in
my fight against Communists, even if I had wanted to?" The Nazi
leader devoted much of the interview to discussing the communist
threat that he blamed on the country's massive unemployment.
"You have—let me see—how many unemployed? Eight million?
Ten million?" Hitler queried Ybarra. "Well, suppose all these millions of American unemployed were Communists taking their
orders from Russia." That was exactly the situation Hitler said he
was facing. "Germany has six million Communists," he observed,
"10 percent of our total population."

"Here is what I wish would happen," Hitler said, making his
point with a knee tap. "That Americans might understand these
special German problems." Hitler wanted Americans to understand the malaise and desperation that had gripped Germany during the Weimar Republic. He calculated there had been 224,000

suicides in the country since the signing of the Treaty of Versailles fourteen years earlier. That was forty per day. Here Hitler paused. He gazed into the distance. "Into his face came some of that mystical quality that has helped him to drive audiences to hysteria," Ybarra noted. Hitler continued: "If only all Americans could come over here to Germany," he said. "They would look about and ask themselves where is this revolution, where is this terror, where is all this destruction and chaos I've heard about?" With that, he rose from his chair and ended the interview.

The impact of Hitler's efforts was immediate and measurable. The German ambassador in Washington reported that he had spent an hour with Roosevelt the day after Hitler's Reichstag appearance and that the American president "spoke warmly of the speech by the Reich chancellor." Roosevelt pointed out that American public opinion of Hitler, which had reached a low point in recent months, had improved by 40 percent.

A week later, Hitler assembled several key cabinet members, including Neurath and Goebbels, along with several other party colleagues, foremost among them Rosenberg, to discuss his strategy for securing the "foreign propaganda" gains he had just made and initiating a sustained and calculated campaign to repair the German image abroad. Hitler handed the floor to Goebbels. "The purpose of today's meeting is to differentiate the areas of responsibility between the ministry of propaganda and the foreign office," Goebbels explained. "The first priority of the Reich Ministry for Propaganda and Public Enlightenment must be influencing public opinion abroad." But he wanted everyone to understand that such an initiative was going to cost money, a great deal of money. "For this purpose we will need a larger budget than the one necessary for internal propaganda," Hitler said, noting the need for expert capacity in this sector. "The Reich ministry needs to be put in the position to be able to respond immediately to any threats from abroad. For this purpose, sending attachés to the key German representations abroad will be necessary. These attachés will have the same status as military attachés."

Neurath saw precisely where this was going. The Nazis had compromised the security services by introducing the SA and SS as "assistant police." Here, they were not only infiltrating the foreign office by seeding embassies with "press attachés," but also seeking to plunder its budget. Two weeks earlier, when this issue was raised at a meeting in the propaganda ministry, it had been recommended that the entire foreign office's press section, along with its budget, be transferred to Goebbels. Now, in the presence of Hitler and ministers and advisers, Neurath drew a line. He was willing to represent Hitler's muscular, even belligerent foreign policy, helping engineer German withdrawal from the League of Nations and the abrogation of foreign treaties and commitments, but he would not sacrifice a ministerial budget line.

"The foreign office cannot get by without its own press office," Neurath stated flatly. "If the press office is subsumed into the Reich Ministry for Propaganda and Public Enlightenment, there will as a result be an urgent need for the foreign office to create a new office for these purposes." He insisted that his diplomats required a regular service by which German foreign policy could be conveyed to the foreign press and, likewise, the foreign press could be analyzed when German foreign policy was being formulated.

These were exactly the types of divisive confrontations Hitler had sought to avoid in his cabinet meetings. He had sat quietly listening to Goebbels and Neurath spar, but now he intervened. "From these deliberations it has been determined that in order to influence the public opinion abroad, a means will be necessary that is not yet available to us at the moment," he said. "A new organization needs to be developed that will create its own method of working." Having addressed the needs of Goebbels, one of his most effective ministers, he now sought to mollify Neurath. "Of course the foreign office cannot function without the instrument of the press office, because its work provides the foreign office with the foundations upon which political decisions are made." But, Hitler said, the "advancement of our ideals" abroad, especially in developing a "defense mechanism against rumors of atrocity," could only be achieved by the creation of a special capacity. "We need to find a way whereby the activity of the foreign office's press department is not shut down," he said, "but that still gives the Reich Ministry for Propaganda and Public Enlightenment sufficient influence."

Hitler underscored the necessity for his government to shape international public opinion "through the systematic application of a wide variety of propaganda techniques, especially in regard to the foreign press." Neurath acquiesced. "The question of responsibility is relatively easy to solve," he said. "The officials of the press department in the foreign office should give factual information, but not create any propaganda." That would be left to Goebbels and his team. There followed a squabble over specific budgets and allocations that Hitler interrupted with brisk remarks: "For a well-functioning propaganda apparatus no cost is too high. The press department of the foreign office will in future restrict itself to its previous areas of activity. The Reich Ministry for Propaganda and Public Enlightenment, now establishing its own press department, will take over the responsibility of making active foreign propaganda." Hitler closed the meeting by underscoring the vital and urgent necessity of responding to the increasingly negative foreign opinion and its impact on the national economy. "We find ourselves in a position of isolation from world politics that we will only be able to escape if we improve the sentiments toward us abroad."

Two days later, Hitler received heartening news when Schacht visited the Reich Chancellery to report on his meetings in Washington with Roosevelt and senior members of the State Department. Schacht had managed to have four personal meetings with Roosevelt in the course of a single week, during which the president appeared to be open and willing to listen. Schacht had explained to him the necessity of German suspension of credit payments, the need to suspend civil liberties, and the decision for Germany to begin rearming itself. Roosevelt was cautious but understanding. At their final meeting, the president asked Schacht to join him on the sofa and said with warm assurance, "You have made an excellent impression here because you have spoken openly and freely in every regard."

Schacht believed he had tipped American sentiments, he told Hitler, but it was now imperative "that our foreign propaganda must be made much more vigorously." America was a democracy and its president was ultimately swayed by public opinion, which in turn was influenced by the press. It was vital that Berlin be able to respond immediately, effectively, and responsibly to accusations of atrocity and terror. "The Reich government needs to be in the position to denounce any information that is incorrect appearing in the newspapers, immediately," Schacht told Hitler.

14

Death Sentence

SHORTLY AFTER FIVE O'CLOCK in the late afternoon of May 24, as Adolf Hitler sat with Goebbels and Neurath, crafting their foreign propaganda offensive, Josef Hartinger received a report of yet another killing in Dachau. It was the first such call in nearly two weeks and came in an uneasy atmosphere. The rash of arrests and detentions of prominent and common folk alike had compelled the general public to grow increasingly cautious. A critical comment about Hitler or his new government would be answered with "Watch out or you will end up in Dachau." The popular proverb that included "Silence is golden" was refitted to the changing times: "Silence is silver, speaking is Dachau." A bedside prayer included the invocation, "Dear Lord, O make me dumb, / Lest to Dachau camp I come!"

"Many fear to talk because a remark critical of the Nazis might send one to Dachau, the great concentration camp for political prisoners near Munich," a *New York Times* correspondent reported that spring. "Munich's quiet is entirely too intense to be natural." In the Hofbräuhaus, where the halls usually "reverberated with the roar of a vast multitude," a subdued and tense atmosphere prevailed.

It reminded the reporter of the "hushed peace" on the streets of Moscow. "The same serious hushed manner is everywhere," the *Times* noted, "even in private homes." The same could be said of the second-floor corridors at Prielmayrstrasse 5, where the subtle menace of deputy prosecutor Heigl and his swastika pin was omnipresent.

Most of Hartinger's colleagues had gone home for the day by the time the call came from the Dachau police. Hartinger rang Dr. Flamm's office, only to be told that he too had already departed. Hartinger called Flamm at home, informed him of the Paragraph 159 death, and instructed him to drive immediately to the camp. Hartinger then asked a fellow Munich II prosecutor, Dr. Lachenbauer, who was still in the office and, like Flamm, had his own car, to drive him to Dachau. Within the hour, the investigators were assembled at the camp. The shooting victim was a twenty-eight-year-old attorney from Munich, Alfred Strauss. He had allegedly attempted to escape while being escorted by the camp guards on a walk near a swimming area for the camp personnel that was under construction near the gravel pit outside the wire compound.

Strauss had been taken into protective custody on March 27 for "unethical exercise of his profession," though rumor had it that his detention had been personally ordered as an "act of revenge" by Hans Frank, with whom Strauss had had repeated courtroom confrontations. Strauss's detention had been reviewed on April 21, and even though there was no evidence of a "criminal act," he was retained, and on May 11 transferred to Dachau.

Hartinger and his team were led beyond the wire compound to the pit. Strauss lay crumpled on the ground, a pool of fresh blood forming a crescent around his head from the single bullet wound that had brought him down. He was a young, fragile man who reminded Hartinger of Benario. Johann Kantschuster, the SS guard who had shot Strauss, was on hand. Kantschuster was large, tall, and handsome, probably the same age as Strauss, but with a

demeanor that struck Hartinger immediately. "I remember especially well that he had the expression of a depraved individual,"
Hartinger recalled. Flamm agreed. "We were both of the opinion
that his face belonged in a police album of criminals." Kantschuster
explained to Hartinger that Dr. Nürnbergk had instructed him to
take Strauss for an evening walk. The two men had exited the wire
compound and were approaching the gravel pit when suddenly
Strauss bolted, Kantschuster said. Kantschuster shouted for him to
stop, as regulations required, then drew his pistol and fired two
shots. Kantschuster estimated that Strauss was eight meters away
when he fell.

As Hartinger studied the slain young man and the blood-
soaked soil, he was troubled not only by Kantschuster's impeccable aim, but also by the incongruous circumstances. Strauss was
dressed in a shirt and trousers but with only one sock and leather
slippers with open backs. It struck Hartinger as curious that a man
would go for a walk in slippers, especially with only one sock. In
addition to the bullets in the back of his head, Strauss also had a
wound on the back of his bare foot. Hartinger decided to have
Flamm conduct a forensic examination. "Above all I wanted to
know whether the corpse showed other signs of abuse," Hartinger
said.

Hartinger ordered the SS guards to carry Strauss back to the
camp, where he was placed in an empty shed and stripped of his
clothing. Flamm set to work with his usual precision. Beyond the
wound on the foot, he found lacerations across Strauss's back. His
buttocks were bandaged to cover a deep gash.

Hartinger ordered an autopsy, which Flamm conducted the following morning. The cause of death was readily evident: "paralysis of the brain" as a result of one bullet that had passed through
Strauss's skull and another that had lodged in the right side of his
skull. More revealing was the trajectory of the bullet. Flamm determined the bullet had been fired "at an angle from the lower back

skull to the upper right" in the style of an execution. Unable to determine the exact distance of the shooting, Flamm took tissue samples for further "chemical and microscopic analysis."

For the past six weeks, Hartinger had sought and failed to meet the Wintersberger standard, not with the shooting of Benario, Goldmann, and the two Kahns, nor with the hanging of Hunglinger or the slashed wrists of Dressel. Not even the corridor murder of Götz had moved Wintersberger to action. But finally, a week after the alleged escape attempts by Schloss and Hausmann and a day after the shooting of Strauss, the chief prosecutor had begun to show interest in this isolated and tortured corner of his jurisdiction.

"It was sometime in May or June 1933 that rumors were finding their way into the open that detainees in the Dachau Concentration Camp were being shot," Wintersberger remembered. "SS guards from the camp had evidently not been keeping as tight-lipped as they should have in local establishments in Dachau. In my opinion it was the fact that stories of these killings in the Dachau Concentration Camp were finding their way into the public that as of this point the camp administration began reporting the deaths to the prosecutor's office." A day after the Strauss shooting, word came that another detainee, Karl Lehrburger, had been shot during an alleged assault on an SS man. This time Wintersberger decided to take matters into his own hands. He arrived at the concentration camp with the full authority of the Munich II prosecutor's office, and, of course, in the company of Dr. Flamm. Wintersberger and Flamm were led to the Arrest Bunker, where Lehrburger, a twenty-eight-year-old communist from Nuremberg, had been shot. Hans Steinbrenner claimed that the detainee had attacked him with a table knife during a routine inspection of the detention cells. Lehrburger's corpse had already been removed, but traces of the shooting were very much in evidence. The walls were spattered with fresh blood from the exit wound. A plate-size puddle of blood glistened on the concrete floor where Lehrburger had fallen.

Wintersberger was given the report and Steinbrenner's deposition prepared by the camp administrator, Josef Mutzbauer.
According to the Mutzbauer protocol, Steinbrenner had entered
Lehrburger's cell and found the detainee trying to hide a letter
in a water pitcher. When Steinbrenner attempted to look into the
pitcher, Lehrburger allegedly seized his bread knife and attacked
him. Steinbrenner pulled his pistol and fired a single shot. It caught
Lehrburger square in the forehead. Lehrburger collapsed to the
floor. In compliance with regulations, Steinbrenner went immediately to the commandant's office to report the incident to Wäckerle,
who in turn instructed him to provide a deposition to Mutzbauer.

Dr. Flamm's forensic examination confirmed that the death
had been caused by a single bullet fired at close quarters: between
ten and twenty centimeters. Lehrburger's corpse showed no signs
of abuse. Flamm saw no need for an autopsy. Wintersberger and
Flamm departed the facility as crisply as they had come.

That evening, toward eight o'clock, Steinbrenner went to see
Anton Schöberl, who kept the "reporting sheet" of detainees in the
Arrest Bunker. "You can strike Lehrburger from the list," Steinbrenner said. "He died today. I shot the sow Jew. He tried to attack
me." Schöberl remembered Steinbrenner, an SS man who prided
himself on his capacity for atrocity, looking "disturbed." Indeed,
Steinbrenner had spent the past two days visited by uncharacter-
istic hesitation and doubt. He had lashed and pummeled detainees
into unconsciousness, but until that point he had never killed a man
with the clear-eyed, unmitigated intent required by a pistol shot to
the head. On the same day that Hilmar Wäckerle had dispatched
Kantschuster to shoot Strauss, he had called Steinbrenner into his
office and instructed him to kill Lehrburger. Agents of the Nuremberg political police had visited the camp and informed Wäckerle
that Lehrburger, who had arrived on the same transport as Strauss
and had somehow slipped through the screening process, was a
Jew. Lehrburger had tried to hide in a top-tier bunk in his barracks

hoping not to be recognized by the visitors from Nuremberg, but had nonetheless been discovered and dispatched to the Arrest Bunker. Now Wäckerle wanted him dead.

Steinbrenner knew that the commandant brooked no opposition. Wäckerle had dismissed Anton Vogel when he refused an order to shoot Strauss. "I refused and explained that I was here as a manager," Vogel recalled, "and if he needed an executioner, he had better look for someone else." Wäckerle told Steinbrenner that Lehrburger was a Soviet Russian agent who had been trained in bacteriological warfare at the Cheka school in Russia. "It was suspected that there was a second or third similar agent who had not been apprehended whom they did not want to have alerted through a trial," Steinbrenner later recalled, "and in addition they did not want to cause disquiet in the general public. It was therefore necessary to have him shot immediately."

The next morning, Erspenmüller came to see Steinbrenner. He wanted to know why Steinbrenner had not carried out Wäckerle's order. Steinbrenner confessed that he had never actually killed a man before. He did not know how. "There is nothing easier," Erspenmüller told him. He laid out the story involving tearing up a letter, the table knife, and the supposed attack. "When the investigators come," he continued, "tell them that while you were inspecting the cell you noticed that Lehrburger put something in his jug and when you leaned over to look inside you saw that Lehrburger had a knife in his hand and wanted to stab you, at which point you shot in self-defense."

Erspenmüller reminded Steinbrenner of the SS oath he had sworn to blind obedience—quoted verbatim by Warren Farr to Sir Geoffrey Lawrence twelve years later in Nuremberg—and ordered him to carry out orders as instructed. Steinbrenner despaired. He knew that another SS man had been beaten for disobedience but still could not bring himself to shoot Lehrburger.

That evening, around five o'clock, Erspenmüller confronted

Steinbrenner yet again. This time he screamed. He ordered Stein-brenner to shoot Lehrburger immediately. If he did not obey, Erspenmüller threatened, it would be his turn. Steinbrenner steeled himself. He marched to the Arrest Bunker, down the nar-row corridor, unlocked Lehrburger's door, and burst into the cell. Lehrburger rose as Steinbrenner entered. Steinbrenner raised his pistol and shot his victim in the middle of the forehead. Lehr-burger collapsed without a word. Steinbrenner stared at him for a moment. There was no movement. He then arranged the room in accordance with Erspenmüller's suggestions, closed the cell door, and marched to the commandant's office to inform Wäckerle that his orders had been carried out as instructed.

Wäckerle told Steinbrenner that he could expect to be ques-tioned either by a prosecutor or by the *Mordkommission*. He should simply repeat what Erspenmüller had told him to say. Stein-brenner provided a deposition to Mutzbauer, who passed it on to Wintersberger.

Wintersberger saw no ground for further investigation. Lehr-burger was dead and there were no witnesses. The inspection of the cell and Dr. Flamm's examination did not contradict the tes-timony provided by Steinbrenner. As in the case of Götz, the SS testimony could not be refuted.

The next day, a report arrived that yet another Dachau detainee, Sebastian Nefzger, had committed suicide in his cell in the Arrest Bunker. The fifty-three-year-old salesman from Munich had been delivered to Dachau on May 11, along with Hans Beimler and the six spies that Reinhard Heydrich had ferreted out of the police files. The one-page report from Mutzbauer provided the precise circum-stances of Nefzger's reported suicide:

> In accordance with the instruction of May 26, 1933, of the con-centration camp commandant, I report the following:
> In the night of May 25 to 26, 1933, Nefzger committed sui-cide in his cell by slitting the artery on his left wrist.

At 5:40 in the morning on May 26, 1933, while making their rounds, Corporal Winhard and SS guard Steinbrenner found Nefzger lying dead on the floor of his cell.

On viewing the corpse I was able to determine that Nefzger first tried to commit suicide by hanging himself, which was evidenced by the strangulation marks on his neck. Nefzger used the leather strap from his artificial leg, which appeared to have torn due to his weight. It seems that Nefzger then, as already mentioned, slashed his wrist.

Since the camp doctor and forensic expert Dr. Nürnbergk determined that the cause of death was clearly evident, the authorities were not notified.

It was as clear a violation of the Criminal Procedure Code as Hartinger could have imagined. Not only had the body been removed but the administration had waited forty-eight hours before reporting the incident.

The following day, Dr. Nürnbergk confirmed the incident in a six-line medical report. "The forensic examination of the detainee Nefzger, Sebastian, salesman in Munich, Schommerstrasse 17, born January 10, 1900, in Munich, Catholic, married. It was determined that there were no outside persons involved in his death," Dr. Nürnbergk recorded. "It is without question that the death resulted from loss of blood caused by the slicing of the artery on the left hand." Hartinger called Dr. Flamm and instructed him to conduct his own forensic examination.

The next morning at nine o'clock, Flamm's phone rang. It was Dr. Nürnbergk wanting to know why a forensic examination was being requested when he had already provided a signed statement. Flamm said he was simply acting on instructions from the prosecutor's office. If Nürnbergk wanted to know why Flamm was being sent, he should talk to Hartinger.

Flamm then set off to Dachau in his car. Nürnbergk was waiting for him when he arrived. He was visibly unsettled. He again wanted to know why Flamm was conducting a forensic examination when he had already provided a report and it was clear that death was due to suicide. Flamm repeated that he was simply following orders. Flamm had Nefzger's corpse photographed frontally, then rolled over and photographed from behind, recording the deep pattern of lacerations that covered the entire back as if from some primitive induction rite. Flamm also had close-up photographs taken of the slashed wrist, with the tendons and tissue clearly visible and still moist with blood.

Flamm set to work. He noted a man "of powerful build and well fed" but with a mercilessly abused body with lacerations across the back, buttocks, and legs, traces of dried blood around his lips, and strangulation marks around the neck. In particular, he noted "a gash on the left hand with a deep gaping wound that sliced the tissue and left three slices in the bone." It struck Flamm as unusual that a man committing suicide would slash his wrist hard enough three times to score the bone. By 2 p.m., Flamm had completed his forensic examination and had determined that it would be necessary to conduct a full autopsy the next day.

As Flamm prepared to leave, Nürnbergk stopped him. He said he had a question. He had just learned that Jewish burial rituals provided for Jews to conduct their own medical examinations of the deceased. Nürnbergk mentioned the case of a Jew, Wilhelm Aron, who had died of "heart failure" and for whom he had issued the death certificate. Nürnbergk said that his medical opinion had sufficed in that case. Munich II had simply placed Aron in a sealed coffin and sent it back to his family in Bamberg. Nürnbergk now wondered whether there was any way to prevent the delivery of the bodies to Jewish families or prevent them from opening the coffin.

On Monday afternoon, Flamm and three other Hartinger colleagues met with Mutzbauer, who told them he had seen Nefzger in Cell 4 lying on his back on the floor in a pool of blood. The table knife was lying nearby, smeared with blood. Nefzger's artificial leg was also lying on the floor. On the right wall, hanging from a hook three or so meters above the floor, were the straps from his artificial leg. The straps were torn in half, apparent evidence of a failed attempt to hang himself.

Flamm commenced with his autopsy at four o'clock, again noting the unusual incisions on the bone. It was typical in such cases for there to be one or more exploratory incisions as the person tested for veins and arteries to slice, but it was highly unusual for a person to slash his wrist with three consecutive incisions with such force. More suspicious still was the inordinate amount of blood that Flamm discovered when he examined Nefzger's skull. "The left temporal side is saturated to a great extent with dark clotted blood," Flamm recorded. "The right temporal muscle is full of blood." When Flamm removed Nefzger's skull he also found it saturated with blood. "After removing the cranium including the upper half of the brain, the lining of the brain was shiny blue," Flamm noted. "The vessels full, in the large artery a great deal of dark fluid and freely flowing blood." This was not the tissue of a man who had bled to death.

Flamm continued to work through Nefzger's body, organ by organ, limb by limb. Nearly three hours later, he had finished. His conclusions were definitive:

I. The results of the autopsy exclude as the cause of death bleeding from the gash on the left arm.

II. The gash on the left wrist shows three cuts into the bone. There are no test cuts. These findings speak against the assumption that this was a self-inflicted wound.

III. Suffocation appears to be the cause of death. The cause of suffocation could be either from choking or strangulation. The marks on the neck do not correspond to what one usually finds in the case of hanging deaths.

Dr. Flamm completed his autopsy at 6:30 that evening and returned to Munich. His thirty-page, ninety-eight-point autopsy report, coupled with the Mutzbauer memorandum and the Nürn-bergk forensic examination, recounted a macabre nocturnal inci-dent: Two SS men mercilessly lash a crippled war veteran into near unconsciousness, strangle him to death, tie his own prosthetic straps around the corpse's neck, hang the straps from a nail in the wall, have the straps tear under the dead man's weight with the body tumbling to the floor, slash the man's wrist with a bread knife to feign suicide, close the cell door and lock it, only to open it a few hours later to "discover" a victim of a nighttime suicide.

Hartinger understood that prosecuting the SS for premeditated murder and obstruction of justice presented challenges. The Bavar-ian courts were notoriously conservative, as Gumbel had reported in his 1922 study and Wintersberger knew from the "little Hitler trial," and had become increasingly cautious under the new regime. But Hartinger believed that even conservative judges, when con-fronted by evidence of such grotesque horror, could not help but reach the only appropriate verdict. These atrocities could not be dismissed as unfounded rumor or "Jewish-Bolshevik" propaganda. This was hard forensic evidence. Moreover, from a practical point of view, it was being delivered by a state office purged of commu-nists and Jews. These were pure-blooded Aryan forensics, indict-ments, and arrest warrants against equally pure-blooded Aryan criminals on charges of premeditated murder and obstruction of justice.

Hartinger's prosecution strategy was simple. He intended to indict Ehmann for the murder of Hausmann, and Kantschuster for the murder of Strauss. Dr. Flamm's reports and Dr. Merkel's lab results would do the rest. Prosecuting the killers of Schloss and Nefzger was more complicated. Hartinger had forensic evidence proving homicide and correspondence on concentration camp let-terhead indicating obstruction of justice, but no murder suspects. Wicklmayr, Ehmann, Kantschuster, and Steinbrenner had all proven themselves capable of shooting a man point-blank, but there were no witnesses and no one willing to talk. Hartinger planned to indict "unknown perpetrators" for those murders, in the hope that the truth would eventually come out, and in the interim use the murders to implicate Wäckerle, Mutzbauer, and Nürnbergk.

On the evening of May 30, as Hartinger awaited the final lab results of the most recent killings, he prepared a report on the murders he intended to prosecute. He summarized each case in a half-page description, headed by a Roman numeral, that included key details of the circumstances, excerpts from Flamm's autopsies, reference numbers to the corresponding investigation files, and the names of the SS guards involved in each killing. He planned to take the four cases with incontrovertible evidence—Hausmann, Nefzger, Schloss, and Strauss—and bundle them into a series of indictments with the intent of demonstrating a pattern of deaths that suggested the intentional serial killing of detainees with possible chain-of-command involvement. He also included the Götz and Lehrburger killings.

Hartinger finally had the hard evidence that met Wintersberger's standard and, more important, the chief prosecutor's attention. "I had in fact by chance mentioned while we happened to be walking with Minister Counselor Döbig," Hartinger recalled, "that as soon as I received a few more documents that I was waiting for, I would be ready to issue indictments to the judge—at the time, a judicial review of indictments was required—and since he did not respond, I assumed he was in agreement."

ON THURSDAY, June 1, Hartinger met with Dr. Hermann Kiessner, the investigating judge for Munich II, and, in accordance with the Criminal Procedure Code, informed him of the forthcoming indictments. "If the prosecutor's office considers it necessary to undertake a judicial investigation," Paragraph 162 dictated, "the request is to be presented to the investigating judge for the district in which the investigation is to be undertaken." Hartinger was aware that the indictment and arrest process could be perilous and fraught with complications. "As was well known, Nazis were required to report to the party anything that could be of interest," Hartinger said. "I planned that the party would not find out about the indictments until the last possible moment." Hartinger had complete trust in Kiessner, an elderly judge, who immediately agreed to the plan. "Since it was necessary to act quickly and with surprise if things were to succeed," Kiessner recalled, "we both discussed the steps that were to be taken." Hartinger would prepare the indictments and arrest warrants, secure Wintersberger's signature, and then deliver them to Kiessner, who in turn would personally carry the arrest warrants to the homicide department. As a former judge and prosecutor, Hartinger had extensive experience with the police and had complete trust in them, and above all in their "diligence and integrity." Kiessner agreed: "It was clear to both of us that success depended wholly on the homicide department of the police. I was to go to them immediately." The police would be dispatched without delay to Dachau to take Wäckerle, Mutzbauer, and Nürnbergk into custody. "There was no question that the police department commanded great respect, and I relied on the hope," Hartinger wrote, "that this respect would also not be without significance with the National Socialists and even with the SS." Three weeks earlier, the police had used this "respect" to extract Josef Hirsch from Dachau. Hartinger calculated they could do the same with the arrest of Wäckerle.

As Hartinger was finalizing details of his plan with Kiessner, he encountered Wintersberger in the second-floor corridor at Prielmayrstrasse 5. "We started talking and stood by a window," Hartinger later remembered. "During this conversation I informed the chief prosecutor that I would now—I probably said 'today'— dictate the indictment for the four cases." Things were ready to go. "And then the chief prosecutor stated quietly and without any visible emotional reaction: 'I'm not signing anything.'" Hartinger looked at Wintersberger, speechless. "That was one of the greatest surprises of my life," he recalled. "In a word, I was stunned. I didn't ask the reason, since his position was clear. I said nothing more and took my leave."

At that point, Hartinger could have abandoned the indictment process. He already had years of service in the state bureaucracy and was ranked in the "special class" pay scale, earning significantly more than he would in more remote parts of Bavaria. With his excellent performance reviews, he could anticipate an appointment as chief prosecutor within the next five years, possibly even of Munich II itself, and eventually ascend to the presidency of a district court, perhaps even become state attorney general. He also had his family to consider. He was a brief three months short of his fortieth birthday, with an apartment in an elegant quarter of Munich where he lived comfortably with his family. "At the time, my wife was often ill," Hartinger would write. "She was suffering from a long-term heart and nervous disorder that brought her to the edge of her grave, and which was caused primarily by the constant worry and anxiety about my unrelenting fight against Nazi brutalities." In brief, Hartinger had every personal reason to keep quiet and every professional justification to defer to his superior. But as he walked down the hall back to his office, he knew there was only one decision he could take. "It was clear to me, and there was no more reason to reconsider," he said, "that I should act on my plan, to dictate, to submit, and sign the indictments and other paperwork myself."

That evening, Hartinger stayed behind in his office with his trusted assistant, to dictate his murder indictments and arrest warrants against the camp personnel. Hartinger was clear, explicit, and resolute: "I hereby issue a public indictment against unknown perpetrators for the crime of murder according to §211 of the Reich's criminal code. In addition against Wäckerle, H., camp comman-

dant, Dr. Nürnbergk, camp doctor, and Mutzbauer, office administrator, all currently resident in the Dachau Concentration Camp,
for the offense of aiding and abetting according to §257 of the
Reich's Criminal Code."

Hartinger had already issued the indictments for the murders
of Alfred Strauss, Louis Schloss, and Leonhard Hausmann, and
finally Sebastian Nefzger. "Although the accused Wäckerle, Nürnbergk, and Mutzbauer knew of the circumstances and understood
the cause of death, they did not act according to their professional
duty, and furthermore presented the situation as if it clearly dealt
with suicide." Hartinger went on to note that Nürnbergk went
so far as to write to the district court in Dachau on May 27 that
"the possibility of death at the hands of another party is excluded."
Hartinger noted that Mutzbauer had also submitted a false report
when he was in clear possession of the facts. In light of these events,
Hartinger wrote, "I submit a request for the opening of a preliminary judicial investigation and the issuance of an arrest warrant
for the accused because of imminent danger of suppression of evidence." Hartinger returned home late that evening to find his wife
waiting for him. When she asked why he was so late, he said flatly,
"I just signed my own death sentence."

15

Good-Faith Agreements

A S HARTINGER WAS PREPARING the murder indictments and arrest warrants in his office, Karl Wintersberger was in the Wittelsbach Palace cautioning Heinrich Himmler about the imminent judicial action against Hilmar Wäckerle and several other concentration camp SS personnel. Wintersberger provided Himmler with evidence from Hartinger's investigation, including photographs of the abused corpses of both Schloss and Nefzger, as well as evidence related to Hausmann and Strauss. "I pointed out that with these four cases in particular, based on the fact that there was a pressing suspicion of serious criminal acts on the part of members of the camp guards and camp administrators," Wintersberger recorded in his notes from the meeting, "and since this fact had become known to the prosecutor's office as well as the police officials, there is an obligation in serious criminal cases to pursue the matter regardless of the individuals involved."

Wintersberger's news of the Dachau murders came as no surprise to Himmler, but the threat of imminent judicial action certainly did. Since the first killings in April, Munich II had proven to be accommodatingly circumspect in its response. Wintersberger

had not only closed the investigation into the shooting of Benario, Goldmann, and the two Kahns after two weeks, but had also
confirmed the SS account of the deaths, even citing verbatim the
disparaging remarks about the Jews' deportment. Wintersberger
had personally investigated the Lehrburger shooting and that
very day, June 1, closed that case as well. But now Wintersberger
had come with news of potential murder indictments and arrest
warrants.

FOR THE PAST SEVERAL MONTHS, Himmler and interior minister
Wagner had played fast and easy with the law in the name of public
security. When Hans Frank had complained of the overcrowding
of state facilities, Wagner was curt and unapologetic. "In case the
justice officials find that the number of existing prisons is not adequate," Wagner proposed, "I would recommend implementing the
same methods that were used earlier against the masses of incarcerated members of the National Socialist German Workers' Party.
They were known to be locked up in any vacant enclosure without
concern whether there was adequate cover against the effects of
the weather."

A few weeks later, Himmler had announced the opening of the
Dachau Concentration Camp with equal disregard for due process.
"We took these measures without worrying about the petty issues,"
the Munich police chief stated at his press conference, "with the
conviction that we were restoring calm to the people and acting in
their best interest."

Wagner and Himmler meanwhile altered the state security
structures. Wagner appointed Munich police chief Himmler as
a "political counselor" in the interior ministry on March 15, and
two weeks later made him commander of the political police for
Bavaria and placed him in charge of "already existing and planned
concentration camps. Himmler placed Reinhardt Heydrich, as

Warren Farr later noted, in charge of the police files, with horrific consequences, especially for covert agents like Hunglinger and Nefzger.

On May 30, the Dachau Concentration Camp was officially transferred into SS authority. For the previous two months, as has been shown, the SS had served as "assistant police" to the Bavarian state police, under the auspices of Captain Winkler. As commandant, Hilmar Wäckerle had been responsible for the detainees, but Winkler remained in charge of the facility. The May 30 transfer was effected with a formal handover by Winkler to Wäckerle. "The command of the SS guard unit, as well as the other guard and security services in the Dachau Concentration Camp, was transferred today to the SS leadership," the transfer protocol stated. Winkler "officially relinquished" authority with his signature, and Wäckerle "officially accepted" with his. The camp regulations, inventory of weapons, a list of telephone numbers that included the Nazi Party headquarters in Munich (Tel: 54901), and other administrative documents were placed in Wäckerle's hands. Winkler departed. Dachau belonged to Himmler.

But now Wintersberger had arrived with news of imminent judicial intrusion. His appearance in Himmler's office that afternoon came amid rising concerns within the state government over reports of the killings in Dachau. Three days earlier, on the afternoon of May 29, Wintersberger had visited Minister of Justice Friedrich Döbig in his office and had shown him a copy of the camp regulations imposing martial law and providing for capital punishment. Wäckerle had told Wintersberger that he had prepared the regulations on instructions from Himmler, who had subsequently approved them. Wintersberger told Döbig he believed the death penalties violated state law. Wintersberger also informed Döbig of "contradictions" between Wäckerle's account of several recent deaths in the camp and the forensic evidence collected by Flamm. Döbig called Hans Frank and suggested that the minister of justice ask Prime Minister Siebert to place the issue on the agenda of a meeting with state ministers scheduled for May 31.

The next day, when Döbig discussed the matter with Wagner, the interior minister said the circumstances of the shootings required "further clarification" with Himmler and Wäckerle. Since Himmler was indisposed, Wagner called Siebert and told him to strike the matter from the meeting agenda. Wagner then proposed a meeting with Himmler, Wäckerle, Nürnbergk, Wintersberger, and Flamm. Döbig countered that they needed to avoid "any appearance of interference in the pending investigation," and proposed instead that Wintersberger have a quiet conversation with Himmler.

Himmler recognized the danger immediately. The administrative tangle that had allowed Wagner and Himmler to transfer police authority for Dachau to the SS was causing increasing confusion at all levels of state government. Siebert was responsible for Bavaria as prime minister, as was Epp as Reich governor. Wagner shared Nazi Party authority with other Gauleiters in Bavaria, but exercised statewide power as interior minister. Himmler was subordinate to SA chief Ernst Röhm—the SS was an elite unit within the SA—but exercised autonomy as chief of police in Munich. The chaos deepened amid local power struggles.

"The state's authority is threatened by unwarranted attacks on all sides from political functionaries in the normal administrative machinery," one local official despaired in those weeks. "Every local political leader, municipal leader, and district leader issues decrees that interfere with the authority of the lower officials in the ministries." Instructions and ordinances were introduced by regional authorities that undermined ordinances issued by district officials, who in turn issued ordinances that undercut authority down to the smallest local police station. "Everyone arrests everyone," he observed. "Everybody threatens everyone with Dachau." Bavaria was collapsing into administrative chaos. "Even in the smallest police station, the best and most reliable officers are facing uncertainties in the administration," he warned, "that will invariably lead to the devastation and destruction of the state."

AMID THE TUMULT and confusion of that blood-spattered German spring, the violence took an unexpected twist that even Emil Gumbel could not have foreseen. Nazis began killing Nazis.

The half million SA storm troopers had long been of brutal utility to the Nazi cause. They battled Bolsheviks in streets and beer halls. As "assistant police," they helped round up and frequently attacked communists, socialists, and Jews. They also turned on each other. In one incident, on April 22, an SA leader and two storm troopers assaulted an SS man in a guesthouse in the town of Feldmoching, just north of Munich, "because he had earlier insulted the SA people" in the town. The SS man was beaten, ordered to kneel before the SA men and beg for forgiveness, then taken to a hospital, where he spent the next two weeks recovering from the abuses. The SA leader "confiscated" his victim's motorcycle and lent it to another SA man, who drove it for two days then returned it and dumped sugar into the gas tank.

On the day Wintersberger appeared at the Wittelsbach Palace, Himmler was in fact seeking the release of one of his prized SS colonels from a psychiatric ward. In March, SS colonel Theodor Eicke had been taken into protective custody by Josef Bürckel, the Gauleiter in Ludwigshafen, then declared mentally incompetent after staging a hunger strike. Eicke dispatched a series of enraged letters to Himmler, one of them eighteen pages long, protesting his incarceration and reminding the Reichsführer SS of his loyal service. Eicke's psychiatrist wrote to Himmler on April 22 with the assurance that after "several weeks of observation and evaluation" there appeared to be no sign of "mental illness" or "tendencies toward a psychopathic personality," and suggested Eicke could be released.

Himmler knew Eicke to be querulous, paranoid, and violent,

but he was also aware that Eicke was a fanatically loyal and effective member of the SS. Eicke had tripled the size of SS-Standarte 10, from 290 to 1,000 men, in less than a year. Himmler personally promoted him to SS colonel in November 1931 and gave him a book with the personal inscription "Loyalty is eternal." Unwavering loyalty was a fundamental precept of SS membership, as Warren Farr was to point out in Nuremberg, in underscoring the collective guilt that came with SS membership. "We must be honest, decent, loyal, and comradely to members of our own blood and to nobody else," Farr would read verbatim to the tribunal. Loyalty was to be repaid with loyalty.

Himmler provided a 300-mark-per-month subsidy for Eicke's family while Eicke was in the psychiatric ward, and by the end of May was willing to extract the former SS colonel from incarceration. "I intend to use Eicke in some position, possibly with the government," Himmler was to write Eicke's psychiatrist on June 2, "but he must not make things too difficult or impossible for me."

On Tuesday, June 1, as Himmler was preparing to make good on his promise of loyalty to a fellow SS man, Wintersberger informed Himmler that the Munich II prosecutor's office was in possession of incontrovertible evidence of Nazi homicide that was going to compel the prosecutor's office to take action against another one of Himmler's prized SS officers. Himmler studied the photographs of Schloss and Nefzger, listened to the details of the four investigations, weighed the implications. He knew that a state law was being drafted that would grant amnesty to the myriad transgressions perpetrated by the SA and SS over the past several months, including the Dachau murders, but he needed to bide his time.*

---

* The "amnesty law"—the Law for the Discontinuation of Criminal Investigations (*Gesetz über die Niederschlagung strafrechtlicher Untersuchungen*)—was presented in draft form by Hans Frank on July 26, 1933, at a state cabinet meeting, and signed into law on August 2, 1933, by Epp in his capacity as Reich governor. The law did not actually amnesty the crimes but instead provided for the discontinuation of criminal investigations that could harm the reputation of the National Socialist government. It was restricted to crimes committed

"Police Chief Himmler has agreed to give instructions not to create any difficulties for me and my investigative judge while handling the investigations in the Dachau camp," Wintersberger recorded after the meeting, "and to comply with all requests, and that he declares that, of course, he would have no objections regarding my further intentions to pursue investigations into the individual cases."

before July 25, 1933, with the intent of curtailing further criminal excesses by the SS and SA. (Lothar Gruchmann, *Justiz im Dritten Reich 1933–1940: Anpassung und Unterwerfung in der Ära Gürtner*, 2nd ed. [Munich; Oldenbourg, 1990], 332.)

16

Rules of Law

O N JUNE 2, shortly after work hours began, Hartinger arrived
at his office to discover to his astonishment that Wintersberger was now ready to sign the four indictments. As planned,
Hartinger brought the four indictments along with the investigation files to Dr. Kiessner, who was waiting in his office. Kiessner
took time to study Hartinger's indictments, then later that morning, as agreed, delivered them personally to the homicide department of the Munich police. There, Kiessner was surprised to learn
that all "political criminal cases" were henceforth being handled
not by the state police homicide department but by the political
police in the Wittelsbach Palace.

"When I subsequently went to the Political Police, I was
received with smirks and referred to the chief of police," Kiessner
recalled. "My attempt to see him did not succeed, however, since it
was explained to me in the reception area that he was away on business." Kiessner returned to his office and began preparing arrest
warrants to send to Himmler with the investigation files.

Hartinger was furious when he learned that Kiessner had been
to the Wittelsbach Palace. "It would have been an absolute require-

ment to inform me, given the agreement between the two of us," he later said. "We were dealing with a criminal case of a special nature that required from the outset cooperation between the court and the prosecutor's office." Hartinger had trusted Kiessner completely and could only attribute Kiessner's act to "rashness." Kiessner apologized, but the damage was done: Himmler had been alerted. "The appearance of the investigator in the offices of the SS apparently had the consequence that Minister of the Interior and Gauleiter Wagner probably learned of the matter from a party functionary responsible for police administration, and complained to the Bavarian Ministry of Justice," Hartinger recalled, unaware that Wintersberger had briefed Himmler the previous afternoon.

"As I was returning punctually to my office on the afternoon of June 2 from the lunch break, which was generally between twelve and two o'clock in the afternoon, I heard my telephone ringing just as I was unlocking my office door," Hartinger recalled. "When I picked up the telephone, Minister Counselor Döbig was on the line and demanded that I personally bring him the four investigation files with the indictments immediately." Hartinger explained that the files were with Kiessner and reminded Döbig that normal procedure was for indictments to be routed through the attorney general rather than through the minister of justice. "He answered in the negative and insisted that I immediately bring them myself." Hartinger retrieved the files from Kiessner's office and delivered them, as instructed, to the justice ministry. The plan was compromised. Hartinger knew the Nazis would be alerted. There would be no arrests. There would be no headlines.

IRONICALLY, another criminal investigation claimed the news headlines the following day. "As the district party leader of the National Socialist Reichstag faction has learned," the *Völkischer Beobachter* reported, "the investigating judge of the Reich Court,

Reich Court Legal Counsel Vogt, concluded on June 1 the preliminary investigation against the suspects Van der Lubbe, Torgler,
Dimitroff, Popoff, and Tanell for the arson attack on the Reichstag." The editors splashed the revelation in a boldfaced headline,
underlined in red, across the top of the newspaper with the sub-
heading "Indictment for the Reichstag Arson Attack." The article spoke of a communist conspiracy involving Marinus von der
Lubbe, the Dutch communist apprehended at the scene, as well as
Ernst Torgler, chairman of the communist faction in the Reichstag,
and three Bulgarian communists. "This report will henceforth
silence all the groundless slanderers," the newspaper wrote, "who,
on Jewish-Marxist command around the world, have claimed that
Reichstag president and party comrade Göring personally set the
Reichstag on fire."*

Hartinger had calculated that Wäckerle's arrest and resulting headlines would stay the killing in Dachau and blunt any SS
reprisal. "It was clear to both of us that by issuing an arrest warrant we were turning the leaders and members of the SS into bit-
ter enemies," Kiessner recalled, "and placing our jobs, our freedom
and even our lives in jeopardy." The two men now found themselves perilously exposed. In the Munich II offices, there had been
"boundless respect for the courage with which Herr Hartinger
repeatedly entered the lion's den." One person recalled that when
an SS guard halted Hartinger at the camp entrance with the threat
"We will shoot you," Hartinger responded, "Then you'll have to
shoot me. I'm coming in." The "general and serious concern" was
suddenly real and imminent. Steinbrenner recalled that the SS

---

* The Reich Court in Leipzig convicted Marinus van der Lubbe of treason in December
1933, but acquitted the other four defendants. Van der Lubbe was beheaded in January 1934.
Mainstream historiography assumes that Van der Lubbe acted alone, and dismisses both the
theory of a communist conspiracy as well as Nazi complicity; however, the issue remains a
point of continued speculation. In 1946, Hans Gisevius, a former member of the Gestapo,
provided details of alleged Nazi involvement, as did a 2001 book based on previously unex-
plored Gestapo archives in Moscow: Alexander Bahar and Wilfried Kugel, *Der Reichstagsbrand* (Berlin: Quintessenz Verlag, 2001).

began making plans to have Hartinger "taken care of." "I told my husband repeatedly that he should burn all his notes that could be dangerous if there was a house search," Hartinger's wife later said. "He refused to burn his register of the occurrences in the Dachau camp, because he hoped that the perpetrators could in fact one day be brought to justice."

Amid the crisis, Wintersberger appeared to have a change of heart. The chief prosecutor's reluctance over the previous two months vanished. Wintersberger had closed the investigation into the shooting of the four Jews in Dachau on April 12, which required disregarding the eyewitness testimony of Erwin Kahn and affirming the SS account. He had delayed or terminated subsequent Dachau murder investigations. On the day Wintersberger met with Himmler, June 1, he closed the books on the Lehrburger shooting "because Wicklmayr's assertions cannot be disproved at present." But suddenly, a day after refusing to sign the indictments and arrest warrants, Wintersberger gave his full support to securing the return of the files. "I really do not know what was wrong with Wintersberger on that afternoon," Hartinger wondered years later, "because after that he was fully behind me with the investigation and did everything possible." Wintersberger reissued the four indictments with his own signature and called Döbig in the justice ministry demanding the return of the investigation files. Döbig informed Wintersberger that the cases had already been forwarded to Wagner in the ministry of the interior. "I explained to Minister Counselor Döbig that without the files I was not in a position to continue the necessary investigation," Wintersberger noted in his files. Hartinger and Kiessner tried to reconstruct the investigation files. "This could not be carried out," Kiessner remembered, "since the autopsy protocol, which was the decisive basis for the case, was not available in a second copy."

But the files were in fact in good hands. "I had Reich governor General von Epp call a meeting," Hans Frank later told the Nuremberg tribunal, "where I produced the files regarding the killing and pointed out the illegality of such an action on the part of the SS and stated that representatives from the German public prosecutor's office had always been able to investigate any death which involved a suspicion that a crime had been committed and that I had not become aware so far of any departure from this principle in the Reich." The meeting, which took place on June 2, pitted Siebert, Epp, and Frank against Wagner and Himmler. Himmler was instructed to put an end to the killings and to undertake "personnel changes" within the camp.

As Hartinger intended, the indictments caused "considerable unrest" within the Bavarian state government and eventually in Berlin. "After that I continued protesting against this method to Dr. Gürtner, the Reich minister of justice, and at the same time to the attorney general," Frank continued. "I pointed out that this meant the beginning of a development which threatened the legal system in an alarming manner. Heinrich Himmler eventually referred the matter to Adolf Hitler, who intervened personally in the matter. The proceedings were ordered to be quashed," Frank recalled. "I handed in my resignation as [Bavaria's] minister of justice but it was not accepted."

Amid the judicial wrangling, the killings in Dachau ceased. There were no Paragraph 159 deaths in Dachau reported during the month of June. The same held true for the first and second weeks of July. On July 15, Hilmar Wäckerle was dismissed as camp commandant. The news came in a terse, one-line missive from Himmler. "I am assigning you as of July 15 to the position of district officer in SS Unit 10," it read, "and am hereby relieving you of your position as Adjutant I/29."* The force of the law had cracked the sworn bond of SS loyalty.

---

* The SS Unit 10 was headquartered in Stuttgart and under the command of SS lieutenant Johann-Erasmus Baron von Malsen-Ponickau, who had received the first SS guards in Dachau in his capacity as head of the Munich "assistant police."

In the last week of July, when a reporter for the *New York Times* came to Dachau, he found the camp transformed from the time of the previous visit, three months earlier. The woodlands surrounding the Würm Mill Creek had been clear-cut, leaving a wide perimeter around the camp. The isolated clearing where Benario, Goldmann, and the two Kahns had been shot had been transformed into a fully operational shooting range. The swimming pool, not far from where Alfred Strauss had died, was now complete. The new commandant was Theodor Eicke, apparently rehabilitated.

Eicke, middle-aged, thick-necked, with a full face, somewhat ruddy, had the hard, disciplined glare of a paymaster accustomed to parsimonious allocation. Familiar with budgets, staffing, and security from previous employment, Eicke was appalled by what he encountered on arrival. "In the entire facility there were only three men who knew how to use a machine gun," Eicke claimed. "My men were housed in drafty factory halls. We were plagued by poverty and misery."

Eicke received a paltry 230 marks per month as camp commandant. "We were considered a necessary evil who did nothing except cost money; irrelevant men behind barbed wire," he said. "I literally had to beg for money by the penny from the state budget to pay my officers and their guards." Worse still, Eicke found that Dachau was being used as a dumping ground for troublemakers from SS units across southern Bavaria, transforming the facility into a "collecting pot of problem cases" that was rife with "disloyalty, embezzlement, and corruption." Eicke said he dismissed sixty men within his first month on the job and sought to mentor those who remained. "I went energetically and happily about my work, I turned guards into junior officers and junior officers into officers," he remembered. "Within a few weeks, a common willingness for sacrifice, deprivation, and a warm camaraderie created a model of behavior from which emerged a perfect esprit de corps. We did not become arrogant, because we really had nothing; behind the barbed wire we quietly went about our duties and ruthlessly removed anyone from our ranks who showed the slightest trace of disloyalty. Thus was formed and nurtured a guard unit in the quiet of the concentration camp. Their ideals were loyalty, bravery, and duty."

The new spirit pervading Dachau was already much in evidence when the *Times* reporter arrived in late July. The reporter, who referred to it as an "educational camp," was particularly impressed with Eicke, who presented himself less as a military-style commandant and more as a "rest camp" administrator. It was his job, he said, to run an orderly facility, not to determine why or for how long a man was to be incarcerated. This had not been the case, he said, under the previous camp administration, which had been notoriously lax. Eicke had imposed discipline and order on detainees and guards alike. "This, both the prisoners and the camp's commander Herr Eicke, agreed, was truer now than before," the reporter observed. "Now camp life has settled into the organized routine of any penal institution."

Eicke assigned SS lieutenant Hans Lippert, who had replaced Erspenmüller as deputy commandant, to tour the facility with the *Times* reporter. Lippert showed him the machine guns mounted in the watchtowers, the barbed wire, the armed guards stationed along the walls, the clean barracks. "For their own comfort, the men see that any pig among them is cleaned up and stays clean," Lippert said. The detainees snapped to attention each time they entered a barrack. The SS personnel were still quartered in barracks as spartan as those of the detainees. But there were noticeable improvements. Some buildings had been refurbished as workshops where craftsmen were put to work at their particular trade. The reporter saw tailors sewing gray prison uniforms, bootmakers producing boots, woodworkers building doors and windows, and locksmiths crafting various fittings. There was even a studio with a skylight where artists made crayon sketches on Nazi themes, medallions featuring Hitler, and metal swastikas. Hitler portraits sold for

50 pfennigs each. The detainees ranged from seventeen-year-old boys to white-haired old men. "All types were represented—sturdy peasants, sturdy laborers and bespectacled intellectuals," the reporter noted, as well as "faces usually attributed to a city's underworld," and all looking "sour, grim, sullen, sad or merely apathetic."

The complaints had not changed. Many said they did not know why they were there. They did not know how long they would be detained. The reporter heard vague rumors of "disciplinary cells" but did not see them himself. He saw some work details with men stripped to the waist clearing brush beneath the blazing afternoon sun, watched over by armed guards, but the majority seemed to be languishing in the camp. "Most of them were lying in the grass and some were in the shade of the few available trees," he wrote, "[. . .] some playing chess, a few reading books, most simply doing nothing. It was an almost idyllic picture of a rest camp."

By all appearances, Hartinger had stayed the homicidal impulses of the new government. "It was certainly an achievement that Wäckerle was gone," Hartinger later said. "Of course, I could not have known that his successor would be even worse."

THE SUMMER LULL IN KILLING was illusory, of course. In mid-August, Franz Stenzer, who had nearly been struck by the bullet that killed Josef Götz, was shot in an alleged escape attempt. He was followed in September by Hugo Handschuch, a twenty-three-year-old, who was said to have died of a heart attack. In October, there were two alleged suicides, the voluntary camp doctor, Dr. Delwin Katz, and another detainee, Wilhelm Franz, an office worker from Munich. The following month, Fritz Bürck was shot in the head, chest, and stomach when he allegedly assaulted SS sergeant Wilhelm Birzle near one of the camp latrines. Hartinger registered another two suicides by hanging in early 1934.

Dachau's death toll hitched and lurched in the months and years to come, averaging twenty killings annually, with a brief slump in 1936, the year the Olympic Games came to Germany, then ballooned monstrously with the outbreak of war as Dachau's myriad atrocities were franchised across the continent. Back in 1922, Emil Gumbel had warned that a society that condoned individual homicide risked condoning mass murder. "These so-called handcrafted murders are effective in contained circumstances, but only here," Gumbel had observed. Expressing bitterness and resignation at the public indifference to "political murder," he anticipated, with chilling prescience, more ambitious forms of killing. "For this," Gumbel wrote, "different and better methods of an industrialized nature will be required."

The single-shot executions initially applied to Benario, Goldmann, and the two Kahns were repeated a millionfold with the mobile killing units that followed the path of the German armies across eastern Europe. The burning of corpses, like those of Willy Aron and the uncounted, unnamed Jews in Dachau's abandoned munitions shed, were to be conducted in high-performance, coke-stoked crematory facilities. The process of strangulation—first tested on Louis Strauss on the night of Monday, May 17, 1933—was enhanced through a crystallized chemical asphyxiate sold commercially as Zyklon B, transforming a homicidal act that originally required little more than brute force into an industrialized process involving closed ventilation systems, airtight chambers, and faux showerheads that consumed the lives of millions of men, women, and children across the continent.

We will never know the potential consequences or the course of events had the Hartinger indictments been delivered that June. The arrest of Wäckerle and his subordinates by the Bavarian state police would have come amid the final negotiations for the concordat in Rome. The domestic embarrassment, coupled with international outrage over forensic evidence of premeditated serial killing, possibly with chain-of-command responsibility, may well have compelled Epp and ultimately Hindenburg to act. "It would have been a great success for me had the arrests succeeded," Hartinger later wrote. Hartinger insisted that these were not mere "fantasies." "As I later learned," he said, "there were discussions in this direction, but the 'good spirits' did not prevail."

In the end, the murder indictments may have failed to deliver on the hope Hartinger invested in them, but they did underscore the potential for change in the early days of the Third Reich, before the seemingly unimaginable had become seemingly inexorable. Hartinger may have lacked the aristocratic bearing of Raoul Wallenberg. He certainly possessed neither the charm nor the wiles of Oskar Schindler. He was little more than a balding, middle-aged civil servant, with a wife and five-year-old daughter. But like these two heroes of Holocaust rescue, Hartinger demonstrated the potential of personal courage and determination in a time of collective human failure. After the war, when attempts were made to honor him, Hartinger dismissed the efforts out of hand. "I was only doing what my sense of duty and my professional oath demanded," he said.

Epilogue

The Hartinger Conviction

I N THE SUMMER OF 1945, an intelligence officer with the U.S.
Army was rifling through the office of Adolf Wagner when he
came across a cache of files locked in a desk drawer. Wagner's office
had been left untouched since June 1942 when the state interior
minister had suffered a stroke to which he had succumbed two
years later. The files contained hundreds of pages of original documents, all dated from May and June 1933, and included the murder
indictment and arrest warrant for Hilmar Wäckerle and several of
his subordinates. The files were transferred to Nuremberg, a city
that for more than a decade had provided the backdrop for the
swastika-swathed pageants of the Third Reich, and now served as
the setting for the International Military Tribunal, where the prosecution team was preparing for the upcoming trial. The neighboring town of Fürth, virtually untouched by the bombings that had
devastated Nuremberg, provided quarters for many of the jurists.

When President Harry S. Truman first approached Supreme
Court Justice Robert Jackson about serving as chief prosecutor,
Jackson had envisioned Adolf Hitler in the dock as defendant, possi-
bly along with Benito Mussolini, and several key Hitler lieutenants,

such as Hermann Göring, Joseph Goebbels, Heinrich Himmler, and Martin Bormann. In the final weeks of the war, Jackson saw his list of suspects eviscerated. On April 30, Hitler committed suicide in his Berlin bunker, followed a day later by Goebbels. Himmler popped a cyanide tablet in his mouth almost immediately after being detained by British intelligence officers. Bormann had vanished, leaving only Göring among the senior Nazis to stand trial and compelling Jackson to recalibrate his prosecution strategy. According to a calculation made by Warren Farr, the second tier of Nazi leaders included 1,000 potential criminal suspects, followed by surviving Gauleiters and their staffs, numbering an estimated 4,000, with another 21,000 local officials, and 2,000 more "group leaders," 60,000 "cell leaders," and another 300,000 "block leaders," for a total of 463,048 potential criminal suspects. This was excluding 400,000 lesser members of the Nazi Party leadership among the four million officially registered party members.

The undertaking was as dubious as it was daunting, a fact that was evident to all, including the defendants. "You can't indict a government and its organizations as criminal," Hans Frank observed from his prison cell. "The concept of the Reich government is a hundred years old. The general staff is hundreds of years old." Frank admitted that the case of the SS was different, since "it was started with the party and by the party." "But it's quite impossible to indict or convict an organization as criminal if it has in its membership millions of innocent people."

But that is exactly what Jackson had decided to do. He indicted twenty-four prominent Nazis—of whom twenty-one made it into the dock—each responsible for a particular sector of the government, then demonstrated the criminal nature of the National Socialist German Workers' Party and its affiliated entities as a way of netting the broadest swath of defendants. Jackson divided assignments among the Russian, French, British, and American jurists, and charged Farr with the task of "criminalizing" the SS. Throughout the summer and autumn of 1945, the prosecution teams combed through more than 100,000 documents taken from offices, archives, sealed vaults, salt mines, and ash heaps. Farr immediately recognized the value of the Dachau murder indictments.

The bundling of the four cases permitted Farr to demonstrate a systematic, chain-of-command process with explicit homicidal intent on the part of the SS within weeks of the Nazi seizure of power. "The significance is that you have, one after the other, murders committed within a short space of time," Farr explained to the tribunal that December. "And, in each instance, an official report by the camp commander or the guard as to the cause of death which was completely disproved by the facts." Farr read from the indictment file for the murder of Alfred Strauss (Document 641-PS), then turned to the indictment for the murder of Leonhard Hausmann (Document 642-PS), only to be interrupted by the tribunal president.

"I don't think you need to read the details."

"I will offer it without reading it."

The murders of Louis Schloss (Document 644-PS) and Sebastian Nefzger (Document 645-PS) were dismissed with equal curtness, but Farr went on to make his point. "These four murders committed within the short space of two weeks in the spring of 1933, each by different SS guards, are but a few examples of SS activities in the camps at that very early date," he explained. "Indeed, that sort of thing was officially encouraged."

Farr returned the next morning to continue his prosecution, underscoring the homicidal nature of the camp command structure, citing from the camp regulations, again quoting from Himmler, and observing that seven of the defendants sitting in the dock had been senior members of the SS. Then he got to his point. "As an organization founded on the principle that persons of 'German blood' were a 'master race' it exemplified a basic Nazi doctrine," he said. "It served as one of the means through which the conspirators

acquired control of the German government. The operations of the
SD and SS Totenkopf Verbände [Death's Head Units] in concentration camps were means used by the conspirators to secure their
regime and terrorize their opponents. . . . In the Nazi program of
Jewish extermination, all branches of the SS were involved from
the very beginning." Farr again emphasized that service in the SS
was voluntary and that terror was integral to its mission. "It was,
we submit, at all times the exclusive function and purpose of the
SS to carry out the common objectives of the defendant conspirators," he concluded. "Its activities in carrying out those functions
involved the commission of the crimes defined in Article 6 of the
Charter. By reason of its aims and the means used for the accom-
plishment thereof, the SS should be declared a criminal organization in accordance with Article 9 of the Charter."*

With Farr's phase of the prosecution complete, the Munich
prosecutor's files were returned to the Bavarian state ministry of
justice. "The enclosed files were found in the desk of former Gauleiter Adolf Wagner," an accompanying memorandum explained.
"These appear to be indictments signed in 1933 that were never
delivered. The documents clearly show that the German judges
at the time pursued the murderers in the SS circles; but that their
efforts failed in the face of the overwhelming power of the political
leadership. These cases can at least serve as valuable vindication for
judges today, and perhaps even permit the prosecution to be taken
up again."

The files lingered in the state ministry of justice for nearly a
year, eventually finding their way to the attention of Munich's
chief of police, Franz Xavier Pitzer, who then forwarded them, on
December 31, 1946, to the Munich II prosecutors' offices, where
they came into the hands of Hartinger's former Munich II col-

---

* Article 6 of the Charter of the Nuremberg Military Tribunal defines Crimes Against
Peace, War Crimes, and Crimes Against Humanity; Article 9 empowers the tribunal to
declare "any group or organization" and its members as criminal.

league Anton Heigl. In early 1934, Heigl had been dismissd from the Munich II office by the National Socialists when his earlier socialist affiliations were discovered, but Heigl had now turned this to his advantage with the American occupation forces, who were impressed with his excellent command of English and his status as a "victim" of the Nazi regime. He was returned to Munich II as deputy prosecutor. He recognized the Hartinger files immediately and decided to inform his former colleague.

At the time, Hartinger was serving as a district judge in his hometown of Amberg, east of Nuremberg. In March 1934, he had been transferred from Munich II, which removed the Dachau Concentration Camp from his judicial authority. Wintersberger was also transferred a few months later, effectively terminating the investigations. During the war, Hartinger served for a time in the east and then on the western front, where he was taken prisoner by the Americans in the autumn of 1944 and spent the next two years in a prisoner-of-war camp. Eventually he returned to civil service. Now, in early 1947, he received a letter from Heigl informing him that his Dachau indictments had suddenly reappeared. Hartinger received the courtesy with mixed feelings. Heigl made no pretense of the fact that he regularly reported on Hartinger to the Nazis, as if it had been part of the normal course of things. "A sign of a sick world," Hartinger later lamented. "Yes, the world was ill, and unfortunately especially the German people."*

Hartinger traveled to Munich, where Heigl offered to let him have a look at the papers he had found. "I took them with me back to Amberg and had multiple copies made of all the files," Hartinger recalled. He had lost the files once; he was not going to lose them again. He had the files notarized on May, 17, 1947, then returned the originals to Heigl, who reactivated the criminal investigation,

---

* Heigl thrived in postwar Germany. He remained in Hartinger's former position until 1948, when he became chief prosecutor for Munich II, and in 1952 he was elected Munich's chief of police, where he remained until his death in 1963.

though most of the suspects included in the Hartinger indictments were now dead.

Wäckerle's office administrator, Josef Mutzbauer, had fallen victim to the very machinery he had helped put in motion. In the spring of 1934, in a moment of lapsed judgment, he mentioned to his SS driver that he was weary of the "swindle" being perpetrated in Dachau. The driver dutifully reported the remark. Mutzbauer was arrested and placed in the Arrest Bunker. The next day he was found hanged in his cell. There was no investigation. Dr. Werner Nürnbergk continued to serve as a camp doctor until March 1934, when he was replaced by Dr. Hans Meixner, but Nürnbergk retains the grim distinction of being the first SS doctor to serve in a Nazi concentration camp.

Following Wäckerle's dismissal as camp commandant, when he was dispatched by Himmler to Stuttgart, Wäckerle married a local beauty, Elfriede Rupp, nine years younger and the daughter of a local veterinarian. Wäckerle was eventually transferred to the nearby town of Ellwangen, where he was involved in helping establish the first armed SS units, the precursor of the Waffen SS, before being transferred to Hamburg. During the war, he served as a colonel in the Waffen SS Viking Division, participating in the invasions of Poland, the Netherlands, and the Soviet Union. He was as fearless and ruthless as he had been in the First World War, committing acts of atrocity and heroism with equal conviction. In the Netherlands, he led an advance unit in the capture of a key railway station, earning an Iron Cross First and Second Class for bravery, and sustaining a bullet wound along the way. A photograph taken a day after the battle shows him bandaged and brimming with pride, his blood-spattered uniform draped over his shoulder. He died two years later during the first weeks of the invasion of the Soviet Union, shot in the head by a Russian soldier when he opened the hatch of a crippled Russian tank. "With the passing of SS colonel Wäckerle we have lost a man whose entire life since his earliest youth was dedicated to the fatherland," an obituary in an SS newspaper read. The tribute made no reference to Wäckerle's distinction as the first commandant of the Dachau Concentration Camp.

In May 1945, American soldiers captured Hans Steinbrenner on the Austrian border with Bavaria. Steinbrenner had spent the previous twelve years in the service of the SS. He would say in a postwar interrogation that he had been transferred from Dachau after Wäckerle's departure and served with an honor guard at the Wittelsbach Palace, at the ministry of the interior, and at the shrine to the "martyrs" of the Beer Hall Putsch, on Odeonsplatz. Steinbrenner returned to Dachau in mid-1934 to train SS recruits, and went on to service at the Lichtenburg and Buchenwald concentration camps. "From September 1939 until the collapse of Germany," he told the investigators, "I served with several divisions of the Waffen SS in campaigns in Holland, Belgium, France, and in Russia on several fronts." After his capture by the Americans, Steinbrenner escaped briefly and sought refuge with his wife. She turned him over to the police and filed for divorce. Steinbrenner was subjected to severe interrogation by the Counterintelligence Corps (CIC) and Military Intelligence Service (MIS) that left him disabled. "The behavior of the Allied soldiers, of the CIC and MIS officials after the war, which included atrocities I experienced to my own person," Steinbrenner said, "showed that the soldiers of the democratic states in the world, the soldiers who fought in the name of Jesus Christ, would not have behaved any differently than our own soldiers. Their acts did nothing to awake any remorse in my soul, but created only a sense of undying hatred." Steinbrenner was eventually handed over to German authorities.

Once in German hands, Steinbrenner was willing to talk. He admitted that Benario, Goldmann, and the two Kahns had been murdered, and spoke of the fear of prosecution that haunted the SS guards following these first killings. "I need to note that back then if the *Mordkommission* from Munich, which on such occasions conducted inspections of the crime scene and other investigations, had been more thorough and decisive from the outset," Steinbrenner said, "the commission would have had to have determined that these Jews had been murdered, not shot trying to escape. This would have had the consequence of preventing further and similar transgressions." Steinbrenner was initially charged in the shooting of the four men, but the charges were dropped due to conflicting witness testimony. Steinbrenner confessed to the Lehrburger murder, but was vague about his role in other excesses, including the death of Willy Aron. "In any event, I never lashed a detainee so long that blood ran from his buttocks down to his ankles," he insisted. He also exposed himself to be the "unknown perpetrator" in the death of Louis Schloss.

On March 10, 1952, following a four-day trial that involved more than six hundred depositions and testimonies, including formal statements by Wintersberger and Hartinger, Steinbrenner was acquitted in Schloss's murder, due to lack of evidence, but was charged with the "crime of bodily harm in the performance of duty." For the death of Willy Aron, he received a life sentence, and in the case of Karl Lehrburger, the court judged Steinbrenner as having acted under the duress of Erspenmüller's threats and Wäckerle's orders and therefore sentenced him to ten years.

Steinbrenner spent the next decade in the state penitentiary in Landsberg am Lech, where Hitler and his fellow Nazis were imprisoned following the 1923 putsch. From Landsberg, Steinbrenner sent Hartinger an eight-page typewritten letter in which he spoke not only of his role as perpetrator but also as victim. "I am certainly aware that all the suffering and injustice committed in the concentration camps could not go unpunished," Steinbrenner wrote, "but on closer examination of the situation it must also be acknowledged that the individual, without any intentionality on his part, or any criminal or perverse intent, was implicated through nothing more than his absolute belief in the future of Germany, that he was misled, harassed, and fanaticized, and without any close connection to a religious community. These guilty individuals are in fact those who were most deceived, and one should not demand from them that they bear the consequences that have been spared those senior to them." Hartinger did not respond. Steinbrenner was released on May 31, 1963, in deteriorating health, and transferred to a convalescent facility near Berchtesgaden. He hanged himself the following year, still unrepentant.

Karl Wicklmayr appeared to be more forthcoming. "As far as I can remember, during my time in Dachau," he told the police in 1948, "I killed the detainees Götz, Dressel, Schloss, Nefzger, and Strauss on orders of Wäckerle, who was commandant at the time." Wicklmayr recalled shooting Götz with his .8 pistol, and slashing Dressel's wrist with a knife, as he did with Nefzger. "I still remember Nefzger today," he said, "because he was a detainee with an amputated leg." Wicklmayr underscored the fact that he committed the killings completely on his own. He also hanged Louis Schloss in his cell on Wäckerle's orders. "I ambushed Schloss," he said. "He offered no resistance and I hanged him from the wall." Wicklmayr could not remember, however, whether he pounded a hook into the wall or whether there was something already there. "On Wäckerle's orders, I also shot the detainee Strauss," he said. "I was walking with Strauss in the camp and killed him with a bullet to the head. I had him walk ahead of me and fired the shot from behind to fake an escape attempt. As in each of the other cases, I reported to Wäckerle that I had carried out his orders." Wicklmayr eventually retracted portions of his confession. He had not, in fact, killed Alfred Strauss. He also claimed he had not shot Josef Götz. Some considered him deranged. In the end, Wicklmayr was sentenced to six years in prison for "complicity in manslaughter."

Hartinger took satisfaction in seeing Nazi war criminals brought to justice, but he was less certain in apportioning guilt to those who had been complicit but not criminal. Hartinger himself had undergone a judicial review (*Spruchkammerverfahren*)* after the war and been acquitted of any complicity in the Nazi regime. Indeed, a former Munich II colleague, Josef Wintrich, who had become president of the German Constitutional Court in Karlsruhe, suggested that Hartinger go public with an account of his efforts in the spring of 1933. Bavaria's prime minister, Dr. Hanns Seidel, urged Hartinger not to do so. "Look, Hartinger, we have enough to do dealing with the present without looking into the past," Seidel told him. "Let's look to building the future, not losing ourselves in the past." Hartinger followed Seidel's advice. He remained silent on the matter for the next thirty years.

In January 1984, a few months after his ninety-first birthday, Hartinger received a letter from Bavaria's minister of justice asking him to commit his recollections to record as part of a general history the state was preparing. This time, Hartinger agreed. He was willing to reveal everything he could remember, but he was hesitant to pass judgment. "The human being is complicated," he observed, "and in complicated times this can lead to confusion." He faulted Hans Frank for having been complicit in atrocities he could have prevented. "Like the generals who served Hitler, he was powerless in the face of these criminals," Hartinger observed. "But just because one is without power does not mean one needs to be without courage and ultimately without character. Shouldn't one try to find some way to make a difference, even in such hopeless circumstances, without necessarily jeopardizing one's life?"

Hartinger reflected in particular on the flawed character of two personal associates from those years. "Until now I have spared two men whom I regarded highly, but who probably would not have

---

* The *Spruchkammerverfahren* were judicial hearings administered in the American, British, and French occupation zones as part of the denazification process. Unlike regular courts in which the prosecution needed to prove guilt, the defendants were required to offer evidence of their innocence. Karl Wintersberger was judged to have been a *Mitläufer* (collaborator), and was fined 1,099.35 reichsmarks. Josef Hartinger was absolved of any guilt or collaboration.

stayed employed after the war, if I had told everything," he said in justifying his four decades of silence. "In other words, I would probably have sacrificed two otherwise flawless colleagues to the Nazi moloch after the fact."

Just as Hartinger did not want to commit an injustice against others for transgressions of the human spirit by speaking during their lifetime, now he did not wish to do injustice to history through continued silence. The two men were now dead. No harm could be done to their careers. He was now prepared to provide details as candidly as he could and as his memory would permit at his age. The first man was Anton Heigl. The second was Karl Wintersberger.

The latter's refusal to sign Hartinger's proposed indictment had been, as Hartinger said, one of the greatest surprises of his life. Now, nearly a half century later, the then ninety-year-old Hartinger was still trying to comprehend the moment. "It is possible that the chief prosecutor added, after refusing to sign, 'You'll need to sign that yourself.'" Hartinger could not recall for certain. "I suppose this is because I left immediately even though it would have been natural to point out that he had recently expressed no objection to the indictment." Still, Hartinger wanted to accord his former superior, long since dead, the benefit of the doubt. "I can't help but believe that Wintersberger was simply overwhelmed," he speculated. "What was wrong with him on June 1 and 2, 1933? Normally he wasn't like that. Why didn't he speak with me on either of these two days? Why didn't he tell me about the meeting with Himmler?" Hartinger ultimately ascribed Wintersberger's refusal to sign to his cautious nature. "I wanted to act rashly, because I felt it was a matter of urgency," Hartinger said of the June 1 indictments. "Others wanted to wait and took refuge in holding meetings."

Wintersberger's postwar judicial review, like Hartinger's, recognized his courageous efforts to confront early Nazi atrocity, but Wintersberger's personnel file in the Bavarian State Archives was less forgiving. In a letter from November 1934, Wintersberger touted his long-standing service to the Nazi movement. He denounced as "libelous" the depiction of his aggressive 1924 prose-cution of the Assault Troop Hitler. Instead, he recalled his sympathy for the "national, youthful enthusiasm" of the forty defendants. He asserted that during the trial he argued that the defendants might have been "wrong in the legality of their actions," but they had believed they were acting within the law. He went on to recount his decade-long prosecution of communists, Social Democrats, and critics of Adolf Hitler. He boasted that in one case the left-wing *Münchner Post* had criticized "my 'national socialist' leanings exhib-ited during the trial."

Wintersberger also underscored his particular service to Hit-ler. When a journalist, Werner Abel, accused Hitler of funding the Nazi movement with foreign capital, Wintersberger delivered exculpatory evidence for the Nazi leader. "It is thanks to my thor-ough investigation that Abel was convicted of libel," he observed. (Abel was sentenced to three years in prison and was eventually transferred to Dachau, where, just before completing his three-year sentence, he allegedly hanged himself.) Wintersberger concluded his five-page missive with a crisp *"Sieg Heil!"* Like most Germans of the era, he gradually accommodated himself to the new regime.

There remained for Hartinger one figure of sterling character whose memory he retained with near reverence. "Finally I need to fulfill a duty of piety," Hartinger wrote in closing. "In my accounts I mentioned the name of the forensic physician Dr. Flamm once. If I have spoken about the incidents that occurred at Dachau during his time in office, the mere mentioning of his name does not do him justice. Without Flamm I would not have stood a chance. He—one simply has to say it this way—sacrificed himself in a way that was exemplary for any forensic doctor." Sitting in his home in Amberg on that Saturday afternoon in the deep winter of 1984, Hartinger could recall vividly those moments when he and Flamm stood with Wäckerle and Steinbrenner and Nürnbergk over the corpses of those first victims. "When I think about the hatred with which the SS men glared at him while [he was] examining the corpses and performing autopsies," he wrote, "I still get chills down my spine." Flamm never flinched. He never relented. "For me Flamm was a model of behavior," Hartinger said.

On May 3, 1934, Eicke had dispatched a stern missive to Wintersberger expressing, "in the form of the sharpest protest possible," his objections to Flamm's continued intrusions. It surprised Eicke that there were still individuals like Flamm even after the "synchronization" of the legal system. He suspected Flamm of motives that were not in alignment with the government. He also said he was making Himmler himself aware of Flamm's intrusions. Wintersberger stood his ground in Flamm's defense and alerted the ministry of justice to Eicke's letter. "It contains such serious, insulting attacks and veiled threats against Court Medical Examiner Dr. Flamm," Wintersberger wrote, "that the engagement of higher authorities is urgently needed." That spring, Flamm was nearly killed when hidden explosives were detonated in a shed where he was supposed to undertake a forensic examination.

In July, the SS attempted to kill Flamm again, this time in his Munich apartment. "It was only thanks to the circumstance that on the night in question, he was not in his Munich apartment but with his mother in Augsburg," Friedrich Döbig recalled; "otherwise he too would have fallen victim to the SS." On July 20, 1934, Flamm was transferred from Munich II and assigned as a physician to the Stadelheim penitentiary. Four months later he was dead. "He died, as far as I ever learned, under fairly questionable circumstances," Hartinger recalled. "It was rumored that the SS was not completely innocent in this affair." By then, there was no one left with the courage or determination to investigate.

HARTINGER COMPLETED HIS MEMOIRS on February 4, 1984. He passed away six months later, shortly after his ninety-first birthday.

APPENDIX

The Hartinger Registers

During the writing of this book, I found myself returning repeatedly to the two registers Josef Hartinger compiled during his criminal investigations in the spring and autumn of 1933. They were for me both eloquent testimony and incontrovertible proof of Hartinger's belief in the transcendent power of justice.

Beyond offering a context-setting snapshot of the sequencing, frequency, and circumstance of the Dachau killings, the entries permit a nuanced understanding of Hartinger's reaction to each killing. Hartinger's choice of details, his inclusion of the names of individual guards, his use of particular phrases and even verb tenses, provide insight into his thought processes. We can see the mind of the investigating prosecutor at work. Hartinger's consistent presentation of the hard facts of each case without any attempt to draw conclusions is notable. That was to be left to the courts.

The first register, which includes six names and is dated May 30, 1933, evidently served as the basis for the murder indictments Hartinger signed on June 1, 1933. The second register is undated and preserves Hartinger's effort to provide a complete and chronological record of the camp deaths, beginning with the shooting of Benario, Goldmann, and the two Kahns on April 12, 1933, and concluding with the final entry in March 1934, just before Hartinger's transfer from Munich II. It should be noted that Hartinger makes occasional errors in regard to the spelling of names and listing of professions, for example, Dirnagl instead of Dürnagl. In addition, the second register contains at least one potential oversight worth mentioning, namely Dr. Albert Rosenfelder. Rosenfelder was a prominent Jewish attorney from Nuremberg known for his legal battles with Julius Streicher and Streicher's anti-Semitic newspaper, *Der Stürmer*. Rosenfelder was taken into protective custody in March 1933 and transferred to Dachau on April 13, 1933. He was placed in the Arrest Bunker in July, along with Dr. Delwin Katz, Wilhelm Franz, and Josef Altmann, following their collective attempt to smuggle written accounts of SS atrocity out of the camp. Rosenfelder appears to have vanished at the same time that Katz and Franz allegedly hanged themselves. It remains uncertain whether he escaped or was murdered, thus explaining his absence from Hartinger's list.

I WOULD LIKE to make a few observations about the translation. Hartinger identifies the professions of several victims with the term *Kaufmann*, which can be variously translated as "salesman," "merchant," or "businessman." I have used the generic term "salesman," except in cases where it appears the victim had his own business, as in the case of Louis Schloss. Hartinger identifies Ernst Goldmann as a *Reisender*, which can be variously understood as a tourist, a traveling salesman, or a wayfarer. Since Goldmann was resident in Fürth and unemployed, I use the term "itinerant." Hartinger similarly misidentifies Rudolf Benario, describing him as first as a *Diplom-Volkswirt*, trained in business or economics, and then as a *Diplom-Landwirt*, trained in agriculture, when in fact he held the title *Doctor rerum politicarum*, a doctor in political economy. I have retained Hartinger's designations, and have also included the original file numbers, for example, with Sebastian Nefzger: AVZ.: G 851/33.

Register I

Munich, May 30, 1933
Subject:
Deaths in the Concentration Camp Dachau

I.

Götz, Josef, 37 years old, married, mechanic from Munich.

On May 8, 1933, Götz was killed by the SS guard Karl Friedrich Wicklmayr (student of philology) in the corridor of the detention block of the camp. The shot to the left temple was fired with a pistol. According to Wicklmayr's testimony, Götz, who had been ordered to bring pillows and a straw bed from one cell to another, attacked the guard twice while passing. On the first occasion, Wicklmayr pushed the aggressor back. However, when he lunged at him a second time, Wicklmayr fired a shot at him. Götz immediately collapsed, dead. (Page 6. R. of the investigation file G 766/33.)

On May 9, 1933, a forensic examination of the corpse was conducted in the camp by the state medical examiner, Dr. Flamm. Aside from the fatal bullet wound, a gash-like wound, 5 by 1 cm. wide, running horizontally across the left frontal lobe and covered by a scab, was discovered just behind the hairline. (Page 4 R. a.a.O.) The cause of this wound could not be determined as of yet.

II.

Schloss, Louis, 55 [*sic*] years old, widowed salesman from Nuremberg.

On the afternoon of May 16, 1933, the state police were contacted by the police station Dachau, after having received notice that Schloss had hanged himself in a solitary detention cell in the camp. On that same day, a forensic examination of the corpse by the state medical examiner Dr. Flamm took place. (Page 2 of the investigation file A.G. 851/33.) During the examination, it became evident that the body had several lacerations, and since the cause of death seemed questionable, an autopsy was conducted on May 17, 1933. Based on the preliminary assessment, death by hanging could not be proven. A fat embolism and asphyxiation were considered more likely to have been the cause of death as a result of the extensive damage to adipose tissues. (P. 12, d.A.)

It is not known who caused these wounds.

III.

Hausmann, Leonhard, 31 years old, married, laborer from Augsburg.

Hausmann was shot by the SS sergeant Karl Ehmann in the late morning of May 17, 1933. According to the latter, Hausmann and another detainee were to dig up young fir trees in the woods by the camp and carry them to a specific spot for collection. Ehmann was guarding him. Suddenly, he could no longer see Hausmann. Thus he started searching for the detainee and saw him running away, ducking between the trees. Ehmann ran after him, shouted "Halt!" at him several times, and once [yelled] "Stop running," but there was no response. Thereupon Ehmann drew his pistol and, without aiming, fired a shot at the fugitive. Hausmann collapsed, dead. Ehmann claimed to have shot from a distance of ten to twelve meters. On the same day, May 17, 1933, a forensic examination of the corpse was performed under instructions of the state medical examiner Dr. Flamm. It was established that death was caused by a shot through the left chest cavity. (Page 2 R d. Investigation file G 866/33.) According to the examination report, the shot was fired (in contradiction to Ehmann's assertion) at a distance of less than one meter. As reported by state medical examiner Dr. Flamm, Professor Merkel determined that the distance was less than 30 cm.

IV.

Strauss, Alfred, 30 years old, unmarried lawyer from Munich.

Strauss was killed on May 24, 1933, by two shots fired from a Dreyse pistol by the accompanying SS man Johann Kantschuster while he was taking a walk, as prescribed to him by the camp physician, outside the enclosed area of the camp. Kantschuster reported the incident as follows: He had to accompany him. Strauss was walking. Suddenly, Strauss ran for a thicket about 6 meters away from the path. As soon as Kantschuster took notice of this, he shot at the fleeing man twice from a distance of about 8 meters. Strauss collapsed, dead. On that same day, May 24, 1933, a judicial inspection of the site was undertaken. Strauss's corpse lay at the edge of the woods. He was wearing slippers on his feet. One foot was covered by a sock, the other one was bare, evidently due to an injury on the foot. After the inspection of the site, the forensics examination of the corpse took place. Two bullet wounds were found in the back of the corpse's head.

V.

Lehrburger, Karl, 28 years old, unmarried salesman from Nuremberg.

Lehrburger was killed on May 8, 1933, in his single-detention cell by the SS man Hans Steinbrenner by a shot to the forehead. According to Steinbrenner, Lehrburger had made a sudden gesture toward him, which he had interpreted as an attack. Thereupon, he made use of his firearm.

On the same day, a forensic examination of the corpse took place, administered by the state medical examiner Dr. Flamm. The report of the corpse's examination has not yet been submitted to the state prosecutor.

VI.

Nefzger, Sebastian, 33 years old, married salesman, former SS man from Munich.

According to information given by the Dachau district court, Nefzger's death occurred in the night from May 25 to 26, 1933.

On May 27, 1933, the district court of Dachau received the following notification: "Concentration Camp Dachau, Political Department, May 27, 1933. To the district court of Dachau. During the forensic examination of the detainee Nefzger Sebastian's corpse, salesman from Munich, it was determined that the possibility of death at the hands of another party is excluded. His death was without doubt caused by excessive bleeding from the opening of the pulse artery in the left hand. Signed, Dr. Nürnbergk, camp physician."

The district court contacted the prosecutor's office. A forensic examination of the corpse was ordered, and took place that same day. Because death by excessive blood loss seemed suspicious, a judicial autopsy was conducted on May 29, 1933. Based on the verbal report by the state medical examiner Dr. Flamm, the autopsy revealed that Nefzger's death could not be traced back to exsanguination. Rather, death by strangling should be assumed. The reports on the forensic examination as well as the autopsy have not yet been delivered to the prosecutors.

Register II

[undated]
Subject:

Deaths of detainees under protective custody in the Dachau Concentration Camp.

1.

Kahn, Arthur, 21 years old, unmarried. Student from Nuremberg.

Dr. Benario, Rudolf, 24 years old, unmarried. Trained economist from Fürth.

Goldmann, Ernst, 24 years old, unmarried. Itinerant from Fürth.

Kahn, Erwin, 32 years old, married. Salesman from Munich.

(AVZ.: G 613 ff/33)

On April 12, 1933, the student Arthur Kahn from Nuremberg, the trained agriculturist [*sic*] Dr. Rudolf Benario from Fürth, and the itinerant Ernst Goldmann from Fürth were killed by shots fired from pistols by SS man Hans Bürner, SS man Max Schmidt, and SS lieutenant Robert Erspenmüller. Furthermore, the salesman Erwin Kahn from Munich was also so severely wounded by pistol shots that he died on April 16. Benario, Goldmann, and Erwin Kahn lay dead or severely wounded in immediate proximity to where they were working. Arthur Kahn lay at a distance of about 80 m. from the workplace, in the woods.

The three SS men indicated that they fired shots because Arthur Kahn, Benario, and Goldmann had attempted to flee. Erwin Kahn had run into their line of fire.

The proceedings were closed on May 24, 1933, since the claims made by the guards that the men who had been killed had attempted to flee were not deemed implausible.

2.

Hunglinger, Herbert, 53 years old, married. Retired major from Pasing.

(AV. A 53/33)

In the night of April 25/26, 1933, retired Major Herbert Hunglinger from Pasing hanged himself in his solitary confinement cell. There is no doubt that it was suicide.

3.

Dressel, Friedrich, 36 years old, married. Construction engineer from Feldmoching.

(AVZ.: G 744/33)

On the evening of May 7, 1933, the former communist delegate of the state parliament, Friedrich Dressel, from Feldmoching was found dead in his single-detention cell, with his artery slit open. The corpse showed lacerations on the back, the buttocks and thighs, which could be traced back to beatings.

The investigation was discontinued on May 12, 1933, on the assumption it was a suicide.

4.

Götz, Josef, 37 years old, married. Mechanic from Munich.

(AVZ.: G 766/33)

On May 8, 1933, the mechanic Josef Götz from Munich was killed by the SS man Karl Friedrich Wicklmayr. He was killed in the hallway of his cell unit by a gunshot to his left temple with a service pistol.

According to Wicklmayr's account of the incident, Götz had attacked him twice, which was why he fired the shot.

Aside from the bullet wound, the corpse showed a soft tissue wound of 5 cm. in length and with a gash of 1 cm. in width running across the left frontal lobe right behind the hairline.

The cause of this wound could not be determined.

The proceedings were discontinued on June 1, 1933, because Wicklmayr's claims to self-defense could not be refuted.

5.

Schloss, Louis, 55 [*sic*] years old, widowed merchant from Nuremberg.
(AVZ.: G 851/33)

On May 16, 1933, the Nuremberg merchant Louis Schloss is said to have hanged himself in his single cell. The autopsy revealed several lacerations across the body and that the cause of death was most probably not by hanging but from a fat embolism. This probably occurred as the result of damage to the adipose tissue. The investigation is to be discontinued as a result of the Amnesty Decree of August 2, 1933.

6.

Hausmann, Leonhard, 31 years old, married. Laborer from Augsburg.
(AVZ.: G 866/33)

On May 17, 1933, the laborer Leonhard Hausmann from Augsburg was killed by a shot through his left chest cavity fired by SS sergeant Karl Ehmann. Hausmann, according to Ehmann, had attempted to take flight while he was working in the woods near the camp. He was said to have been shot dead at a distance of about 10–12 m.

Investigations made at the forensic institute determined that in fact the shot was fired from a distance of less than 30 cm.

The investigation is to be discontinued as a result of the Amnesty Decree of August 2, 1933.

7.

Dr. Strauss, Alfred, 30 years old, unmarried. Lawyer from Munich.
(AVZ.: G 927/33)

On May 24, 1933, the lawyer Dr. Alfred Strauss from Munich was taking a walk, which had been prescribed to him by the camp doctor, when he was killed by two bullets in the back of his head, fired by the accompanying guard, SS man Johann Kantschuster. According to Kantschuster, Strauss suddenly tried to escape into the nearby thicket whereupon Kantschuster fired two shots at him with his Dreyse pistol at a distance of about 8 m.

Inspections of the area and the corpse showed that Strauss was only wearing leather slippers, that he was only wearing a sock on one foot while the other foot was apparently bare due to an injury on this foot.

The autopsy revealed, apart from the two shots to the head, older lacerations on the right thigh and around the buttocks as well as bruising on the left side of the abdomen.

The investigation is to be discontinued as a result of the Amnesty Decree of August 2, 1933.

8.

Lehrburger, Karl, 28 years old, unmarried. Salesman from Nuremberg.

(AVZ.: G 918/33)

On May 25, 1933, Karl Lehrburger from Nuremberg was killed in his solitary confinement cell by a shot to his forehead, fired by SS man Steinbrenner.

Lehrburger is said to have made a movement that Steinbrenner interpreted as an attack. According to medical findings made during the autopsy, the shot was fired from a distance of 10–20 cm.

The investigation was discontinued on June 1, 1933, because Steinbrenner's claim to self-defense could not be disproven.

9.

Nefzger, Sebastian, 33 years old, married. Salesman, former SS man, from Munich.

(AVZ.: G 928 ff/33)

On May 27, 1933, the district court of Dachau was informed by the Concentration Camp Dachau that the salesman Sebastian Nefzger from Munich took his life in his solitary-confinement cell by slitting open his wrist. He apparently died in the night from May 25 to 26, 1933.

Through an autopsy it was determined that he had died from asphyxiation, caused by strangling and beating. The investigation is to be discontinued as a result of the Amnesty Decree of August 2, 1933.

10.

Stenzer, Franz, 33 years old, unmarried. Railroad worker from Pasing.

(AVZ.: G 1703/33)

On August 22, 1933, while the railroad worker Franz Stenzer from Pasing was going for a walk near the camp, the SS sergeant Rudolf Dirnagl, who was accompanying him, shot a bullet through his skull and killed him.

According to Dirnagl's testimony, Stenzer was fleeing, which is the reason Dirnagl ran after him and fired at him. Dirnagl claims to have fired the shot at a distance of five meters. However, after a preliminary forensic examination by the forensics institute, the shot appears to have been fired from a distance of less than one meter.

The investigation was discontinued on December 21, 1933, because SS sergeant Dirnagl's claims that Stenzer had fled and Dirnagl thus had the right to fire at him could not be disproven.

11.

Handschuch, Hugo, 23 years old, unmarried. Craftsman from Munich.

(AVZ.: G 1848/33)

On September 6, 1933, the craftsman Hugo Handschuch from Munich was buried in the Dachau cemetery. The corpse was brought from the concentration camp to the Dachau morgue in a coffin that had been nailed shut. The opening of the coffin had been strictly forbidden.

Following a complaint issued by the mother of the deceased man, exhumation and an autopsy were conducted. These investigations revealed that the death had been caused by excessive abuse. Thus far, the investigations have yielded evidence that the abuses on Handschuch began immediately after his arrest in the night of August 22/23, 1933, in the Brown House in Munich. From there Handschuch was taken to the police prison in Ettstrasse on the evening of August 23. What happened next with Handschuch has not yet been determined. The Bavarian political police are requested to investigate further into this issue.

12.

Franz, Wilhelm, 34 years old, unmarried. Salesman from Munich.
Dr. Katz, Delwin, 46 years old, married. Doctor from Nuremberg.

(AVZ.: G 2138/33)

A report by the Political Police on October 18, 1933, indicated that on October 17, 1933, the salesman Wilhelm Franz from Munich, and in the following night Dr. Delwin Katz from Nuremberg, hanged themselves in their respective solitary detention cells. During the autopsy conducted on October 20, 1933, it was discovered that both men had died of asphyxiation, caused by strangling and beating by another person. Furthermore, the corpse of Franz showed several fresh lacerations on the head and in particular abundance on his torso and arms. Around the wounds there was extensive bleeding and fragmentation of the adipose tissue so that his demise could also have been caused by a fat embolism. Further investigations are in progress.

13.

Bürck, Fritz, 40 years old, married. Textile worker from Memingen.

(AVZ.: G 2436/33)

On the afternoon of November 28, 1933, the detainee Bürck who was in protective custody was killed near one of the camp latrines by SS staff sergeant Wilhelm Birzle. He was hit by three bullets (through the heart, the stomach, and the head) with a Mauser pistol cal. 7.63. According to Birzle, he had escorted him to the latrine and was confronting him about some misbehavior earlier that day.

Thereupon, Bürck lunged at his neck to grab it and, after he was pushed away, evidently tried to attack him again. That is when Birzle shot him three times with his pistol. The investigation was discontinued on December 16, 1933, since Birzle's account could not be disproven. In accordance with the commandant's concentration camp regulations, under those circumstances he had the right and even the obligation to use his firearm in defense.

14.

Altmann, Josef, 43 years old, unmarried. Salesman from Dolling.

P.A. [mailing address] Mühldorf a. /Inn.

(AV.: G 260/34)

On the evening of February 12, 1934, around 20:30, the detainee Altmann, who was in protective custody, was found hanged in his solitary-confinement cell. The autopsy conducted on February 14, 1934, gave no evidence of a secondary person having been involved in his death. The investigations were discontinued on February 17, 1934, because there was no suspicion of an outside party.

15.

Hutzelmann, Wilhelm, 37 years old, married. Salesman from Nuremberg.

(AV.: G 353/34)

On the afternoon of February 25, 1934, the detainee Hutzelmann, in protective custody, hanged himself in a secluded part of the camp. The autopsy on February 27, 1934, yielded no signs of an outside party. The investigations were therefore discontinued on March 6, 1934.

NOTES

The story of Josef Hartinger and the first Dachau murders is a small story that holds a correspondingly small but—I would assert—significant place in the much larger story of Hitler's seizure of power and all that followed. As with most microhistories, many of the sources were discovered in unlikely and occasionally obscure places, or in the interstices of the more frequently visited sources and archives.

The narrative framework for this story derives from two extended letters written by Hartinger on January 16 and February 11, 1984, at the request of the then Bavarian state justice minister, August Lang. The thirty-two-page typewritten transcription proved to be a rich source of historical and human insight.

I also drew significantly from the personnel files and postwar judicial inquiries (*Spruchkammerverfahren*) of Karl Wintersberger (Bamberg, 1947) and Josef Hartinger (Amberg, 1948), as well as Hartinger's original investigation files for the murders committed in April and May 1933. The postwar trials of former SS concentration camp guards, in particular Hans Steinbrenner. Karl Wicklmayr, Anton Hoffmann, and Karl Ehmann, were also a major source. Dr. Nikolas Naaff, the investigating judge (*Untersuchungsrichter*), assembled more than seven hundred eyewitness testimonies (former detainees, state policemen, SS men, et al.) from 1946 until 1953. In addition, the published memoirs and diaries of a wide range of individuals, from Hans Kallenbach to Hans Beimler to Josef Goebbels, Hans Frank, and Hjalmar Schacht, provided further detail and context.

As one might expect from firsthand accounts, especially those with a political agenda (such as Kallenbach's and Beimler's) or those recalling events long after the fact, there are frequent contradictions and alternative versions of specific incidents. I have tried to be vigilant in selecting those accounts for which there is either corroborating evidence or testimony, but I wish to acknowledge that there may be cases where alternative versions may be equally valid.

The various depositions, testimonies, protocols, and interrogations used as evidence in the trial are available in the State Archives in Munich (Staatsarchiv München).

The testimonies are indicated below with the name of the witness (or perpetrator in the case of Steinbrenner, Wicklmayr and Ehmann) and refer to the Hans Steinbrenner case (*Betrifft: Hans Steinbrenner wegen Kriegsverbrechen*) unless otherwise indicated.

The following abbreviations correspond to the archives:

Bay HStA	Bayerisches Hauptstaatsarchiv (Bavarian State Archives)
BayHStA Abt IV	Bayerisches Hauptstaatsarchiv—Kriegsarchiv (Bavarian State Archives, War Archives)
DaA	Archiv KZ-Gedenkstätte Dachau (Dachau Memorial Site Archives)
StAM	Staatsarchiv München (State Archives Munich)
StAM Stanw	Staatsarchiv München, Staatsanwaltschaft beim Landgericht (State Archives Munich, Prosecutor's Office Archives)
StAAm	Staatsarchiv Amberg (State Archives Amberg)
StAB	Staatsarchiv Bamberg (State Archives Bamberg)
SB	Staatsbibliothek München (State Library Munich)
USHMM	United States Holocaust Memorial Museum Archives

PRELUDE TO JUSTICE

3 **"During the past weeks"**: *Trial of the Major War Criminals Before the International Military Tribunal, Nuremberg, 14 November 1945—1 October 1946*, vol. 4, "Twenty-Third Day, Wednesday, 19 December 1945, Afternoon Session," 161. Publication abbreviated to *IMT* in further endnotes. For online access to the proceedings, see the Avalon Project at Yale University: http://avalon.law.yale.edu/subject_menus/imt.asp.

4 **"The wrongs which we seek to condemn"**: "Opening Address for the United States by General Prosecutor Justice Robert H. Jackson," November 21, 1945, *IMT*, vol. 2, "Nazi Conspiracy and Aggression," 25.

4 **the phalanx of twenty-one defendants**: The attitudes of the defendants are recorded in the official court transcript, and are also preserved in the black-and-white film footage of the proceedings. Telford Taylor, *The Anatomy of the Nuremberg Trials: A Personal Memoir* (New York: Alfred A. Knopf, 1992), contains vivid descriptions of the individual defendants. An additional source is *The Nuremberg Interviews: An American Psychiatrist's Conversations with the Defendants and Witnesses*, ed. Robert Gellately (New York: Alfred A. Knopf, 2004), the posthumously published transcripts of U.S. Army psychiatrist Leon Goldensohn, containing one-on-one interviews with the main war criminals. See also G. M. Gilbert, *Nuremberg Diary* (New York: Da Capo, 1995; originally published 1947 by Farrar, Straus). Gilbert was a prison psychologist and kept a journal of his discussions with the prisoners, quoting them in some cases verbatim. The memoirs of Dr. Hans Frank, *Im Angesicht des Galgens* [In the Shadow of the Gallows] (Munich-Gräfelfing: Friedrich Alfred Beck Verlag, 1953), written in the months before he was executed, also provides useful insights into the attitude of a major war criminal. An alternate interpretation of Frank's contritition in Nuremberg can be found in the memoir *Der Vater: Eine Abrechnung*, by his son Niklas Frank (Munich: Goldmann Verlag, 1993).

4   **"Hitler gave us orders"**: Keitel told this to Leon Goldensohn in an interview on April 6, 1946. Goldensohn, *The Nuremberg Interviews,* 160.

4   **"as an ersatz for Himmler"**: Gilbert, *Nuremberg Diary,* 5.

4   **"a lawyer by profession"**: Jackson's opening address, November 21, 1945, *IMT,* vol. 2, 120.

4   **"We must never forget that the record"**: Jackson's opening address, November 21, 1945, *IMT,* vol. 2, 101.

5   **Telford Taylor**: Taylor, *Anatomy of the Nuremberg Trials,* 205.

5   **"Farr had his troubles"**: Ibid., 206.

5   **"About a week or ten days ago"**: Warren Farr prosecution, December 19–20, *IMT,* vol. 4, 161–88. All further exchanges cited in these paragraphs are from these pages.

8   **"Document 641-PS"**: For Documents 641-PS, 642-PS, 644-PS, and 645-PS relating to the Dachau killings, see *IMT,* vol. 26, 171–89.

1 CRIMES OF THE SPRING

13   **In the spring of 1933**: The term *Hitlerwetter* was used inchangeably with *Führerwetter.* "Yesterday rain still threatened, but today the sun is shining," Joseph Goebbels wrote in his diary on May 1, 1933. "Real Hitler weather!" *Joseph Goebbels Tagebücher, Band 2: 1930–1934,* ed. Ralf Georg Reuth (Munich: Piper Verlag, 1999), 797.

14   **"My responsibilities included"**: Letter from Josef Hartinger to the Bavarian state minister of justice, August R. Lang, Munich, January 16, 1984, DaA 20.108.

15   **an unprecedented wave of arrests**: Cited from among surviving entries in the Munich II case register. See *Beratungsserie München II 1899–1960: München II 1933–1934* (Munich: Generaldirektion der Staatlichen Archiv Bayerns, undated).

15   **"Hitler is a foreigner"**: Cited from among hundreds of entries in *Archivinventare Band 3, Sondergericht München Teil 1: 1933–1937* (Munich: Generaldirektion der Staatlichen Archiv Bayerns, undated).

15   **Thousands of others were taken**: Dachau was the only official concentration camp in Bavaria at the time, though state prisons and local jails, as well as warehouses, sports halls, and other facilities, served for temporary detention. The very first concentration camp in Germany was opened on March 3, 1933, in a school in Thuringia. In Bremen, an abandoned river barge was pressed into service. Of the seventy concentration camps established in Germany in 1933, only three were equipped with barracks, barbed wire, and watchtowers, at Papenburg, Emsland, and Dachau. For more on the early concentration camps, see Geoffrey P. Megargee, ed., foreword by Elie Wiesel, *Encyclopedia of Camps and Ghettos, 1933–1945,* vol. 1, *Early Camps, Youth Camps, and Concentration Camps and Subcamps under the SS-Business Administration Main Office (WVHA)* (Bloomington: Indiana University Press, 2009); Jane Kaplan and Nikolaus Wachsmann, eds., *Concentration Camps in Nazi Germany: The New Histories* (London and New York: Routledge, 2010); and Johannes Tuchel, *Konzentrationslager: Organisationsgeschichte und Funktion der "Inspektion der*

Konzentrationslager" 1934–1938 (Boppard am Rhein: Harold Boldt Verlag, 1991).

16 **"those in protective custody"**: Letter from Cardinal Faulhaber to Franz von Epp, April 3, 1933, in Ludwig Volk, ed., *Akten Kardinal Michael von Faulhabers 1917–1945*, vol. 1: 1917–1934 (Mainz: Matthias Grünewald Verlag, 1975), 693.

16 **his "greatest ambition"**: Ibid.

16 **"Most Honorable Herr Cardinal"**: Letter from Wagner to Faulhaber, April 12, 1933, in Bernhard Stasiewski, ed., *Akten deutscher Bischöfe über die Lage der Kirche 1933–1945*, vol. 1: 1933–1934 (Mainz: Matthias Grünewald Verlag, 1968), 124.

17 **Paragraph 159**: See Dr. Otto Schwarz, *Strafprozessordnung mit Gerichtsverfassungsgesetz und den wichtigsten nebengesetzen des Reiches, Preussens und Bayerns*, Dritte, verbesserte und vermehrte Auflage, Stand vom 15. Mai 1933 (Berlin: Verlag von Otto Liebmann, 1933), 146–47. Further references cited throughout the notes as *Strafprozessordnung*.

17 **"As soon as the prosecutor"**: Ibid., 147.

17 **had earned perfect grades**: Performance appraisal, "Meinungsäusserung über den Oberarzt Moritz Flamm. Garnisonlazarett München Station B III," May 20, 1920, in Flamm's military personnel file, BayHStA Abt. IV OP 739.

18 **"Particularly noteworthy is"**: Ibid.

18 **"At the front [Flamm] became"**: Ibid.

18 **Flamm was accused**: For Flamm's complaint, see the letter in his military personnel file: "Betreff: Beschwerde des Oberarzt Moritz Flamm. An Reichsbefehlstelle Bayern; Absender: Generalarzt," September 19, 1919.

18 **After two years with Flamm**: Letter from Josef Hartinger to August R. Lang, January 16, 1984.

19 **After the war**: On November 7, 1918, King Ludwig III of Bavaria was deposed and Bavaria declared its independence from the Reich as the People's State of Bavaria (*Volksstaat Bayern*), which in turn led to the establishment of the Soviet Republic (Bayerische *Räterepublik*) in April 1919. The Battle of Dachau was fought on April 16, 1919, between the troops of the Bavarian Red Army and ad hoc military forces sent to depose the Bolshevik government. Two weeks later, right-wing Bavarian militia units, known as Freikorps, or Free Corps, supported by Reichswehr (regular army) units dispatched from Berlin, overthrew the Bolshevik government and returned Bavaria to the Berlin government as the *Ordnungszelle Bayern*, or the "orderly cell" of Bavaria.

20 **"Since 1920"**: "Arbeitsbeschaffungsmöglichkeit in den Deutschen Werken," *Dachauer Zeitung*, January 25, 1933.

20 **"The facility seemed uncanny"**: Eugen Mondt, *Künstler und Käuze: Aufzeichnungen aus dem Dachau der 20er Jahre* (Munich: Süddeutscher Verlag, 1979).

21 **"On the water tower"**: "Neues Leben in dem Deutschen Werken?," *Dachauer Zeitung*, March 21, 1933.

21 **On Monday, March 20**: Hans-Günter Richardi, *Schule der Gewalt: Die Anfänge des Konzentrationslagers Dachau 1933–1934: Ein dokumentischer Bericht* (Munich: C. H. Beck Verlag, 1995), 36–37.

22 **"These are to be armed"**: Letter from Josef Hartinger to August R. Lang, Munich, February 11, 1984, DaA 20.109.

23 "authorities and officials of the police": *Strafprozessordnung*, 147–48.

23 He was told that the four: The scene as described by Erspenmüller is recounted in Wintersberger's report of the incident, "Tötung flüchtiger Gefangener im Sammellager Dachau," April 24, 1933, USHMM 1995 A. 104: 67–69.

23 the deputy camp commandant: Robert Erspenmüller's name is occasionally miscited in testimonies as Erpsenmüller or Erbsenmüller. In the camp, he was sometimes referred to as *"die Erbse,"* meaning "the pea."

24 "One of the stretcher-bearers": Testimony of Josef Gabriel, "Zeugenvernehmungsprotokoll aufgenommen in der gerichtlichen Voruntersuchung gegen Birzle Wilhelm," Weilheim, January 23, 1953, StAM Stanw 34465.

24 He asked to see a rabbi: Ibid.

24 The corpses had been unceremoniously: Testimony of Emil Schuler, Nuremberg, March 29, 1951, StAM Stanw 34464/3.

24 Their heads were shorn: "Tötung flüchtiger Gefangener im Sammellager Dachau," April 24, 1933, USHMM 1995 A. 104: 67–69.

24 Arthur Kahn, the medical student: Ibid.

25 Dr. Rudolf Benario, a political scientist: Ibid.

25 Ernst Goldmann, more robust: Ibid.

25 "Your guards are very good shots": Transcript of Hans Steinbrenner's interrogation, Garmisch, August 19, 1948 . DaA 22.031. At that time Steinbrenner had already undergone a number of interrogations and was being held in internment in Garmisch. Steinbrenner does not specify the exact context in which Flamm made this remark to Wäckerle, but I have taken the liberty of situating it during their first encounter.

25 "They started beating the Jews: For Gesell's account, see Hans-Günter Richardi, *Schule der Gewalt*, 62.

26 "they were beaten horrifically": For Scharnagel's account, see Siegfried Imholz, "Der Mord an Ernst Goldmann in Dachau am 12. April 1933," 6: http://www.der-landbote.de/Downloads/Der%20Mord%20an%20Ernst%20Jakob %20Goldmann.pdf.

26 Around three o'clock: Richardi, *Schule der Gewalt*, 89.

27 "On the critical day": Testimony of Heinrich Ultsch, Nuremberg, March 6, 1950, StAM Stanw 34462/4.

27 " 'You come along too' ": Ibid.

27 He handed the four of them spades and picks: Ibid. In his postwar interrogation, Steinbrenner mistakenly said that he had selected five Jewish detainees and that he had selected them at random. There are also varying accounts as to the exact time and circumstances of the selection process, though there is general agreement that the incident took place in the late afternoon toward dusk of April 12. See the transcript of the Steinbrenner interrogation, Garmisch, August 19, 1948.

27 "Everybody stop!": Richardi, *Schule der Gewalt*, 89.

27 According to Gessell: Ibid.

28 "a terrified young man pressed hard": Letter from Josef Hartinger to August R. Lang, February 11, 1984.

28 "my assessment of the personalities": Ibid.

2 LATE AFTERNOON NEWS

29 **Leo and Maria Benario were preparing a package**: Letter from Leo Benario to the administration of the Dachau Concentration Camp, April 13, 1933, personal archive of Michael Schneeberger, Kitzingen, Germany, reprinted on page 12 in *Birken am Rednitzufer—eine Dokumentation über Dr. Rudolf Benario am 12. April 1933 im KZ Dachau ermordet*, Schulprojekt der Hauptschule Soldnerstrasse, Stadt Fürth, 2003.

29 **Since the town jail was too small**: Siegfried Imholz, "Der Mord an Ernst Goldmann in Dachau am 12. April 1933," 6: http://www.der-landbote.de/Downloads/Der%20Mord%20an%20Ernst%20Jakob%20Goldmann.pdf.

30 **"Among the individual students"**: Letter from the rector of the Friedrich Alexander University in Erlangen, "An das Staatsministerium für Unterricht und Kultur," December 12, 1932, Archive of Erlangen University, reprinted in *Birken am Rednitzufer*, 7.

31 **"Dr. Siegmund Bing, had frequented"**: Marianne Mohr, "Dr. Siegmund Bing, Nürnberg," Rijo Research, August 24, 2013. http://www.rijo.homepage.t-online.de/pdf/DE_NU_JU_bing.pdf.

31 **They packed Rudolf's winter coat**: For a listing of the package contents, see the letter from Leo Benario to the administration of the Dachau Concentration Camp, April 13, 1933, reprinted in *Birken am Rednitzufer*, 12.

31 **By the seventeenth century, Fürth**: For a description and brief history of Fürth's Jewish institutions, see "Jüdische Geschichte in Fürth": http://www.fuerth.de/home/tourismus/geschichte/juedische-geschichte-in-fuerth.aspx.

32 **"Maria was the daughter"**: Rolf Seubert, "Mein lumpiges Vierteljahr Haft . . . ," in *Alfred Andersch "Revisited": Werkbiographische Studien im Zeichen der Sebald-Debatte*, ed. Jörg Döring and Markus Joch (Berlin: Walter de Gruyter Verlag, 2011), 81. For a history of the Bing family see Ignaz Bing, *Aus meinem Leben* (Hamburg: Wellhausen & Marquardt Medien, 2004).

33 **"This branch seems destined"**: *Advocate of Peace* 75, no. 7 (July 1913): 149.

34 **"When someone claims"**: *Adolf Hitler: Reden, Schriften, Anordnungen: Februar 1925 bis Januar 1933*, ed. Institut für Zeitgeschichte, 5 vols. in 12 parts (Munich: Institut für Zeitgeschichte, 1992–98), vol. III, 680.

35 **"Student Benario"**: "Aus der Asta," *Erlanger Nachrichten*, January 18, 1930.

35 **"I do not think there is anything"**: Speech given at Erlangen University, November 13, 1930. *Adolf Hitler: Reden, Schriften, Anordnungen: Februar 1925 bis Januar 1933*, ed. Institut für Zeitgeschichte, 5 vols. in 12 parts (Munich: Institut für Zeitgeschichte, 1992–98), vol. IV, 105.

37 **"the big cleanup of Bavaria begins!"**: Imholz, "Der Mord an Ernst Goldmann in Dachau," 6.

38 **"The all-too-well-known communist and Jew Benario"**: "Ruhige Nacht in Fürth: Beginn der Generalsäuberung," *Fürther Anzeiger*, March 10, 1933.

38 **"The retired editor and guest lecturer"**: Seubert, "Mein lumpiges Vierteljahr Haft . . . ," 84.

38 **"To restore a national and professional civil service"**: For the full text of the law (in German), see "Gesetz zur Wiederherstellung des Berufsbeamtentums": http://www.documentarchiv.de/ns/beamtenges.html.

39 "For the moment I am still safe": See Klemperer's diary, April 12, 1933. Victor Klemperer, *I Will Bear Witness: A Diary of the Nazi War Years, 1933–1941*, trans. Martin Chalmers (New York: Modern Library, 1999), 14.

39 "to give my son Rudolf Benario from the contents": Letter from Leo Benario to the administration of the Dachau Concentration Camp, April 13, 1933.

39 THREE COMMUNISTS SHOT: "3 Kommunisten bei einem Fluchtversuch aus dem Dachauer Konzentrationslager erschossen," *Fürther Anzeiger*, April 13–14, 1933.

40 "several more detainees have been released": "Aus der Schutzhaft entlassen," *Amper-Bote*, April 14–15, 1933.

3 WINTERSBERGER

41 "I did not hesitate to give my opinion": Letter from Josef Hartinger to the Bavarian state minister of justice, August R. Lang, February 11, 1984, DaA 20.109.

41 his deputy possessed "many years of experience": Hartinger's performance review, "Dienstliche Würdigung 1931," in his personnel file, state prosecutor's office, BayHStA MJu 26797.

42 Wintersberger ran Munich II: Letter from Josef Hartinger to August R. Lang, February 11, 1984.

42 "needed to have a complete overview": Ibid.

42 "iron diligence": Wintersberger's performance review, "Dienstliche Beurteilung durch den Präsidenten des Landgerichts München I," May 22, 1931, BayHStA MJu 26443.

42 In his study: Emil J. Gumbel, "Die Einnahme von München," in *Vier Jahre politischer Mord* (Berlin-Fichtenau: Verlag der Neuen Gesellschaft, 1922).

43 "Of the thirty-five jurisdictions": Ibid., 125.

43 "In another era": Ibid., 147–48.

43 Hitler's plans came to an abrupt halt: Ian Kershaw, *Hitler, 1889–1936: Hubris* (New York: W. W. Norton, 1998), 211.

44 "You may pronounce us guilty": "Vor dem Volksgericht: Vierundzwanzigster Verhandlungstag," in *Hitler: Sämtliche Aufzeichnungen, 1905–1924*, ed. Eberhard Jäckel and Axel Kuhn (Stuttgart: Deutsche Verlags-Anstalt, 1980), 1216.

44 A few weeks after Hitler's courtoom triumph: For the verdict against Assault Troop Adolf Hitler, see "Urteil vom Volksgericht für den Landgerichtsbezirk München I in der Strafsache Berchtold Josef und 39 Genossen wegen Beihilfe zum Hochverrat, u.a.," April 28, 1924, StAM JVA 12436. The trial records were destroyed during the bombing of Munich in the Second World War, but a notarized copy of the final verdict survived.

44 "not relevant in terms of the guilt": Ibid., StAM JVA 12436: 10.

44 "the little Hitler trial": In 1933, one Assault Troop defendant, Hans Kallenbach, published a memoir of his time in prison, *With Hitler in Landsberg Prison*, and devoted an entire chapter to the Wintersberger prosecution. Hitler himself provided an introduction to the book. Hans Kallenbach, *Mit Adolf Hitler auf Festung Landsberg* (Munich: Verlag Parcus & Co., 1933).

45 While Hitler's trial: Kallenbach, *Mit Hitler auf Festung Landsberg*, 19.

45   the number of shattered windowpanes: Ibid., 23–24.
45   He chronicled the Assault Troop's subsequent march: Ibid., 29.
45   "all means of judicial rhetoric": Ibid., 33.
46   "Decree for Public Order": See "Dritte Verordnung des Reichspräsidenten zur Sicherung von Wirtschaft und Finanzen und zur Bekämpfung politischer Ausschreitungen," October 6, 1931: http://www.documentarchiv.de/wr/1931 /wirtschaft-finanzen-ausschreitungen_reichspraesident-vo03.html#t7.
46   a growing number of assaults on Jews: James Waterman Wise, *Swastika: The Nazi Terror* (New York: Harrison Smith and Robert Haas, 1933), 55.
46   "For us, the citizen of the Jewish faith": Peter Longerich, *Heinrich Himmler: Biographie* (Munich: Siedler Verlag, 2008), 160.
46   "In Chemnitz the Jewish lawyer": "Jüdische Rechtsanwalt emordet: S.A. zur Aufdeckung der Tat eingesetzt," *Völkischer Beobachter*, April 13, 1933.
47   Two of them were "tall, slender, and blond": Ibid.
47   "*Das machen die nicht*": Letter from Josef Hartinger to August R. Lang, February 11, 1984.

4 WITNESS TO ATROCITY

49   One bullet had penetrated his skull: For Kahn's medical record, see "Kranken Hauptbuch Nr. II/173 Krankeitsgeschichte Erwin Kahn," StAM Stanw 34465: 81–87.
49   "The injured man stated": Ibid.
50   It was here that Joseph Lister: LMU Klinikum der Universität München, official website: http://www.klinikum.uni-muenchen.de/Klinik-fuer-Allgemeine -Unfall-Hand-und-Plastische-Chirurgie/de/ueber-uns/historischerRueck blick/index.html.
50   Kahn was taken into protective custody: For details of Erwin Kahn's arrest, see Rolf Seubert, "Mein lumpiges Vierteljahr Haft . . . ," in *Alfred Andersch "Revisited": Werkbiographische Studien im Zeichen der Sebald-Debatte*, ed. Jörg Döring and Markus Joch (Berlin: Walter de Gruyter Verlag, 2011), 89–90.
51   "You probably came to Stadelheim": Letter from Erwin Kahn to his wife, Eva, March 23, 1933, StAM Stanw 34465: 115.
51   "I have but a single wish, to finally be": Letter from Erwin Kahn to his wife, Eva, March 30, 1933, ibid., 116.
51   "I don't know why I was arrested": Letter from Erwin Kahn to his parents, April 5, 1933, ibid., 117.
52   Erwin Kahn mistakenly responded: Testimony of Heinrich Ultsch, Nuremberg, March 6, 1950, StAM Stanw 34462/4.
52   someone screamed for him to stop: Testimony of Emil Schuler, Nuremberg, March 29, 1953, StAM Stanw 34464/3.
52   "Average-sized man": Erwin Kahn's medical record.
52   "Condition is basically unchanged": Ibid.
53   "My husband went on to explain": Testimony of Eva Euphrosina Ehlers (Eva Kahn), "Niederschrift aufgenommen in der Voruntersuchung gegen Burner, Hans, ua. wegen Mord," February 4, 1953, StAM Stanw 34465.
53   "Fever rising": Erwin Kahn's medical record.

53 His breathing grew labored: Ibid.

53 "Nevertheless, these twenty-eight": Pfanzelt's letter of April 17, 1933, to the Ordinariat München. See the chapter by Thomas Kempter about the practice of religion in the first days of the camp, "Die ersten Gottesdienste und die Erlaubnis zur Beichte," in his thesis "Gott Feiern in Dachau: Die Feier der Eucharistie im KZ Dachau" (Diplomarbeit, Albert-Ludwigs-Universität Freiburg/Breisgau, September 2005), 39.

53 In Nuremberg, Bernhard Kolb: Bernhard Kolb's manuscript "Die Jüden in Nürnberg: Tausendjährige Geschichte einer Judengemeinde von ihren Anfängen bis zum Einmarsch der amerikanischen Truppen am 20. April 1945." The manuscript was edited with an introduction by Gerhard Jochem in 2007 and published online with the title *Bernhard Kolb: Die Jüden in Nürnberg 1839–1945.* Kolb also mentions the deaths of Benario, Goldmann, and Erwin Kahn, as well as several other Jewish detainees who died in Dachau, though some of his observations are based on hearsay and not always accurate. For the full text, see: www.rijo.homepage.t-online.de/pdf/DE_NU_JU_kolb_text.pdf.

54 "the camp administration wanted to conceal": Ibid., 21.

54 Kahn had been a political activist: Letter from Herbert Kahn to Gertraud Lehmann, December 15, 1993, in which he wrote that "my brother was a medical student in Würzburg and was at the time of his arrest during the Easter holiday in Nuremberg. He was also active in the anti-Nazi movement in Würzburg." See Seubert, "Mein lumpiges Vierteljahr Haft . . . ," 88.

54 he was taken into protective custody: Ibid., 87.

54 The manifest identifies: Ibid.

54 "When the news came": Author's telephone interview with Lothar Kahn, February 19, 2014.

54 "According to newspaper reports": The article was referenced in Arthur Kahn's student record at the University of Würzburg, 1933; see Seubert, "Mein lumpiges Vierteljahr Haft . . . ," 87.

55 Siegfried and Meta Goldmann: Ibid., 85.

55 "With great sadness": Obituary in *Fürther Tagblatt,* April 18, 1933, reprinted in *Birken am Rednitzufer—eine Dokumentation über Dr. Rudolf Benario am 12. April 1933 im KZ Dachau ermordet,* Schulprojekt der Hauptschule Soldnerstrasse, Stadt Fürth, 2003, 1.

55 The cause of death was determined: E-mail from Professor Wolfgang Eisenmenger, with detailed comments to the author, January 9, 2014.

55 "Hartinger was very nice to me": Testimony of Eva Euphrosina Ehlers (Eva Kahn), February 4, 1953, 69–70.

56 "Nevertheless, [Hartinger] advised me": Ibid.

5 THE STATE OF BAVARIA

59 The headline-making news: "Die neue nationalsozialistische Regierung in Bayern," *Völkischer Beobachter,* April 13, 1933.

59 On the last Monday: Frederick T. Birchall, "Incendiary Fire Wrecks Reichstag; 100 Red Members Ordered Seized; Alleged Communist Said to Confess Setting Blaze as Main Chamber Is Ruined—Cabinet Drafts Law to Bar Dis-

seminating Proscribed News Abroad: INCENDIARY FIRE WRECKS REICHSTAG: FAMOUS REICHSTAG BUILDING, DAMAGED BY NIGHT FIRE," special cable to the *New York Times*, February 28, 1933. For eyewitness accounts and documentation of the fire, see Walther Hofer, Edouard Calic, and Christoph Graf, eds., *Der Reichstagsbrand: Eine wissenschaftliche Dokumentation* (Veröffentlichungen des Internationalen Komitees zur Wissenschaftlichen Erforschung des Ursachen und Folgen des Zweiten Weltkrieges), vol. 1 (1972); vol. 2 (1978).

60 "That can only be an attack by the communists": Franz von Papen, *Der Wahrheit eine Gasse* (Munich: Paul List Verlag, 1952), 302.

60 "The burning of this symbol": Robert Jackson's opening address, November 21, 1945, *IMT*, vol. 2, 110.

60 "Based on the confiscated materials": For minutes of the meeting, see "Ministerbesprechung 28. Februar 1933," in *Akten der Reichskanzlei: Regierung Hitler 1933–1938. Teil I: Die Regierung Hitler*, vol. 1 (January 20 to August 1933), ed. Karl-Heinz Minuth (Boppard am Rhein: Harald Boldt Verlag, 1983), 128–29. The volume is further noted as *Reichskanzleiakten*.

60 "Hitler said they were tendentious": Otto Meissner, *Staatssekretär unter Ebert, Hindenburg, Hitler: Der Schicksalsweg des deutschen Volkes, 1918–1945* (Hamburg: Hoffmann und Campe, 1950), 283.

61 "including freedom of the press": "Verordnung des Reichspräsidenten zum Schutz von Volk und Staat ['Reichstagsbrandverordnung'],'" February 28, 1933: http://www.documentarchiv.de/ns.html.

62 "the conditions incorporated in the German national constitution": Richard Kessler, *Heinrich Held als Parlementarier: Eine Teilbiographie 1868–1924* (Berlin: Duncker & Humblot, 1971), 394.

62 "The recent developments in public affairs": Letter from Heinrich Held to Hindenburg, February 4, 1933, in *Reichskanzleiakten*, vol. 1, 45.

62 Held was especially disquieted by "rumors": Ibid.

63 There was serious concern among Hitler's ministers: "Ministerbesprechung 28. Februar 1933," in *Reichskanzleiakten*, vol. 1, 132.

63 "We are masters of the Reich": March 5, 1933, entry in *Joseph Goebbels Tagebücher, Band 2: 1930–1934*, ed. Ralf Georg Reuth (Munich: Piper Verlag, 1999), 773.

64 "we will now tackle Bavaria": March 8, 1933, entry, ibid., 775.

64 A plan was designed to destabilize: Ibid.

64 On the morning of March 9: Kurt Preis, *München unterm Hakenkreuz: Die Hauptstadt der Bewegung zwischen Pracht und Trümmern* (Munich: Ehrenwirth, 1980), 21.

64 "I categorically reject this request": Ibid., 19–20.

65 "The cabinet has decided not to follow": Ibid., 20.

65 "General von Epp has just assumed": Ibid.

65 "Since the restructuring of Germany's political situation": Ibid., 21.

65 "In order to prevent": Ibid., 23–24.

65 when Held arrived at work: Karl Schwend, *Bayern zwischen Monarchie und Diktatur: Beiträge zur bayerischen Frage in der Zeit von 1918 bis 1933* (Munich: Richard Pflaum Verlag, 1954), 541.

66 "These rough characters": T. R. Ybarra, "Says Hitler," *Collier's Weekly*, July 1, 1933, 17.

66 "Epp's Second March": "Epps zweiter Einmarsch in München," *Völkischer Beobachter,* March 10, 1933.

67 the ministry itself was being dissolved: "Die neue nationalsozialistische Regierung in Bayern: Abschaffung des Aussenministeriums, Schaffung einer Staatskanzlei," *Völkischer Beobachter,* April 13, 1933.

67 "Everything that has been achieved": "Die Gleichschaltung—die beste und glücklichste Lösung für Deutschland," *Völkischer Beobachter,* April 14–15, 1933.

67 "We owe the former Bavarian State Government": Letter from Cardinal Faulhaber to Heinrich Held, April 3, 1933, in Ludwig Volk, ed., *Akten Kardinal Michael von Faulhabers 1917–1945,* vol. 1: 1917–1934 (Mainz: Matthias Grünewald Verlag, 1975), 695.

68 Faulhaber dispatched a "pastoral instruction": "Pastorale Anweisungen Faulhabers," ibid., 700.

68 "Right after the putsch": Letter from Josef Hartinger to the Spruchkammer, September 19, 1946, Nuremberg, StAAm 589.

69 "Whenever the three of us were": Letter from Josef Hartinger to the Bavarian state minister of justice, August R. Lang, February 11, 1984, DaA 20.109.

70 "It was naïve to think": Ibid.

70 Reinhard Heydrich, as the new head of Department VI: Peter Longerich, *Heinrich Himmler: Biographie* (Munich: Siedler Verlag, 2008), 159.

70 "Himmler's dual capacity": See Warren Farr's prosecution, December 20, 1945, *IMT,* vol. 4, 186.

71 "the position of a judge": Frank, *Im Angesicht des Galgens* (Munich-Gräfelfing: Friedrich Alfred Beck Verlag, 1953), 135.

71 "I assumed responsibility": Ibid., 134.

71 "I considered all of them": Letter from Josef Hartinger to August R. Lang, February 11, 1984.

6 RUMORS FROM THE WÜRM MILL WOODS

72 a Jewish merchant named Max Neumann: For details on the Max Neumann, Kindermann, and Krel cases, see James Waterman Wise, *Swastika: The Nazi Terror* (New York: Harrison Smith and Robert Haas, 1933), 54. For a detailed account of early Nazi atrocities, see: *SA-Terror als Herrschaftssicherung: "Köpenicker Blutwoche" und öffentliche Gewalt im Nationalsozialismus,* ed. Stefan Hördler (Berlin: Metropol Verlag, 2013).

73 "I could count only until the tenth stroke": Ibid., 54–55.

73 The German Foreign Office: Ibid., 53.

73 "The Reich minister": "Mitteilungen des Reichsministers des Auswärtigen," in cabinet meeting of March 7, 1933, *Reichskanzleiakten,* vol. 1, 166.

73 "The cracking sound hit us": Rolf Seubert, "Mein lumpiges Vierteljahr Haft . . . ," in *Alfred Andersch "Revisited": Werkbiographische Studien im Zeichen der Sebald-Debatte,* ed. Jörg Döring and Markus Joch (Berlin: Walter de Gruyter Verlag, 2011), 70.

73 "That is fascism": Hans-Günter Richardi, *Schule der Gewalt: Die Anfänge des Konzentrationslagers Dachau 1933–1934: Ein dokumentischer Bericht* (Munich: C. H. Beck Verlag, 1995), 90.

73 "If something happens to me": Ibid.

74 "I saw three men in front of me": Testimony of Emil Schuler, Nuremberg, March 29, 1951, StAM Stanw 34464/3.

74 the detainee had related the entire incident: Interrogation of Hans Steinbrenner, Garmisch, August 19, 1948, DaA 12.288.

74 "I received the order": Testimony of Matthias Grel, Tutzing, November 9, 1950, StAM Stanw 33462/7.

75 A message was smuggled: "Dachau: The 1st Concentration Camp," Holocaust Education and Archive Research Team: http://www.holocaustresearch project.org/othercamps/dachau.html.

75 Louis Lochner of the Associated Press: Andrew Nagorski, *Hitlerland: American Eyewitnesses to the Nazi Rise to Power* (New York: Simon & Schuster, 2012), 124–25.

75 Edgar Mowerer of the *Chicago Tribune*: Ibid., 125.

75 "If there had been anything left of me": Ibid.

76 "Permission to make the visit": "Nazis Shoot Down Fleeing Prisoners," *New York Times,* April 23, 1933, 22. Subsequent quotes and descriptions refer to the *New York Times* article referenced here.

76 "Today, I would like to thank": Letter from Cardinal Faulhaber to Hilmar Wäckerle, April 26, 1933, in Ludwig Volk, ed., *Akten Kardinal Michael von Faulhabers 1917–1945,* vol. 1: 1917–1934 (Mainz: Matthias Grünewald Verlag, 1975), 718.

77 "My guards consist of 120 storm troop men": Ibid. According to Richardi, the number of SS men in Dachau on April 20, 1933, was 217. See Richardi, *Schule der Gewalt,* 55.

81 In a three-page report: Wintersberger's official report, "Tötung flüchtiger Gefangener im Sammellager Dachau," April 24, 1933, USHMM 1995 A. 104: 67–69.

82 In those same days: Seubert, "Mein lumpiges Vierteljahr Haft . . . ," 107.

7 THE UTILITY OF ATROCITY

83 The camp's alarm and communication system: For a memo on the need to update the facility's security and electrical systems, see "Präsidium der Regierung von Oberbayern an Kommando der Schutzpolizei. Betreff: Lagerwache Dachau," Munich March 27, 1933, DaA 4118.

84 "possibilities for enemy assault": Regulations by the Bavarian state police, "Abwehr von Angriffen," BayHStA Lapo Kdo. Bd. 8.

84 "The first measure": Ibid.

84 "Wäckerle . . . was constantly afraid of an attack": Testimony of Emil Schuler, Nuremberg, March 29, 1951, StAM Stanw 34464/3.

84 "As the battle commences": Gerhard Schmolze, ed., *Revolution und Räterrepublik in München 1918/19 in Augenzeugenberichten* (Düsseldorf: Karl Rausch Verlag, 1969), 381.

85 "We will meet again": The speech took place on February 12, 1933. See Christopher Dillon, "We'll Meet Again in Dachau: The Early Dachau SS and the Narrative of Civil War," *Journal of Contemporary History* 45, no. 3 (2010): 544.

85 "A very energetic police captain": Memorandum, "Präsidium der Regierung von Oberbayern an Kommando der Schutzpolizei. Betreff: Lagerwache Dachau," Munich, March 20, 1933, DaA A-4118.

85 That same day: Rolf Seubert, "Mein lumpiges Vierteljahr Haft . . . ," in *Alfred Andersch "Revisited": Werkbiographische Studien im Zeichen der Sebald-Debatte,* ed. Jörg Döring and Markus Joch (Berlin: Walter de Gruyter Verlag, 2011), 63.

85 Unwilling to subject the detainees: Hans-Günter Richardi, *Schule der Gewalt: Die Anfänge des Konzentrationslagers Dachau 1933–1934: Ein dokumentischer Bericht* (Munich: C. H. Beck Verlag, 1995), 69.

86 "The prisoners were treated decently": Testimony of Johann Kugler, Passau, April 26, 1951, StAM Stanw 34464/3. See also Kugler deposition, Passau, February 10, 1933, StAM Stanw 34465.

86 "We worked with the soldiers": Richardi, *Schule der Gawalt,* 56.

86 "the imprisonment of the detainees was unlawful": Ibid., 52.

86 "We have not come here": Ibid., 54.

87 "Yes, that was horrible": Ibid.

87 "guards were to strictly refrain from assaulting prisoners": Testimony of Hermann Weyrauther, Traunstein, March 13, 1951, StAM Stanw 34465.

87 "knock off a few Jews": Ibid.

87 "I was walking": Testimony of Wilhelm Brink, Munich, October 18, 1950, StAM Stanw 34462/7.

87 "The transfer is to take place": Protocol, Munich, April 7, 1933, BayHSta Lapo Kdo. Bd. 8.

87 "For security and training": Ibid.

88 "The first time I saw Wäckerle": Interrogation of Hans Steinbrenner, Garmisch, August 19, 1948, DaA 12.288.

88 "When Hitler took over power": Curriculum vitae, "Lebenslauf Hilmar Wäckerle," May 15, 1936, DaA 38.634.

88 "I was with the party": Ibid.

89 The transport from Fürth and Nuremberg: Seubert, "Mein lumpiges Vierteljahr Haft . . . ," 76.

89 "I should note in this context": Testimony of Emil Schuler, Nuremberg, March 29, 1951, StAM Stanw 34464/3.

89 The SS men exercised: Richardi, *Schule der Gewalt,* 89.

90 Franck designed the camp registration system: Testimony of Otto Franck, Kaiserslautern, October 24, 1951, StAM Stanw 34464/3.

90 "an entire shift of guards": Testimony of Emil Schuler, March 29, 1951, StAM Stanw 34464/3.

90 "They [the SS guards] did not know": Richardi, *Schule der Gewalt,* 62.

91 On April 25, Wäckerle received: Dachau transport list dated April 24, 1933. International Tracing Service. Doc ID 9908504, 1.1.6.1, ITS Digital Archives.

92 "people who . . . served as spies within the NSDAP": Transport list: Bayerische Politische Polizei, Munich, April 24, 1933, USHMM, Doc 9908504#1.

92 "Beimler, number 7": Ibid.

93 "the time will come to end all anguish": Protocol mentioning Beimler, "Bayrischer Landtag. 4. Sitzung vom 17 Juni 1932," DaA A-1279: 82–86.

93 "The corpses were plundered": *Münchner Neueste Nachrichten,* May 3, 1919.

The article is based on hearsay and presents an inaccurate account of the incident. It does, however, capture the traumatic response to the Luitpold High School incident. Within right-wing circles, the event became the defining moment of the Soviet Republic of Bavaria, as suggested in the number of books on the subject, including *Der Geiselmord in München: Ausführliche Darstellung der Schreckentage im Luitpold-Gymnasium* (Munich: Hochschul-Verlag, 1919) and *Ein Jahr bayerische Revolution im Bild* (1919) by Heinrich Hoffmann, Adolf Hitler's future photographer. Hoffmann published this "photographic report" with 130 images that included the high school, the courtyard execution site, and the prominent personalities who were shot.

93 **Steinbrenner recalled that Wäckerle**: Dillon, "We'll Meet Again in Dachau," 546.

8 STEINBRENNER UNLEASHED

94 **Steinbrenner approached one man who was suffering**: Testimony of Fritz Irlbeck, Marktredwitz, October 24, 1950, 34439.

94 **drove his knee into the stomach**: Ibid.

95 **Steinbrenner headed the *Schlägergruppe***: "Abschrift, Landesausschuss der pol. Verfolgten in Bayern an das Bayerische Staatsministerium der Justiz. Herrn Dr. Lachenbauer: Angehörige der sogenannten Schlägergruppe in Dachau," March 18, 1948, StAM Stanw 34464/1.

95 **"After a few strokes"**: Testimony of Hans Steinbrenner, Garmisch, August 19, 1948, DaA 12.288.

95 **Kasimir Dittenheber, who worked**: Testimony of Kasimir Dittenheber, February 15, 1950, StAM Stanw 34439.

95 **"Steinbrenner placed the greatest value"**: Testimony of Friedrich Schaper, Kriminalaussenstelle Coburg in Kronach, July 27, 1948, StAM Stanw 34464/3.

95 **"the spiritual leader of all abuses"**: Testimony of Willibald Schmitt, Munich, November 3, 1950, StAM Stanw 34464/2.

95 **to Wäckerle, he was simply "Hans"**: Testimony of Josef Hirsch, Munich, December 27, 1949, StAM Stanw 34439.

95 **Steinbrenner set his men upon**: Unless otherwise noted, the description and dialogue presented in this chapter relating to Beimler's incarceration and treatment in the camp is taken from Beimler's memoir first published in August 1933 in the Soviet Union in German: *Im Mörderlager Dachau: Vier Wochen unter den braunen Banditen* (Moscow and Leningrad: Verlagsgenossenschaft ausländischer Arbeiter in der UdSSR). The forty-seven-page book appeared in English the same year with the title *Four Weeks in the Hands of Hitler's Hell-Hounds: The Nazi Murder Camp of Dachau* (New York: Modern Library). The book was reissued in 2012 and includes a biography on Beimler by Friedbert Mühldorfer: Hans Beimler, *Im Mörderlager Dachau: Um eine biographische Skizze ergänzt von Friedbert Mühldorfer* (Cologne: Papy Rossa Verlag, 2012).

96 **Andreas Irrgang was on the same transport**: Testimony of Andreas Irrgang, February 14, 1951, StAM Stanw 34464/2.

97 **They entered the wire enclosure**: Police sketch of the bunker by Emil Schuler included in the investigation files, Hans Steinbrenner, StAM Stanw 34439.

97 "If I wasn't wrapping a blanket": Interrogation of Hans Steinbrenner, Garmisch, August 19, 1948, DaA 12.288.

98 The word *"Wache"*: Beimler, *Im Mörderlager Dachau,* 45.

101 "Only after Hunglinger's brother agreed": Deposition of Josef Hartinger, "Abschrift von Abschrift Landesgerichtsdirektor Hartinger, Betrifft Vorgänge im Konzentrationslager Dachau," Amberg, July 13, 1949, DaA 8834.

9 THE GUMBEL REPORT

102 In 1922, Emil Gumbel: Emil J. Gumbel, *Vier Jahre politischer Mord* (Berlin-Fichtenau: Verlag der Neuen Gesellschaft, 1922).

102 In the town of Perlach: Ibid., 27–42.

103 "How are such things possible": Ibid., 87.

103 the "psychological brutalization": Ibid., 146.

104 application of the law on "protective custody": Ibid., 90.

104 "Don't make such a scene": For details on the case of Max Mauer, shot on October 31, 1921, ibid., 116–18.

104 "According to the law of March 20": Ibid., 117–18.

105 "The murderer goes free": Ibid., 149.

105 Between 1919 and 1921: Ibid., 147.

106 "If we are to find a satisfactory": Ibid., 92.

106 "They are making themselves culpable": Ibid., 147.

106 His father had served: The Wittelsbach rulers first attained the title of king in 1806, when they were so named by Napoleon. For details on Hartinger's family background, see his personnel file with the prosecutor's office, BayHStA MJu 26792.

106 "Cannonier Josef Hartinger": Hartinger's personnel file, prosecutor's file.

107 Hartinger's "technical abilities": Performance review of officers, 6th Bavarian Field Artillery Regiment, February 23, 1918, BayHStA Abt.IV, OP 16158.

108 "The bursting of shells": "Die grosse Schlacht in Frankreich," in *Bayrisches Feldartillerie Regiment 10,* 128–64, BayHStA Abt.IV ABsw3777.

108 Bavaria's Military Service Medal: Hartinger's performance review, "Dienstliche Würdigung Joseph Hartingers durch den Generalstaatsanwalt des Oberlandesgerichts München und den Oberstaatsanwalt des Landgerichts München II," June 1, 1931, personnel file, prosecutor's office. BayHStA MJu 26797.

108 Hans Steinbrenner was just thirteen: Christopher Dillon, "We'll Meet Again in Dachau: The Early Dachau SS and the Narrative of Civil War," *Journal of Contemporary History* 45, no. 3 (2010): 546–47.

109 By Gumbel's calculation: Gumbel notes that this calculation does not include the greater Munich area. Gumbel, *Vier Jahre politischer Mord,* 31.

109 placed the number at one thousand: Ibid.

109 Hartinger had enlisted: Hartinger enlisted in the Freikorps Hilger in Amberg. See also Hartinger's military personnel file, BayHStA Abt.IV, Freikorps 154. By April 1919 he was living at Blütenstrasse 14/I in Munich, and had enrolled as a student in the law faculty of the Ludwig Maximilian University.

109 He resigned from his Freikorps: Hartinger's personnel file, prosecutor's office, BayHStA MJu 26797.

109 "the ethics in demanding": Alexandra Ortmann, "Vom 'Motiv' zum 'Zweck.' Das Recht im täglichen Wandel—das Beispiel der Reichsstrafprozessordnung 1879," in *Wie wirkt Recht? Ausgewählte Beiträge zum ersten gemeinsamen Kongress der deutschsprachigen Rechtssoziologie-Vereinigung an der Universität Luzern, 2008,* ed. Michelle Cottier, Josef Estermann, and Michael Wrase (Baden-Baden: Nomos Verlag, 2010), 417.

109 "The accused is not obliged": Ibid.

110 "most frequently cited after the Bible": "Das A-B-C des Angeklagten," in Kurt Tucholsky, *Kritiken und Rezensionen: Gesammelte Schriften 1907–1935,* vol. 7 (Reinbek bei Hamburg: Rowholt Verlag, 1975), 20–24.

110 "I have no personal resources": Request form "Bezirkskommando II Munich," April 5, 1921, BayHStA Abt.IV.OP 16158.

110 "Hartinger's critical financial situation": Letter from "Versorgungs-Amt I. München an Militär-Fonds-Kommission," May 17, 1921, BayHStA Abt.IV.OP 16158.

110 500-mark student subsidy: "Nachweisung über die Einkommens- und sonstige Verhältnisse des Unterzeichneten . . . ," May 25, 1921, BayHStA Abt. IV.OP 16158.

110 "a number of responsibilities": Hartinger's performance review by First Prosecutor Himmelstoss (first name not recorded), "Abschrift: Dienstliche Würdigung durch den I. Staatsanwalt Himmelstoss für Josef Hartinger," Hartinger personnel file, prosecutor's office, September 30, 1925, BayHStA MJu 26797.

110 "His gift for sharp analysis": Ibid.

111 "In my position as a prosecutor": Letter from Josef Hartinger to the Spruchkammer, Nuremberg, September 19, 1946, StAAM 589.

111 "special class": Letter from Josef Hartinger to the Spruchkammer, Amberg, February 14, 1948, StAAm 589.

10 LAW AND DISORDER

113 "During the night from May 8 to 9": "Flucht aus dem Konzentrationslager Dachau," *Dachauer Zeitung,* May 11, 1933.

114 "After consultation with the officials": Police report, "Abschrift Bayerische Politische Polizei," May 1, 1933, DaA 17.269.

114 "absolutely nothing abnormal was observed": Ibid.

114 Surveying the transport list: Transport list, "Bayerische Politische Polizei," May 3, 1933, DaA 17.270.

115 "On that day": Testimony of Emil Schuler, Nuremberg, March 29, 1951, StAM Stanw 34464/3.

115 "Where is Dressel? That swine": Hans Beimler, *Im Mörderlager Dachau: Um eine biographische Skizze ergänzt von Friedbert Mühldorfer* (Cologne: Papy Rossa Verlag, 2012), 57.

116 "What, you bastard": Ibid., 58.

116 "And you, you coward": Ibid.

116 "Why is that young guy there?": Ibid., 58–59.

117 "one of the real bosses": Testimony of Josef Hirsch, Munich, December 27, 1949, StAM Stanw 34439.

117 "Hard, really hard": Ibid.
117 "Götz, the troublemaker, is in there": Beimler, *Im Mörderlager Dachau*, 59.
117 During a separate interrogation: Ibid.
117 Steinbrenner returned the next day: Beimler, *Im Mörderlager Dachau*, 59–60.
118 "Turn around!": Ibid., 60.
118 "He has five days": Ibid.
118 "An hour later Dressel": Testimony of Friedrich Schaper, July 27, 1948, Coburg in Kronach, StAM Stanw 34464/3.
118 "In that same moment": Ibid.
118 "Hey, Beimler, how long": Beimler, *Im Mörderlager Dachau*, 64.
119 "Will you look at that!": Ibid.
119 "So! Now you see how": Ibid., 65–66.
119 "Let me tell you something": Ibid., 66.
120 "Both [Dressel's] arteries": Testimony of Emil Schuler, Nuremberg, March 29, 1951, StAM Stanw 34464/3.
120 "I've heard you want to hang yourself": Beimler, *Im Mörderlager Dachau*, 66–67.
120 "I don't want my son always to be reminded": Ibid.
120 "I wouldn't ask a man": Ibid.
121 "So I told the commandant": Ibid.
121 "Beimler was in the cell": Testimony of Josef Hirsch, Munich, December 27, 1949, StAM Stanw 34439.
121 "Get the hell out": Ibid.
121 "Just wait, you are dead dogs": Ibid.
121 "no longer mentally normal": Ibid.
122 "Afterward I had to clean the stall": Testimony of Rudolf Wiblishauser, Sonthofen, February 22, 1950, StAM Stanw 34462/4.
122 strips of the *Völkischer Beobachter*: Ibid.
122 "Gradually, those in the front": Sworn statement of Dr. Walter Buzengeiger, Ulm, June 1945, StAM Stanw 34464/4.
122 "As we later learned": Ibid.
122 Max Holy, the "decent communist": Max Holy is listed on the transport list, May 3, 1933. Testimonies in the Hans Steinbrenner case contain numerous accounts of the Beimler escape, most notably the one by Josef Hirsch (testimony, December 27, 1949). See also Anna Sophie Lindner's unpublished memoirs in which she recounts her help in providing Beimler with a place to stay and then arranging his transport to Czechoslovakia, DaA 17991.
123 "a series of lucky breaks": Beimler, *Im Mörderlager Dachau*, 69–70. In 1983, Dorothea Dressel, the widow of Fritz Dressel, provided a less dramatic but more plausible account, claiming that Beimler had been helped by Max Holy, who had arranged the escape and had Beimler delivered to the Dressel household at five o'clock on the morning of May 9 and then taken to Munich and eventually smuggled across the Czechoslovak border to Prague and then to Moscow. Beimler went on to fight in the Spanish Civil War, where he was killed in December 1936.
123 "Shortly thereafter": Hirsch also said, "This captain was exceedingly decent to us, and I would like to maintain outright that he saved my life, because

by this [transfer] order he saved me from further abuse and, above all, from being shot." Testimony of Josef Hirsch, Munich, December 27, 1949.

123 **Wicklmayr took responsibility:** See Hartinger's register, May 30, 1933, in the Appendix.

123 **"I opened the door and saw":** Interrogation of Hans Steinbrenner, Garmisch, August 19, 1948, DaA 12.288.

123 **"You are lucky":** Ibid.

123 **"It looks like a slaughterhouse":** Testimony of Max Holy, Hersching, May 18, 1949, StAM Stanw 34439.

123 **Detainee Friedrich Schaper:** Testimony of Friedrich Schaper, Tettau, November 29, 1949, StAM Stanw 34464/4.

124 **Kasimir Dittenheber worked:** Testimony of Kasimir Dittenheber, Munich, February 15, 1951, StAM Stanw 34439.

11 A REALM UNTO ITSELF

125 **"My father is on the city council!":** "Biographie Willy Arons (1907–1933)," on the website "Willy-Aron-Gesellschaft Bamberg e.V.": http://www.willy -aron.de.

125 **He gripped Aron's head:** Steinbrenner recalled that Aron's head was wrapped in bedding but could not recall whether he was the one who held Aron's head or participated in the whipping. See interrogation of Hans Steinbrenner, Garmisch, August 19, 1948, DaA 12.288.

125 **His father, Judicial Counsel:** Andreas Dornheim and Thomas Schindler, *Wilhelm Aron (1907–1933) Jude, NS-Gegner, Sozialdemokrat und Verbindungsstudent* (Bamberg: Schriftenreihe des Historischen Verbands Bamberg, 2007), vol. 40. Dornheim and Schindler undertook an in-depth study of the city of Bamberg's "first Nazi victim," Wilhelm Aron. Unless otherwise cited, the quotations and descriptions relating to Willy Aron in this chapter refer to this work.

126 **The conservative *Bamberger*:** *Bamberger Volksblatt*, December 3, 1932.

126 **The *Freistaat*, a local:** *Freistaat*, December 9, 1932.

127 **"Epidemic of Abortions":** *Bamberger Volksblatt*, October 12, 1932.

128 **"Should he be released":** Letter from "Präsidenten des Landgerichts Bamberg an den Präsidenten des Oberlandesgerichts Bamberg," April 22, 1933, StAB K 100.

129 **"Special Regulations":** See Karl Wintersberger's letter to the Bavarian ministry of justice, May 29, 1933, which included the regulations (*Sonderbestimmungen*), DaA 18.736/6.

130 **"The jurisdiction within the camp":** Ibid.

130 **"Here we have the Jewish pig Schloss":** For a description of Schloss's treatment see Hans-Günter Richardi, *Schule der Gewalt: Die Anfänge des Konzentrationslagers Dachau 1933–1934: Ein dokumnetischer Bericht* (Munich: C. H. Beck Verlag, 1995), 89.

131 **"He had barely gotten off the truck":** Testimony of Emil Schuler, Nuremberg, March 29, 1951, StAM Stanw 34464/3.

131 **"Aron, Wilhelm," he yelled out:** Hans-Günter Richardi, *Schule der Gewalt*, 100. See also Eugen Oehrlein's testimony, StAM Stanw 34462/2.

131 "We were called in there": See Oppenheimer's letter, "Schreiben des ehemaligen Dachauer KZ-Häftlings Justin Oppenheimer an den Generalstaatsanwalt München aus Israel," November 3, 1951, in Dornheim and Schindler, *Wilhelm Aron*, 109.

132 Oppenheimer, who stood beside Aron: Ibid.

132 "Get up, you Jewish swine!": Ibid.

132 "When I came into the room": Testimony of Karl Leonhardt, Erlangen, November 1, 1951, StAM Stanw 34464/2.

132 "His buttocks had been lashed": Several witnesses provided testimony during the Steinbrenner trial. See testimonies of Josef Götz (a different Josef Götz than the one killed in the camp), November 3, 1950, StAM Stanw 34464/2; Johann Schumann, October 14, 1951, StAM Stanw 34464/3; and Wilhelm Zauzich, November 6, 1950, StAM Stanw 34462/7.

132 "During the morning visit": Testimony of Friedrich Schaper. "Vernehmungsniederschrift durch die Kriminalaussensteller Coburg in Kronach, Strafakte des Anton Vogel," July 27, 1948, StAM Stanw 34464/3.

133 "Get up!" Aron did not: Ibid.

133 "Rumors had it that": Testimony of Hans Steinbrenner, Garmisch, August 19, 1948, DaA 12.288.

133 "I could still recognize Aron": Testimony of Anton Schöberl, Hilpoltstein, October 17, 1951, StAM Stanw 34464/3.

134 "had been intentionally torched": Testimony of Hans Steinbrenner, Garmisch, August 19, 1948, DaA 12.288.

134 The official cause of death: Dornheim and Schindler, *Wilhelm Aron*, 43.

134 Aron's body was placed: Ibid.

134 "The corpse of junior attorney": *Bamberger Volksblatt*, May 13, 1933.

135 "a fine of 150 marks": "Reichstransport Minister gegen Tierquälerei," *Völkischer Beobachter*, May 11, 1933.

135 "In response to repeated complaints": Ibid.

135 Dr. Moritz Flamm declared himself: Letter from Dr. Moritz Flamm to the president of the district court Munich II, May 13, 1933, Rechtsmedizin Universität München, Archive Prof. Dr. Eisenmenger.

135 Flamm was responding: Letter from the president of the district court Munich II to Dr. Moritz Flamm, April 21, 1933, regarding "Reichsgesetz zur Wiederherstellung des Deutschen Amtentums," Archive Prof. Dr. Eisenmenger.

136 A swastika flag fluttered: When the SS first arrived in Dachau in late March and hoisted a swastika flag, state policeman Herman Weyrauther forced them to remove it. See Weyrauther's March 13, 1951, testimony. In fact, the SS had the right to hoist the flag as permitted by Hindenburg's decree of March 12, 1933, under the paragraph heading "Flaggenerlass."

136 "The director of administration for the prosecutor's office": Letter from Josef Hartinger to the Bavarian state minister of justice, August R. Lang, January 16, 1984, DaA 20.108.

136 The investigation materials: I was unable to locate Hartinger's investigation file into the shooting of Benario, Goldmann, and the two Kahns (1933 File Number: G 613 ff/33). The only extant record is the final report by Wintersberger, dated April 24, 1933, formally closing the investigation.

137   As evidence vanished: See Hartinger's register in the appendix.
137   "On April 12, 1933": Ibid.
137   In recording the observations: Ibid.

12   EVIDENCE OF EVIL

139   suicide of a fifty-three-year-old: Protocol, "Konzentrationslager Dachau Politische Abteilung an die Staatsanwaltschaft für den Landgerichtsbezirk-Munich II: Betreff Schloss Louis," signed by Hilmar Wäckerle, May 16, 1933, DaA 8832.
139   "Schloss was a detainee": Ibid.
140   A middle-aged man: For the official report of Schloss's death, plus a sketch of him hanged in his cell, see "Protokoll aufgenommen in Sachen Schloss Luis [sic], verw. Kaufmann aus Nürnberg hier dessen Selbstmord durch Erhängen. Dachau, Conzentrationslager [sic], 16. Mai, 1933," May 17, 1933, DaA 8832.
140   "camphor and a cardial injection": Ibid.
140   "I was the one who cut": Testimony of Karl Kübler, Augsburg, July 26, 1950, StAM Stanw 34462/6.
141   "On the glans": "Protokoll aufgenommen in Sachen Schloss Luis [sic], verw. Kaufmann," May 17, 1933, DaA 8832.
141   "Whether the cause of death": See Schloss entry in Hartinger's register in the Appendix.
141   Two attendants stood nearby: Invoice dated May 30, 1933, for 26.30 reichsmarks for the costs of "Leichenwärter, Leichenfrau, Leichentransport, Benutzungsgebuehr für Sektionsraum: Geschäftstelle des Amtsgerichts Dachau an die Staatsanwaltschaft München II," DaA8832.
141   Frontal photographs: "Vorder- & Rückansicht des verstorbenen Kaufmanns Louis Schloss. Aufgenommen im Auftrage der Staatsanwaltschaft im Leichenhaus in Dachau," May 17, 1933, DaA 8832.
142   "marks from hanging on the": Schloss autopsy report, "Protokoll aufgenommen in Sachen Leichenschau und Leichenöffnung in Sachen Schloss Luis [sic]," May 17, 1933, DaA 1471.
142   Ehmann was notorious: Christopher Dillon, "We'll Meet Again in Dachau: The Early Dachau SS and the Narrative of Civil War," *Journal of Contemporary History* 45, no. 3 (2010): 550.
142   "Guards were standing": Karl Ehmann's deposition, "Protokoll aufgenommen in Sachen Hausmann Leonhard hier dessen Tod durch Erschiessen auf der Flucht am 17.5.1933 in Concentationslager [sic] Dachau," May 18, 1933, DaA 8833.
142   "He just glanced back at me": Ibid.
143   "In the war I was": Ibid.
143   "The corpse had obviously not been touched": Max Winkler's deposition, ibid.
143   Another SS man: Ludwig Wieland's deposition.
143   "The terrain on which Hausmann was": Ibid.
144   "a sketch of the scene": Report from Gendarmerie headquarters Dachau to prosecutor's office Munich II, May 18, 1933, signed by Police Chief Johann Bielmeier. Report includes sketch. DaA 8833.

144 "Since the forest": Ibid.
144 "the size of a plate": "Protokoll aufgenommen in Sachen Hausmann Leonhard," Dachau, May 18, 1933, StAM Stanw 7014.
145 "The autopsy has shown": Schloss autopsy, May 17, 1933.
146 "I had one hope": Letter from Josef Hartinger to the Bavarian state minister of justice, August R. Lang, January 16, 1984, DaA 20.108.
146 "Basically, I was intent": Ibid.

13 PRESIDENTIAL POWERS

149 "Dachau has been known": "Dachau, der bekannteste Ort in Deutschland," *Dachauer Zeitung*, May 23, 1933.
150 "These pizzles were": Testimony of Paul Hans Barfuss, Munich, April 11, 1950, StAM Stanw 34439.
151 "The situation is threatening": "Vermerk des Ministerialrats Willhun über den Stand und die Aussichten der deutschen Warenausfuhr," *Akten zur deutschen auswärtigen Politik, 1918–1945, Serie C: 1933–1937, das Dritte Reich: Die ersten Jahre, Band 1, 2: 16. Mai bis 14. Oktober 1933* (Göttingen: Vandenhoeck & Ruprecht, 1971), 148. Further cited as *Akten zur Deutschen Auswärtigen Politik.*
151 "Recently the situation has been exacerbated": "Der Reisverkehrsminister an Staatssekretär Lammers, Betrifft: Unterstützung der Seeschiffahrt," May 23, 1933, in *Reichskanzleiakten*, vol. 1, 475–76.
151 "foreign policy interests take priority": Ministerial meeting minutes, April 7, 1933, "Ausserhalb der Tagesordnung: Deutsch-holländische Handelsvertragsverhandlungen," in *Reichskanzleiakten*, vol. 1, 236.
152 "When I saw him filmed": Victor Klemperer, *I Will Bear Witness: A Diary of the Nazi War Years, 1933–1941*, trans. Martin Chalmers (New York: Modern Library, 1999), 7–8.
152 Otto Meissner, his chief: Otto Meissner, *Staatssekretär unter Ebert, Hindenburg, Hitler: Der Schicksalsweg des deutschen Volkes, 1918–1945* (Hamburg: Hoffmann und Campe, 1950), 385.
152 "like a corporal following": Theodor Eschenburg, "Die Rolle der Persönlichkeit in der Krise der Weimarer Republik: Hindenburg, Brüning, Groener, Schleicher," *Vierteljahrshefte für Zeitgeschichte 9*, issue 1 (January 1961): 6.
153 "the resolute mien of a dictator": Thomas Russell Ybarra, *Hindenburg: The Man with Three Lives* (Cornwall, NY: Cornwall Press, 1932), 5.
153 "in its hour of great despair": For Hindenburg's last will and testament (*politisches Testament*), see Walther Hubatsch, *Hindenburg und der Staat: Aus den Papieren des Generalfeldmarschalls und Reichspräsidenten von 1878 bis 1934* (Göttingen: Musterschmidt Verlag, 1966), 382.
153 The key objective: Ibid.
153 "The Reich president in reply": "Aufzeichnung über die Besprechung des Herrn Reichspräsidenten mit Adolf Hitler am 13. August 1932 nachmittags 4.15," in Hubatsch, *Hindenburg und der Staat*, 338.
154 "I really don't know what could still go wrong": Franz von Papen, *Der Wahrheit eine Gasse* (Munich: Paul List Verlag, 1952), 289.
154 "Hitler was smart enough": Ibid., 326.

155 "from the nightmarish spectacle": Hindenburg's letter of April 26, 1933, to Prince Carl of Sweden references the prince's letter of April 4, 1933 . See "Der Reichspräsident an den Präsidenten des Schwedischen Roten Kreuzes, Prinz Carl von Schweden," *Reichskanzleiakten*, vol. 1, 391.

156 "After the blood sacrifices": For Löwenstein's letter to Hitler, April 4, 1933, see "Der Reichsbund judischer Frontsoldaten an den Reichskanzler," *Reichskanzleiakten*, vol. 1, 296–98.

156 "I pleaded successfully with Hindenburg": Testimony of von Papen, June 17, 1946, IMT, vol. 16, 276.

156 "Dear Herr Reich Chancellor": Letter from Hindenburg to Hitler, "Gegen die Entlassung kriegsbeschädigter jüdischer Justizbeamter," Berlin, April 4, 1933, in Hubatsch, *Hindenburg und der Staat*, 374.

156 "all officials, judges, teachers, and lawyers": Ibid.

157 "Thus far Prussia has": Papen, *Der Wahrheit eine Gasse*, 323.

157 "For more than seventeen years": Letter from Carl Melchior, "Carl Melchior an den Reichspräsidenten," Hamburg, May 6, 1933, in *Reichskanzleiakten*, vol. 1, 430–32.

158 The Nazi Party program: "Program of the National Socialist German Workers' Party", The Avalon Project, Yale University, http://avalon.law.yale.edu /imt/nsdappro.asp.

158 "In the long years of party struggle": Papen, *Der Wahrheit eine Gasse*, 325. See also Cabinet meeting minutes, "Betrifft: Auslandspropaganda," *Reichkanzleiakten*, May 24, 1933, 477–79.

158 "The world will learn": Goebbels diary, April 1, 1933, *Joseph Goebbels Tagebücher, Band 2: 1930–1934*, ed. Ralf Georg Reuth (Munich: Piper Verlag, 1999), 790.

159 Pope Pius XI and his close adviser: Ludwig Volk, *Das Reichskonkordaat vom 20 Juli 1933* (Mainz: Matthias-Grünwald Verlag, 1972), 64.

159 "His Holiness greeted my wife": Papen, *Der Wahrheit eine Gasse*, 314.

159 "Roosevelt and Hitler both entered office": Hjalmar Schacht, *76 Jahre meines Lebens* (Bad Wörishofen: Kindler und Schiermeyer Verlag, 1953), 390.

160 Rosenberg had aspired: Ernst Piper references Rosenberg's aspiration in *Alfred Rosenberg: Hitlers Chefideologue* (Munich: Karl Blessing Verlag, 2005), 287. Neurath's testimony in Nuremberg confirmed Hindenburg's insistence that Neurath remain foreign minister. See June 22, 1946, IMT, vol. 16, 600.

160 "My grandfather": Testimony of Neurath, June 22, 1946, IMT, vol. 16, 593.

160 In March, Hindenburg signed: Ministerial meeting minutes, "Ausserhalb der Tagesordnung: Flaggenerlass," March 11, 1933, *Reichskanzleiakten*, vol. 1, 195.

160 "creation of the APA": John P. Fox, "Alfred Rosenberg in London," *Contemporary Review*, July 1, 1968, 6.

160 "We in this country": Fox, "Alfred Rosenberg in London," 8.

161 "Germany had lost the sympathy": "Simon and Hitler Envoy in Angry Session: German's Visit Is Denounced in Commons," *New York Times*, May 11, 1933.

161 "in honor of": Fox, "Alfred Rosenberg in London," 9.

161 "a deliberate protest": "British Minister Warns the Reich of 'Sanctions' If It Bolts on Arms: Hailsham Threatens Action Under Versailles Treaty—

Rosenberg Denounced in Parliament—Margot Asquith Tells Him Nazi Policies Are Held in Contempt," *New York Times*, May 12, 1933.

161 **in what capacity had Rosenberg come**: Fox, "Alfred Rosenberg in London," 6–11.

161 **London "raged" at**: "London Rages at Hitler Aide: Rosenberg Has Unlucky Day as Visitor in Britain; Wreath Laid on Cenotaph Dumped into River; Objection to His Admission to Country Raised," *Los Angeles Times*, May 12, 1933.

161 **"The government of this representative"**: John Steele, "Rosenberg Has Another Sad Day in London: Reds Denounce Hitler at Envoy's Hotel," *Chicago Daily Tribune*, May 13, 1933.

162 **"A number of incidents"**: Testimony of Alfred Rosenberg, April 15, 1946, *IMT*, vol. 11, 454.

162 **The catastrophic state**: For Hitler's May 17, 1933, speech on foreign policy at the Reichstag, see *Akten zur deutschen auswärtigen Politik*, 446.

162 **Hitler addressed the American people**: Andrew Nagorski, *Hitlerland: American Eyewitnesses to the Nazi Rise to Power* (New York: Simon & Schuster, 2012). On the note in the foreign ministry files, see "Aufzeichnung des Oberregierungsrats Thomsen über eine Unterredung des Reichskanzlers mit dem Sonderkorrespondenten von *Collier's Weekly*, Ybarra," May 18, 1933, *Akten zur deutschen auswärtigen Politik*, 461.

162 **"In observing the American attitude"**: T. R. Ybarra, "Says Hitler," *Collier's Weekly*, July 1, 1933, 17.

163 **"His face was solemn"**: Ibid.

163 **"Whatever violence there was"**: Ibid.

163 **"You have—let me"**: Ibid.

163 **"Here is what I wish"**: Ibid.

164 **"spoke warmly of the speech"**: Telegram from German ambassador Luther to the Foreign Office in Berlin, "Der Botschafter in Washington an das Auswärtige Amt,'Hatte 3/4 stündige Unterredung allein mit Präsident,'" May 23, 1933, *Akten zur deutschen auswärtigen Politik*, 475.

164 **"The purpose of today's meeting"**: Ministerial meeting minutes, May 24, 1933, *Reichskanzleiakten*, vol. 1, 477.

164 **"For this purpose, sending attachés"**:Ibid.

165 **"The foreign office cannot"**: Ibid.

165 **"From these deliberations"**: Ibid., 478.

166 **"advancement of our ideals"**: Ibid., 478–79.

166 **"The question of responsibility"**: Ibid.

166 **"We find ourselves"**: Ibid., 479.

167 **"You have made"**: Schacht, *76 Jahre meines Lebens*, 393.

167 **"our foreign propaganda"**: Ministerial meeting minutes, May 26, 1933, *Reichskanzleiakten*, vol. 1, 489–91.

167 **"The Reich government"**: Ibid., 491.

14 DEATH SENTENCE

168 **"Watch out or you"**: The German originals are: "Vorsicht sonst kommst du nach Dachau"; "Sprechen ist Silber. Schweigen ist Gold"; and "Lieber Gott,

mach mich stumm, dass ich nicht nach Dachau kumm." The word *kumm* is Bavarian dialect that derives from the High German *kommen*.

168 "Munich's quiet is entirely": "Tourists Sought by Bavarian Nazis," *New York Times*, July 4, 1933, 6.

169 Hartinger then asked: Letter from Josef Hartinger to the Spruchkammer, Amberg, July 13, 1949, StAAm 589.

169 "unethical exercise of his profession": Reinhard Weber, *Das Schicksal der jüdischen Rechtsanwälte in Bayern nach 1933* (Oldenbourg: Wissenschaftsverlag, 2006), 53.

170 "his face belonged in a police album": Letter from Josef Hartinger to the Spruchkammer, July 13, 1949.

170 "Above all I wanted": Letter from Josef Hartinger to the Bavarian state minister of justice, August R. Lang, January 16, 1984, DaA 20.108.

170 Hartinger ordered an autopsy: See Hartinger's register in the Appendix.

171 "It was sometime in May": Wintersberger testimony, Bamberg, March 7, 1951, DaA 8768.

171 attacked him with a table knife: Deposition of Josef Mutzbauer, "Beglaubigte Abschrift, Betreff: Nefzger Sebastian," May 26, 1933, DaA 8834.

172 the Mutzbauer protocol: Ibid.

172 "You can strike Lehrburger": Testimony of Anton Schöberl, "Zeugenvernehmungsprotokoll Betrifft Zill Egon wegen Kriegsverbrechen," August 20, 1951, StAM Stanw 34462/10.

172 Agents of the Nuremberg: Ibid.

173 "I refused and explained": Testimony of Anton Vogel, "Zeugenvernehmungsprotokoll aufgenommen in der Voruntersuchung gegen Wicklmayr Karl u.a.," January 15, 1951, StAM Stanw 34439.

173 "Lehrburger was a Soviet Russian agent": Interrogation of Hans Steinbrenner, Garmisch, August 19, 1948, DaA 12.288.

173 "There is nothing easier": Ibid.

174 "In accordance with the instruction": Deposition of Josef Mutzbauer, May 26, 1933.

175 "The forensic examination": See memorandum, "Konzentrationslager Dachau Politische Abteilung—An das Amtsgericht Dachau," signed Dr. Nürnbergk, May 27, 1933, DaA 8834.

175 Dr. Nürnbergk wanting to know: "Vormerkung zum Falle Nefzger," signed Dr. Flamm, Munich, June 1, 1933, StAM Stanw 7014.

176 close-up photographs: Photographs from Flamm's autopsy, StAM Stanw 7014.

176 "of powerful build": "Protokoll aufgenommen in Sachen Leichenschau und Leichenöffnung zum Tode des verh. Kaufmanns Nefzger Sebastian aus München im Konzentrationslager Dachau," signed Dr. Flamm, Dr. Mueller, Essel, Brücklmeier, Dachau, May 29, 1933, DaA 8834.

176 As Flamm prepared to leave: Flamm, "Vormerkung zum Falle Nefzger."

176 On Monday afternoon, Flamm: Ibid.

177 "The left temporal side": Nefzger autopsy, see attachment to "Beglaubigte Abschrift Protokoll in Sachen Leichenschau und Leichenöffnung zum Tode des verh. Kaufmanns Nefzger Sebastian."

177 His conclusions were: Ibid.

179 He summarized each case: See Hartinger's register, May 30, 1933, in the Appendix.

179 "I had in fact": Letter from Josef Hartinger to August R. Lang, January 16, 1984.

179 "If the prosecutor's office": *Strafprozessordnung*, 148.

180 "Nazis were required to report": Letter from Josef Hartinger to August R. Lang, January 16, 1984.

180 "Since it was necessary to act": Sworn statement of Dr. Hermann Kiessner, "Eidesstattliche Erklärung," Munich, January 6, 1947, in Hartinger, "Spruchkammerverfahren," StAAm 589.

180 As a former judge: Letter from Josef Hartinger to August R. Lang, January 16, 1984.

180 "It was clear to both": Sworn statement of Dr. Kiessner, January 6, 1947.

180 "the police department commanded great respect": Letter from Josef Hartinger to August R. Lang, January 16, 1984.

180 Three weeks earlier: Hirsch was returned to the concentration camp but was lodged with the other detainees and no longer subjected to the abuses he had experienced in the Arrest Bunker. See Hirsch testimony, January 27, 1949.

180 "We started talking": Letter from Josef Hartinger to August R. Lang, January 16, 1984.

181 "my wife was often ill": Letter from Josef Hartinger to the Spruchkammer, Amberg, February 14, 1948, StAAm 589.

181 "It was clear to me": Ibid.

181 "I hereby issue": Indictment signed by Josef Hartinger for the death of Sebastian Nefzger, June 1, 1933, StAM Stanw 7014.

182 "Although the accused": Ibid.

182 "I submit a request": Ibid.

182 "I just signed my own death sentence": See Helene Hartinger's sworn statement, "Spruchkammerverfahren, Josef Hartinger," Amberg, February 14, 1948, StAAm 589.

15 GOOD-FAITH AGREEMENTS

183 "I pointed out that": Wintersberger report to justice ministry on meeting with Himmler, "Betreff: Ableben von Schutzhaftgefangenen im Konzentrationslager Dachau," June 2, 1933, DaA 18.788. Wintersberger begins his memo with the word *auftragsgemäss*, or "as instructed," indicating that the meeting with Himmler was prearranged and on higher instruction. Given Hartinger's jurisdictional responsibilities for Dachau and his central role in the invesigtation, it is curious that Wintersberger did not inform Hartinger.

184 Wintersberger had personally investigated: Wintersberger memo of June 1, 1933, closing the case on the Lehrburger shooting, DaA 18.727.

184 "In case the justice officials": Hans-Günter Richardi, *Schule der Gewalt: Die Anfänge des Konzentrationslagers Dachau 1933–1934: Ein dokumentischer Bericht* (Munich: C. H. Beck Verlag, 1995), 36.

184 "We took these measures": "Ein Konzentrationslager für politische Gefangene in der Nähe von Dachau," *Münchner Neueste Nachrichten*, March 22, 1933.

184 Wagner appointed Munich police chief Himmler: Johannes Tuchel, *Konzen-*

trationslager: Organisationsgeschichte und Funktion der 'Inspektion der Konzentrationslager' 1934–1938 (Boppard am Rhein: Harald Boldt Verlag, 1991), 122.

185 "The command of the SS guard": "Wachtruppe Übergabe-Protokoll: Konzentrationslager Dachau," May 30, 1933, BayHSta Lapo Kdo. Bd. 8.

185 Wintersberger had visited: For details of Wintersberger's visit to Döbig and Wintersberger's discussion with Wäckerle, see Friedrich Döbig's memorandum titled "Betreff: Konzentrationslager Dachau," June 1, 1933. Appended is Wintersberger's memo "Betreff: Schutzhaftlager Dachau," dated May 29, 1933, with a copy of Wäckerle's regulations (*Lagerordnung*), DaA 18.736.

185 death penalties violated state law: Ibid.

186 "any appearance of interference": Ibid.

186 "The state's authority": Letter to Ludwig Siebert from a deputy SA special commissioner (*Sonderkommissar*), cited in Lothar Gruchmann, *Justiz im Dritten Reich 1933–1940: Anpassung und Unterwerfung in der Ära Gürtner*, 2nd ed. (Munich: Oldenbourg, 1990), 381.

186 "Everyone arrests everyone": Ibid.

187 In one incident: Gruchmann, *Justiz im Dritten Reich*, 384.

187 The SS man was beaten: Ibid.

187 Eicke's psychiatrist wrote: Ibid., 137.

188 Eicke had tripled: Ibid., 131.

188 Himmler personally promoted him: Ibid., 136.

188 "I intend to use Eicke": Ibid., 138.

189 "Police Chief Himmler": Wintersberger report to justice ministry on meeting with Himmler, June 2, 1933, DaA 18.737.

16 RULES OF LAW

190 "When I subsequently": Sworn statement of Dr. Hermann Kiessner, "Eidesstattliche Erklärung," Munich, January 6, 1947, in Hartinger "Spruchkammerverfahren," StAAm 589.

190 "It would have been": Letter from Josef Hartinger to the Bavarian state minister of justice, August R. Lang, January 16, 1984, DaA 20.108.

191 "As I was returning": Ibid.

191 "He answered in the negative": Ibid.

191 "As the district party leader": "Die Voruntersuchungen zum Reichstagsbrand abgeschlossen," *Völkischer Beobachter*, June 3, 1933.

192 "It was clear to both of us": Sworn statement of Dr. Kiessner, January 6, 1947.

192 "boundless respect for the courage": Johan Schütz, *Josef Hartinger: Ein mutiger Staatsanwalt im Kampf gegen den KZ-Terror* (Munich: Bayrisches Staatsministerium der Justiz, 1990), 8.

192 "We will shoot you": "Spruchkammerverfahren Josef Hartinger." Amberg, February 14, 1948, StA AM 589.

193 have Hartinger "taken care of": Letter from Hans Steinbrenner to Josef Hartinger, cited in Otto Gritschneder, "Es gab auch solche Staatsanwälte," *Münchner Stadtanzeiger*, February 24, 1984, 5.

193 "I told my husband repeatedly": Helene Hartinger's testimony (*Eidesstattliche Erklärung*), Amberg, February 14, 1948, "Spruchkammerverfahren Josef

Hartinger." Hartinger's wife was referring to the situation after they had moved to Amberg and found themselves under close scrutiny by local Nazis, but I have taken the liberty of situating this quote in the context of their Munich years.

193 "because Wicklmayr's assertions": Wintersberger memo of June 1, 1933, closing the case on the Lehrburger killing, "Staatsanwaltschaft von dem Landgerichte München II an den Herrn Generalstaatsanwalt bei dem Oberlandesgerichts München Beteff: Ableben des Schutzgefangenen Karl Lehrburger im Kozentrationslager Dachau," DaA 18.727.

193 "I really do not know": Letter from Josef Hartinger to August R. Lang, January 16, 1984.

193 "I explained to Minister Counselor Döbig": A copy dated March 7, 1951, of the original Wintersberger memo to the files dated June 21, 1933. It contains a three-page list with eight entries chronicling his attempts to have the files returned. The last one is dated May 11, 1934. The list is attached to Testimony of Karl Wintersberger, Bamberg, March 7, 1951, DaA 8768.

193 "This could not be carried out": Sworn statement of Dr. Kiessner, January 6, 1947.

193 "I had Reich governor": Testimony of Hans Frank, April 18, 1946, IMT, vol. 12, 5.

194 Himmler was instructed: Hans-Günter Richardi, Schule der Gewalt: Die Anfänge des Konzentrationslagers Dachau 1933–1934: Ein dokumentischer Bericht (Munich: C. H. Beck Verlag, 1995), 113.

194 "After that I continued protesting": Testimony of Hans Frank, April 18, 1946, IMT, vol. 12, 5.

194 eventually referred the matter: Ibid.

194 "I am assigning you as of July 15": Memo from Reichsführer SS to SS-Sturmhauptführer, July 27, 1933, DaA A 4369.

195 "In the entire facility": Eicke letter dated August 10, 1936, Berlin, "An dem Reichsführer-SS," DaA 16444.

195 "considered a necessary evil": Ibid.

195 "I went energetically and happily": Ibid.

196 The reporter, who referred to it as an "educational camp": "Special Correspondent," "Times Writer Visits Reich Prison Camp," New York Times, July 26, 1933, 9. The quotations from the New York Times that follow are taken from this article.

197 "It was certainly": Letter from Josef Hartinger to the Bavarian state minister of justice, August R. Lang, February 11, 1984.

197 He was followed in September: Memorandum of Chief Prosecutor Karl Wintersberger, "Ableben des Schutzhaftgefangenen Hugo Handschuch im Lager Dachau," September 19, 1933, DaA 1588/4.

197 two suicides by hanging: See Hartinger's register, undated, in the Appendix.

198 "so-called handcrafted murders": Emil J. Gumbel, Vier Jahre politischer Mord (Berlin-Fichtenau: Verlag der Neuen Gesellschaft, 1922), 125.

199 "It would have been": Letter from Josef Hartinger to August R. Lang, January 16, 1984.

199 "I was only doing": Ibid.

EPILOGUE: THE HARTINGER CONVICTION

201 In the summer of 1945: Found with the files was a letter from "Polizeipräsident Pitzer an Oberstaatsanwalt beim Landgerichte München II," dated December 31, 1946, StAAm 589: 92.

201 Jackson had envisioned Adolf Hitler: John Q. Barrett, "The Nuremberg Roles of Justice Robert H. Jackson," *Washington University Global Studies Law Review* 6 (2007): 518.

202 According to a calculation: Ibid., 519.

202 "You can't indict a government": Leon Goldensohn, *The Nuremberg Interviews* (New York: Alfred A. Knopf, 2007), 33.

202 He indicted twenty-four: Martin Bormann, head of the *Parteikanzlei* and Hitler's personal secretary, was tried in absentia; head of the German Labor Front Robert Ley committed suicide shortly after the trial began; and industrialist Gustav Krupp von Bohlen und Halbach was deemed too old to stand trial. For a list of the twenty-one who stood trial, see the *Trial of the Major War Criminals Before the International Military Tribunal, Nuremberg, 14 November 1945–1 October 1946 (IMT)* files in the Avalon Project, Yale University, avalon.law.yale.edu.

203 "The significance is that": See Farr prosecution, December 19, 1945, *IMT*, vol. 190.

203 "I don't think you": Ibid.

203 "These four murders": Ibid.

203 "As an organization founded": Ibid.

204 "The enclosed files": Memo with indictments retyped in the letter, StAAm 589: 92.

204 The files lingered: Letter, "Polizeipräsident Pitzer an Oberstaatsanwalt beim Landgerichte München II," dated December 31, 1946.

205 "Heigl made no pretense": Letter from Josef Hartinger to the Bavarian state minister of justice, August R. Lang, February 11, 1984, DaA 20.109.

205 "I took them with me": Ibid.

206 Josef Mutzbauer, had fallen victim: Otto Gritschneder, "Es gab auch solche Staatsanwälte," *Münchner Stadtanzeiger,* February 24, 1984, 5.

206 Wäckerle's . . . was dispatched: For details on Wäckerle's life after Dachau, see obituary, "Standartenführer Wäckerle gefallen . . . ," DaA 38.634.

206 "With the passing": Letter from Steiner, "H-Division 'Viking,'" July 2, 1941, informing the Reichsführer of Wäckerle's death on that day, DaA 38.634.

207 "From September 1939": Testimony of Hans Steinbrenner, Garmisch, August 19, 1948, DaA 12.288.

207 "The behavior of the Allied soldiers": Ibid.

207 "I need to note": Ibid.

208 "I never lashed a detainee so long": Ibid.

208 "I am certainly aware": Letter from Hans Steinbrenner to Josef Hartinger, cited in Gritschneder, "Es gab auch solche Staatsanwälte," 5.

209 "I killed the detainees Götz, Dressel": Testimony of Karl Wicklmayr, "Vernehmungsniederschrift Karl Wickelmayr [*sic*], Landpolizei Oberbayern, Kriminalaussenstelle Mü-Pasing" Garmisch, September 10, 1948, StAM Stanw 34462/1.

209 "I still remember Nefzger": Ibid.

209 "I ambushed Schloss": Ibid.

209 "On Wäckerle's orders": Ibid.

209 Wicklmayr was sentenced to six years: For the final verdict in the Wicklmayr case, July 2 and 3, 1951, see StAM Stanw 2624.

210 "Look, Hartinger": Letter from Josef Hartinger to the Bavarian state minister of justice, August R. Lang, January 16, 1984, DaA 20.108.

210 "The human being is complicated": Ibid.

210 "Like the generals": Letter from Hartinger to Lang, February 11, 1984.

210 "Until now I have spared": Ibid.

211 "It is possible that the chief prosecutor": Ibid.

211 "Wintersberger was simply overwhelmed": Ibid.

211 "I wanted to act rashly": Ibid.

212 denounced as "libelous": Wintersberger letter, "An den Herrn Präsidenten des Oberlandesgerichts Bamberg, Betreff: Beleidigung des Oberlandesgerichtsrats Karl Wintersberger in Bamberg durch die Presse," November 8, 1934, BayHStA MJu 26443.

212 "my 'national socialist' leanings": Ibid.

212 "It is thanks to my thorough investigation that Abel": Ibid.

212 "Finally I need to fulfill a duty of piety," Letter from Hartinger to Lang, January 16, 1984.

212 "When I think about the hatred": Ibid.

213 "the sharpest protest possible": Letter from Theodor Eicke, "An Herrn Oberstaatsanwalt beim Landgericht Mch.II, Begrifft: Dort. Aktz. G506/34," May 3, 1934, DaA 34851.

213 "It contains such serious, insulting attacks": Memorandum from Wintersberger to the Generalstaatsanwalt beim Oberlandesgericht Munich Sotier, "Betreff: Ableben des Schutzhaftgefangenen Martin Stiebel," May 9, 1934, DaA 34852.

213 In July, the SS attempted: Testimony of Friedrich Döbig, August 22, 1951, StAM Stanw 34464/3.

213 "He died, as far as I ever learned": Letter from Josef Hartinger to August R. Lang, January 16, 1984.

APPENDIX: THE HARTINGER REGISTERS

217 Register I, Munich, May 30, 1933: "Wichtige Vorkommnisse im Konzentrationslager Dachau", DaA 34851.

220 Register II, [undated]: DaA 8833.

ACKNOWLEDGMENTS

Three discoveries alerted me to the full significance of the Dachau murders. The first was Josef Hartinger's observation, in his letter of February 11, 1984, that he believed from the outset that Hilmar Wäckerle was ordering the execution of Jews in Dachau. The second was Karl Wintersberger's categorical dismissal of his deputy's suspicion. The third, of course, was the remarkable headline in the Sunday, April 23, 1933, edition of the *New York Times*, reporting on the shootings but failing to mention the names of Rudolf Benario, Ernst Goldmann, and Arthur Kahn, or to investigate the further fate of Erwin Kahn. The reporter literally missed the story of the century.

These four murders gave specificity and substance to the painful and oft-repeated observation that the trail of blood that began in Dachau led ultimately and seemingly inexorably to Auschwitz. It was my goal in writing this book to show that what has come to seem so obvious, even inevitable in retrospect, had been for most contemporary observers unthinkable, including America's leading newspaper of record. I also wanted to demonstrate that if Germany had found more individuals like Hartinger, perhaps history could have been set on a different, less horrific path.

I first tested this idea in an opinion piece for the *International Herald Tribune* in January 2011 under the title "First Killings of the

Holocaust," and awaited qualifiers and corrective missives regarding such specificity in an event of such complexity and magnitude. Instead, I received encouraging responses, not the least from the United States Holocaust Memorial Museum. I thank Serge Schmemann for first giving this story an audience in the pages of the *International Herald Tribune*'s op-ed section.

I would also like to acknowledge three previous chroniclers of the Dachau murders whose work contributed to the framing of the Hartinger story. Hans-Günter Richardi demonstrated the narrative power of eyewitness testimonies in recounting the killings in his superb account of the early Dachau Concentration Camp, *Schule der Gewalt (School of Violence)*. Professor Dr. Lothar Gruchmann underscored for me the centrality, and potential drama, of the judicial processes. Dr. Rolf Seubert provided new and surprising primary source documents in his contribution to a retrospective on the former Dachau detainee and distinguished postwar writer Alfred Andersch.

However, archival materials and eyewitness testimony provided the main substance for this book. The transport manifests of regular deliveries to Dachau, generally twenty-five to thirty detainees at a time, were a source of poignant detail. Here, one could trace the diverse trajectories and occasional collisions of individual fates. I came to see that the world of extremist Bavarian politics could be surprisingly small and personal. The buses from Bamberg, Würzburg, or Nuremberg delivered clusters of friends, sometimes into the vengeance-seeking hands of hometown adversaries. Wäckerle was particularly concerned by a transport from Kempten, where he had spent several years as commander of the local SS unit. Leonhard Hausmann from Augsburg found himself at the mercy and gunpoint of a fellow Augsburger, SS staff sergeant Karl Ehmann. Karl Lehrburger was identified by a visiting team of SS men from Nuremberg. The testimonies of victims and perpetrators alike were, of course, the primary source for this story.

The accounts of atrocity were endless and overwhelming. Here the devil truly resided in the details.

But the material needed to be approached with caution. Human memory is faulty at best, and all the more so when sieved through trauma and time, or, in the case of the Nuremberg defendants, seeking to avoid the gallows. There are frequent divergent eyewitness accounts, even with an incident as central as the shooting of Benario, Goldmann, and the two Kahns. Some claim that the four men were standing in line waiting for mail delivery, others that they were returning from a work detail, and one had them lying in the grass between Barracks II and III talking about a U.S. dollar. Most eyewitnesses saw Steinbrenner lead them to the gate and hand them to Erspenmüller, but others saw Steinbrenner accompany them into the woods. One account had Johann Kantschuster emerging from the trees with a smoking pistol. State police officer Emil Schuler provided the most detailed and credible account, along with a precise sketch of the crime scene, but seemed astonishingly, almost criminally, passive in the face of such blatant atrocity.

I was particularly cautious with Josef Hartinger's accounts, and not just because he was recalling events of a half century after the fact and just beyond his ninetieth birthday. Barbara Distel had met Hartinger when she was director of the Dachau Concentration Camp Memorial Site. She told me he had felt he had not received adequate recognition for his efforts, since most of the attention had gone to Karl Wintersberger. I wondered whether his detailed description of the events, long after all other key participants were dead, was an attempt to position himself for posterity. I was therefore rigorous in seeking corroborating evidence or testimony and did find lapses. Hartinger recalled, for example, that on June 2 he retrieved the files himself from Kiessner's office because Kiessner had gone home for the day. Kiessner recalled that he was sitting in his office when Hartinger came by to collect the files. Hartinger was also unable to square the existence of two signed sets of indictments dated June 1, 1933, one set with his signature and one set with Wintersberger's. I also failed to resolve the contradictions. But Hartinger seemed to be as honest with the material as he could be, and certainly was more generous with his assessment of Karl Wintersberger than the postwar judges who found Wintersberger guilty of complicity.

The surviving autopsy reports by Dr. Moritz Flamm provided crucial evidence for the Hartinger indictments and a central point of reference for this story. I am thankful to Professor Dr. Wolfgang Eisenmenger, the former head of the Institute for Forensic Medicine at the Ludwig Maximilian University of Munich, for generously providing copies of archival material on Dr. Flamm, reviewing the early chapters, and alerting me to the potentially sinister implications of the Erwin Kahn autopsy. I am also thankful to Dr. Claudius Stein at the Archiv und Sammlungen des Herzoglichen Georgianums of the Ludwig Maximilian University of Munich, who helped clarify the identity of Dr. Nürnbergk, and set me on a trail that led from Munich to archives in Erfurt, Weimar, Berlin, and Washington, D.C. It was in D.C. that Dr. Stefan Hördler at the German Historical Institute provided vital corroborating evidence for confirming Dr. Nürnbergk as the camp's first official physician.

The director of the Bavarian State Archives in Munich, Dr. Christoph Bachmann, was particularly helpful in leading me to the surviving documents (most destroyed during the war) from the "little Hitler trial." I would like to express particular and sincere appreciation to Robert Bierschneider, also at the Bavarian State Archives, who was, as in the past, ever helpful in guiding me to some of the most crucial material in the Bavarian state's vast holdings. Anton Knoll provided similar and equally appreciated support in the archive at the Dachau Concentration Camp Memorial Site. A word of thanks is also due to Peggy Frankston and Caroline Waddell at the United States Holocaust Memorial Museum in Washington, D.C., for their diverse and kind assistance.

I also received generous help from archivists in special collections or local archives across Bavaria. In Munich, these included the personnel files and the war service records within the Main Bavarian State Archives, as well as the collections at the Institute for Contemporary History. I would also like to recognize willing assistance at public and private archives in Augsburg, Bamberg, Coburg, and Fürth, and especially in Amberg, where Till Strobel was of particular help with materials on Hartinger. Manfred Lehner gave access to primary source materials on Rudolf Benario collected by the students at the Soldner High School in Fürth. These young people provided an exceptional tribute to the memory of one of the first victims of the Holocaust. Sincere appreciation is also due to Michael Schneeberger for the copy of Benario photo. I owe similar thanks to Daniel Dorsch, head of the Willy Aron Society in Bamberg, as well as Gerald Raab at the Staatsbibliothek Bamberg. Appreciation is also due to Denise Anderson for her extensive efforts at the University of Edinburgh. Lothar Kahn at age ninety kindly shared with me memories of his older brother, Arthur Kahn, and his parents' reaction to their son's death. The German Historical Institute in Paris was an indispensable source for standard reference works, as well as an original copy of Emil Gumbel's insightful and tragically prescient 1922 report on political violence.

Florian Beierl shared, as always, his valuable contacts and primary source materials, and Guido Burkhardt kindly reviewed the sections related to the history of Bavaria. Oliver Halmburger and his team at Loopfilm in Munich, especially Kai Schäfer, were vital in identifying and securing relevant images and photographs. Russell Riley at the University of Virginia located important early accounts of Dachau in the American press, in particular several key articles in the *New York Times*.

The scholars Professor Dr. Johannes Tuchel, Dr. Nikolaus Wachsmann, and Joseph Robert White pointed me in useful directions for my research into the early camps. I appreciate the time and attention provided by Philippe Couvreur, the long-serving registrar at the International Court of Justice in The Hague, who is custodian of the original files of the Nuremberg tribunal. Justice Richard Goldstone, the first prosecutor of the International Criminal Tribunal for Yugoslavia, kindly reviewed the sections related to the prosecution in Nuremberg. Jonathan Duff in Paris read an early draft of the manuscript and provided thoughtful criticism and recommendations.

Jonathan Segal, my editor at Alfred A. Knopf, guided this book with firmness, rigor, and wisdom from start to finish. My agent, Gail Hochman, remains an ongoing source of support and encouragement, assisted by Marianne Merola, who continues to work her magic. And last but defintely not least, Dr. Richard M. Hunt remains a model and mentor, just as he did nearly three decades ago when I served as a teaching assistant in his course on Weimar and Nazi culture at Harvard University. As always, Jonathan Petropoulos in California was there to provide friendship, encouragement, and an unrelentingly scrupulous review of the historical content.

My wife, Marie-Louise, who directs the Holocaust Education and Genocide Prevention program at the Salzburg Global Seminar, first alerted me to the connection between the Dachau murders and the Nuremberg tribunal. For this and for her steadfast support I remain grateful and indebted, happily so, though, as one can imagine, our dinner conversations are not always about the cheeriest of subjects. I also wish to thank our two oldest children, Katrina and Brendan, for their willingness to let me test ideas on them, and in particular our youngest, Audrey, for her extensive help in the final work on the manuscript and additional archival research. Last but not least, I have the pleasure of continuing to acknowledge my mother, who has always been there to encourage my writing and, at a similar age to Joseph Hartinger, seems destined to continue doing so for many years to come.

INDEX

Page numbers beginning with 229 refer to endnotes.

ILLUSTRATION CREDITS

A NOTE ABOUT THE AUTHOR

TIMOTHY W. RYBACK has written for the *Atlantic Monthly*, *The New Yorker*, the *New York Times*, and the *Wall Street Journal*. He is the author of *The Last Survivor: Legacies of Dachau*, a *New York Times* Best Book of the Year 2000, and *Hitler's Private Library: The Books That Shaped His Life*, which has appeared in more than twenty-five editions around the world. He lives in Paris with his wife, and has three grown children.

A NOTE ON THE TYPE

This book was set in Monotype Dante, a typeface designed by Giovanni Mardersteig (1892–1977). Conceived as a private type for the Officina Bodoni in Verona, Italy, Dante was originally cut only for hand composition by Charles Malin, the famous Parisian punch cutter, between 1946 and 1952. Although modeled on the Aldine type used for Pietro Cardinal Bembo's treatise *De Aetna* in 1495, Dante is a thoroughly modern interpretation of the venerable face.

Composed by North Market Street Graphics,
Lancaster, Pennsylvania

Printed and bound by Berryville Graphics,
Berryville, Virginia

Designed by Cassandra Pappas